NEVERTHELESS

I LIVE

NEVERTHELESS
I LIVE

LIVING FREELY IN A BOUND WORLD

I am crucified with Christ: **nevertheless I live***; yet not I, but Christ liveth in me: and the life which I now live in the flesh I live by the faith of the Son of God, who loved me, and gave himself for me.* Galatians 2:20

STEVEN B. CURINGTON

Reformers Unanimous International

PO Box 15732, Rockford, IL 61132

Visit our website at www.reformu.com.

Printed in Canada

Cover design by Tina Morris, Apex Marketing, Rockford, IL

Curington, Steven B., 1965-

Nevertheless I Live : Living Freely in a Bound World / Steven Curington.

ISBN 0-9761498-0

Dedication

Nevertheless I Live is dedicated to three men God used to shape my life.

The first man taught me the value of character and hard work. He is a great father who never gave up on me despite my many failures. He is the gentlest man I know. Without question, no person shaped my *personal* life more than my dad, **Delmar Curington**.

The second man trained me to preach and taught me through example how to live the abundant Christian life. His confidence in me has been the driving force for the development of Reformers Unanimous. He is the most loving man I know. Without question, no person has shaped my *spiritual* life more than my pastor, **Paul Kingsbury**.

The third man enlightened me in how to gain God's power on my life and in my work. He hired me despite my résumé saying I would be a waste of time. As my former employer, I still seek his wise counsel. He is the meekest man I know. Without question, no person has shaped my *professional* life more than my mentor, **Daniel Arnold**.

Acknowledgments

I am especially grateful to my wife, Lori. She never expressed frustration with my countless hours spent on this book.

Many thanks to the RU editorial staff members who have sacrificially given of their time, insight, and expertise to bring this project from bud to full bloom. This book would have remained an impossibility without them.

Thank you Joy, Wendy, and Jeff.

A special thank you to Tina from Apex Marketing. She is a friend and helper to our ministry who has given of her God-given talents to produce a cover design that accurately depicts the crucified Christian life.

Thank you, also, to Bethel Baptist Print Ministry for believing in our mission.

In conclusion, I thank God for His gracious leading during the tenure of this book. My journey began with a desire to teach others about the abundant Christian life, only to find myself transformed as the Holy Spirit matured me to a position of enlightenment that has changed the way I view all my circumstances in life.

Contents

Foreword

Nevertheless I Live is an educational resource for living freely in a bound world. Sadly, many Christians struggle in bondage to sinful habits. Though we are saved from the penalty of sin (eternal separation from God), we often forfeit the freedom that can be found from the power of sin. You *can* live freely from the bondage of sin!

Each chapter of this textbook is taught over a four to six week period in our weekly Reformers Unanimous Addictions Class. It can also be used as a church discipleship course for its members. Our intention is for our students to read this textbook while participating in our 6-8 month discipleship course.

You must realize, though, that this book is not intended to be read like most commercially published books. It is really a textbook. As a result, the repeated verses in different chapters may seem repetitive as you progress. Just remember, however, that repetition is the key to learning. I have found that the truths found in this book, which I have taught for over eight years now, have produced a level of maturity in many of our students that has often never been experienced in the life of many decade old Christians.

May God bless you as we begin our journey to freedom in a bound world.

Chapter 1

One way, One truth, One life, Once to die.

*Jesus saith unto him, I am the way, the truth,
and the life: no man cometh unto the Father,
but by me.* —John 14:6

Throughout our study of living freely in a bound world, we will discuss many truths that have to do with the Christian life. For the most part, we will attack each subject from the assumption that each reader is a Christian, but bound by a stubborn habit or addiction.

However, in chapter one, it is necessary to take the time to introduce readers to the single most important Person in our recovery process. It is not you. It is not your spouse or sponsor, or even your support group. It is our Savior Jesus Christ. In this chapter, we are going to discover how freedom is found by following this Way, Truth, and Life. We will look at God's truth that leads to freedom versus the lie of the world that leads to bondage. We will conclude with an explanation of how God intends for us to enjoy the life He has for you and for me.

Jesus, the Way

Society will tell us there are many different "ways" to overcome an addiction. In my search while away from God, I learned many of them as I attempted my road to recovery in my own power. Let's look at some of their different "ways."

SELF-HELP PROGRAMS

The first "way" used by society to guide us to freedom is through self-help programs. This "way" teaches that we must think higher of ourselves. We must improve our low self-esteem and negative self-image. I personally struggled with addiction for over ten years. I sought counsel from a variety of society's programs. Nearly every time I was told that I had low self-esteem; I had a low opinion of myself. What solution did they offer? I needed to think higher of myself! I needed to realize that I was a good man for making an effort. By being proud of my accomplishments, I would overcome my strongholds.

As a result of this mistake in philosophy, I remained addicted for many years. I had come to believe that if I only thought more of myself, I could be like the others who had been set free from their addictions. This "way" failed, and failed, and failed. It seemed as if the more I tried it the harder I fell.

Why did this "way" fail? When I would begin to feel better about myself, and become proud of my accomplishment of temporary sobriety, and experience any real clean time, I always seemed to stumble shortly thereafter. The reason for my failure is found in Proverbs 16:18. *Pride goeth before destruction, and a haughty spirit before a fall.* The principle being taught here is that if we believe in ourselves to do something that only God can do for us, we <u>will</u> stumble and will eventually be destroyed through our self-centered efforts. Proverbs 29:23 reminds us that, *A man's pride shall bring him low…*

> The principle being taught in Proverbs 16:18 is that if we believe in ourselves to do something that only God can do for us, we will stumble and will eventually be destroyed through our self-centered efforts.

A second mistake with this self-focused philosophy is that my advice was coming from men who were not seeking the "ways" of the Lord. Proverbs 14:12 says, *There is a <u>way</u> which seemeth right unto a man, but the end thereof are the ways of death.* That was part of my problem! I was seeking counsel from men whose motives were good, and although they wanted to help me, their advice was not coming from the Lord. According to this verse the "ways" of man will look right, but the end result will be a premature death. That wasn't the result I was looking for, and I think it's safe to say you aren't either.

What is God's answer to these philosophical errors? First, seek godly counsel. Since man's way and man's advice lead to death (a spiritual and sometimes a premature physical death), we should seek advice from people who get their counsel from God.

Second, reject our self-centered pride and be willing to humble ourselves. It was a glorious day when I got down on my knees and said, *Oh, God, I can't do it by myself! I need your help, Lord! Please help me overcome this habit.* When I was willing to humble myself in the sight of the Lord, <u>then</u> He was willing to lift me up. I realized that I could never do it in my own power. I confessed to God my utter dependence on His power to not only save, but also to deliver. This is a Scriptural principle. James 4:10 reads, *Humble yourselves in the sight of the Lord, and he shall lift you up.* First Peter 5:5-6 teaches that, *God resisteth the proud, and giveth grace to the humble. Humble yourselves therefore under the mighty hand of God, that he may exalt you in due time.* You see, God wants us to humble ourselves, admit we need His help, and give our lives to Him to control.

I have found that there are "steps of action" in the humbling process. As we grow in the Lord, God will reveal various areas of our life that need to be given over to Him. As we continue to surrender, He *will* continue to lift us up. If we do the humbling, He will do the exalting. They work hand-in-hand. It's impossible to have one without the other. My dear friend, if you will humble yourself in your efforts to overcome your habits in your own power and realize you are powerless without God's help, the Scriptures will prove to be true. God will exalt you and lift you out of your addictive lifestyle!

SUPPORT OF BAD FRIENDS

A second "way" that society will try to lead us to freedom is through the support of bad friends. Leaning on our friends as our "way" to freedom can often lead us away from God. They may have our best interest at heart; but if they are not guided by the Lord Jesus Christ, they will be unable to lead us to freedom. Second Corinthians 6:14 says, *Be ye not unequally yoked together with unbelievers: for what fellowship hath righteousness with unrighteousness? And what communion hath light with darkness?* We will explain these verses in detail in a later chapter, but for now I ask you to realize this truth—those living in darkness cannot help us get to the light.

Psalm 1:1 and 6 says, *Blessed is the man that walketh not in the counsel of the ungodly, nor standeth in the way of sinners, nor sitteth in the seat of the scornful. For the LORD knoweth the way of the righteous: but the way of the ungodly shall perish.* According to this verse, if we get advice from bad people, or hang out with bad people, or act like bad people, we will be unhappy and perish. You can follow their leading if you want, but you will not appreciate where it will take you.

GOVERNMENTAL SOCIAL PROGRAMS

A third "way" to freedom taught by society is through governmental social programs. This "way" teaches that the path to freedom is wide and all-inclusive. There are no restrictions on this path and we can bring other habits (cigarettes, foul language, sexual immorality, etc.) with us, as we overcome the ones we don't like. There could be nothing farther from the truth. No real freedom will ever be consistently experienced if we choose to feed one addiction or habit while attempting to starve another. Ephesians 4:22-24 teaches that we are to *put off concerning the former conversation* (or, lifestyle) *the old man, which is corrupt according to the deceitful lusts; And be renewed in the spirit of your mind; And that ye put on the new man, which after God is created in righteousness* (or, right living) *and true holiness* (or, set apart from worldly ways).

I've been to so many programs in an attempt to overcome my various addictions. I was often encouraged to overlook my smoking habits and sexual cravings while attempting to find freedom in "more important" areas. As a result, I would smoke as many cigarettes as I could! The language in those meetings was so dirty that even though I was living in sin, I felt like I needed to take a shower from the filth of the language in the room! The constant critical spirits toward authority and nonstop talking about drinking only left me thirsty!

Why is it that we are willing to abort one unwanted addiction only to end up feeding another unwanted one? It's because we believe the lie that the path to freedom from our bad habits is wide and all inclusive with no restrictions on other "sins."

However, according to our key verse, there is only one way to freedom. That way is not found in our power, or our friends, or our pride, or our "sin swapping." This "way" is found in God's Son, Jesus!

JESUS IS THE ONLY WAY

Our key verse (John 14:6) tells us, *Jesus saith unto him, I am the way...* "The" means the only way! There is no other way that works. In Matthew 7:13 Jesus also said, *Enter ye in at the strait gate:* (He then begins to describe a gate other than that strait gate: He describes the gate that most people walk through) *for wide is the gate, and broad is the way, that leadeth to destruction, and many there be which go in thereat.* Did you catch that? Wide is the gate, and broad is the way (or, many are the ways) that leads to destruction!

Ask yourself these questions. Which gate am I attempting to enter in to find freedom? Which path am I on? Is it a wide gate? Is it a broad way? Will it lead to destruction? Are there many going through that gate? How many have gone this "way" before me and failed? If you have answered "yes" to those questions, you need to change your path from "the way" of the world to "the way" of God's Son.

After Jesus describes the wide gate and broad path that

leads many to destruction, He describes that strait gate in verse 14. *Because strait is the gate, and narrow is the way, which leadeth unto life, and few there be that find it.*

Few there be that find it? Why would the narrow way which leads to freedom from the devil's bondage have the sad description of "few there be that find it?" Because the strait gate is Jesus. His gate is <u>not</u> all-inclusive; everyone is welcome, but many reject this way because it is <u>not</u> dependent on our work. It is completely dependent on the Lord Jesus Christ. It is narrow because there are few people who will give up on their self effort and lean on Jesus. They fail to believe in Him alone to save and change them. Therefore, they fail to find freedom. Jesus is the Only Way, and …*no man cometh unto the Father, but by* [Him].

To help us understand this principle, we are going to use a parable (a story with a truth to be understood) given in John 10:1-10. Throughout this passage, I will dissect and define Bible words. This will help us understand the truths that the Lord intends for us to understand.

> *Verily, verily, I say unto you. He that entereth not by the door into the sheepfold, but climbeth up some other way, the same is a thief, and a robber.* (In other words, there is a sheepfold. It has a door in which you enter. If you try to enter any other way, you are considered a thief and a robber.) *But he that entereth in by the door is the shepherd of the sheep …and the sheep follow him: for they know his voice. And a stranger will they not follow, but will flee from him: for they know not the voice of strangers.* This parable (a story with a truth to be understood) *spake Jesus unto them: but they understood not. Then said Jesus …I am*

the door of the sheep. *All that ever come before me are thieves and robbers* (those who came before must have tried to enter some other way to be considered thieves and robbers, as mentioned earlier in the verse): *but the sheep did not hear them. I am* the door: *by me* (by the door of Jesus) *if any man enter in, he shall be saved* (First saved, then...), *...and find pasture* (or, fulfillment in life; that's freedom in Christ). *The thief* (the person who boasts of some other way) *cometh not but for to steal, and to kill, and to destroy* (That sounds like the destructive nature of our addictions). —John 10:1-10

If you today are struggling with a stubborn habit or addiction, what do these verses mean to you? It's very simple. The strait and narrow gate spoken of in Matthew 7:13-14 is the same door spoken of in this passage- it is Jesus Christ. Now, do you want to enjoy this way of pasture called freedom? It is an absolute freedom from not only the penalty of sin, but from the power of stubborn habits and addiction, as well! To receive this freedom, you must enter in through that narrow gate of Jesus. He is the only way to freedom!

Now who is this thief? The thief is that which tries to convince us that we can find freedom some other way rather than the door. In other words, society's many paths to freedom have been our thief. It has *stolen* our joy, *killed* our potential, and *destroyed* our life. It has robbed us of a happiness that most people don't even know is possible!

I'm sure by now, you may be thinking, "Is it impossible for a person to overcome an addiction through programs in society?" I am sure there are people in society's programs that have overcome various habits and addictions. Yet, I am equally sure that those people have had to put forth an incredible effort of self-discipline. They had to do <u>all</u> the work themselves. And I am sure that it appears to pay off. However, make

> To receive this freedom from the penalty and power of sin, you must enter in through the narrow gate of Jesus.

no mistake about it, they are *not* truly free from the power of that sin. Every day that battle will be with them. They will spend most days fighting that desire on a daily basis, never truly being free.

It would be much like being a slave that has been set free by his master, yet he chose to wear his chains the rest of his life. Sure, he could find another profession and not belong to that master, but he wouldn't be truly freed because he is still bound by what had previously controlled him.

Jesus is the gate that leads to a life of freedom from the bondage of habitual sin, and you have found it! (Matthew 7:13-14) The Devil's going to be after you, but don't get discouraged. This path is the only "way" to freedom. God's Word will be our "navigational tool" to keep us on the right path.

Personally, I've never been so free in my whole life! It's because I went through the right door after spending years trying to enter in so many different ways. I have no shackles to weigh me down; I'm free! If you get on the one right way, you too will find freedom and live an abundant Christian life! (John 10:10)

Jesus, the Truth

Entering in at the right gate and realizing that Jesus is the way is just the beginning. Jesus also reminds us He is the truth. Once again, take note of our key verse, John 14:6. *I am the way, **the truth**, and the life; no man cometh unto the Father but by me.*

The world teaches that there are many different truths that we can believe. But that can't be true! Truth will never conflict with itself. There must be one standard of truth whereby all else is judged. Our key verse tells us that the truth is Jesus Christ. So, how do we discern between what is truth and what is lie? John 17:17 tells us to *Sanctify them* (or, set them apart) *through thy truth: **thy word is truth.*** We are supposed to discern right from wrong by using the Word of Truth, the Bible. Hebrews 4:12 says that *the word of God… is a discerner of the thoughts and intents of the heart.* It will tell us if our thoughts are right or wrong.

Let's look at some of the lies of society. We will then analyze what our "standard of Truth," God's Word, has to say about these lies.

HOW WE LIVE WILL NOT AFFECT OUR RELATIONSHIP WITH A LOVING GOD.

The first lie of society is the false assumption that how we live our lives will not affect our relationship with a loving God. The general philosophy in society's programs is that we need to learn to discipline ourselves in that area of particular weakness, and the other "not-so-bad" areas have no real affect on our shortcomings. But according to 1 John 1:6, *If we say that we have fellowship* (or partnership) *with* [God], *and walk in darkness* (or, spiritual blindness), ***we lie, and do not the truth.*** But on the other end of the spectrum, the very next verse says, *But if we walk in the light* (or, spiritual direction), *as he is in the light* (or, spiritual direction), *we have fellowship one with another, and the blood of Jesus Christ his Son cleanseth us from all sin* (or, our wrong doings). In other words, we cannot reject truths of God's Word and say we are in a right relationship with God. It doesn't work. Sin always breaks fellowship! However, if we seek spiritual direction and deal with areas of sin as God directs us, fellowship is restored and we will walk in a right relationship with Him.

For many years I believed this lie of society. I knew that I had a problem with drinking and with drug addiction. However, I thought if I was able to overcome those two areas of my life, I would

> We cannot reject the truths of God's Word and say we are in a right relationship with God.

be a good person. But that is far from being true. I had deep-seeded sins that were embedded in my heart. I overlooked these sins, refusing to surrender them to the Lord. As these seeds of sin grew, they eventually led to my alcoholism and drug addiction. This lie of focusing on the addiction while overlooking the root cause kept me from focusing on the truth of my addiction. The truth was that I had failed to walk in fellowship with God. That was only going to be restored by walking in the light of spiritual direction found in God's Word. This spiritual direction reveals our heart's sin. As we confess and forsake that sin, our relationship with God will be restored.

THERE IS NO RIGHT FROM WRONG.

A second lie of society is that there is no right from wrong. There was a time in my life, though not a very long period of time, that I thought my lifestyle was not wrong. I was in my early twenties, holding a job, and social drinking, but I wasn't *really* living a bad life. I was enjoying myself, and I convinced myself that there was nothing wrong with my style of entertainment. I was just so sure that it was not sin.

The world teaches us that there is nothing wrong with certain "sins": social drinking, smoking, bad music, casual sex… the list could go on. But 1 John 1:8 and 10 says, *If we say that we have no sin, we deceive ourselves, and the truth is not in us. If we say that we have not sinned, we make him a liar, and his word is not in us.*

The remedy for our sin lies in 1 John 1:9. *If we confess* (or, agree with God about) *our sins* (or, wrong doings), *he is faithful* (or, consistent) *and just* (or, right) *to forgive* (or, to cease to hold to our charge) *us our sins* (or, wrong doings), *and to cleanse us* (or, make us feel better) *from all unrighteousness* (or, sinful behavior).

SOME CAN CLAIM TO BE CHRISTIAN, BUT YET THEIR LIFESTYLE WILL SHOW OTHERWISE.

A third lie of society is that some can claim to be Christian, but yet their lifestyle will show otherwise. First John 2:4 says, *He that saith, I know him* (Jesus), *and keepeth not his commandments is a liar, and the truth is not in him.* Once again, we are focusing on what the Bible says is truth and what the Bible says is a lie. According to this verse, if you say you know Jesus Christ, but yet you don't obey his commandments, you are a liar and the truth (Jesus) is not in you.

If we never grow in our Christian life, or never experience any God-given victory over sin, or if we are unable or unwilling to obey Biblical commandments that especially deal with our wrong doings, it could be that the Truth is not in us! First John 2:3, 5-6 go on to say, *And hereby we do know that we know him* (or, here is how we know if we are a child of God), *if we keep* (or, observe in order to obey) *his commandments. But whoso keepeth his word, in him verily is the love of God perfected: hereby know we that we are in him.*

He that saith he abideth in him (Jesus) *ought himself also so to walk, even as he* (Jesus) *walked.* It is not a power in ourselves to obey, but rather a submission to God's power that produces obedience. *In Him* means, to be under His control. If we are *in Him*, we will keep His Word.

As you begin growing in your Christian life, gaining victory over various habits, developing godly friendships, and serving in your local church, please remember this: there will be other people in society and in churches who will claim to be Christians, but their lifestyle will show otherwise. This could tempt us to give ground to the enemy that we have already re-claimed for the cause of Christ. It is a lie of the world that God doesn't expect obedience from his children. If we abide in Him we ought to walk as Jesus walked.

Though perfection will never be achieved here on earth, we ought to always be growing. Jesus, who was perfect, had to grow in wisdom as a child. As a new child of God, He stimulates growth through revealed sin. When we gain victory, we experience spiritual growth. That's how we can be sure the Truth (Jesus) is in us.

JESUS WAS A GREAT MAN, BUT HE WAS NOT THE CHRIST, OUR ATONING ONE.

A fourth lie of society is that Jesus was a great man, maybe even a prophet. But He was not the Christ, our Atoning One. First John 2:22 says, *Who is a liar but <u>he that denieth that Jesus is the Christ</u>. He is Anti-Christ that denieth the Father and the Son.* According to this verse, whoever says that Jesus Christ is anything less than the Savior of the world is a liar. The truth is found in John 3:16. *For God so loved the world, that he gave his only begotten Son* (Jesus), *that whosoever believeth in him* (Jesus) *should not perish, but* *have everlasting life.* We serve a risen Savior!

Jesus, the Son of God, came to earth as a propitiation (or, payment) for our sins. Because of His perfection and personal freedom from the law of sin and death, He is the only One that can truly set us free from the penalty and power of sin! He paid the debt that we could not pay. Our sin demanded our life, resulting in an eternity in Hell. But His blood was shed for our sake. We need only to accept His payment as our own! Whether we accept it or not, the payment is made. Man's part is only to believe and receive.

CHRISTIANS ARE HYPOCRITES WHO SHOW A LACK OF COMPASSION FOR OTHERS.

A fifth lie of society is that Christians are hypocrites who show a lack of compassion, even a hatred for others—even other Christians. Let's look at two passages out of 1 John.

- First John 3:15 *Whosoever hateth his brother is a murderer...*
- First John 4:19-20 *We love him* (Jesus), *because he first loved us. If a man say, I love God, and hateth his brother, he is a liar: for he that loveth not his brother whom he hath seen, how can he love God whom he hath not seen?*

These verses are saying that an outward evidence of an inward relationship with God is a compassion for others, especially for other children of God. God's children should never be apathetic to the needs and faults of others. It is sad that in some churches we see a lot of inner bickering, criticism, and negativity when discussing needy Christians. This doesn't please God! That type of behavior is of one who is a liar and does not love God.

When I used to attend various addiction programs in

society, people would testify of their "higher power" being the primary reason why they were able to overcome their addiction. I didn't really feel as if I had a "higher power." I thought I loved God, but I didn't have a strong relationship with Jesus Christ. However, as my relationship with Christ grew, I wanted to proclaim His name and let everyone know of the victory that He had given to me. I would go to these various programs and ecstatically testify that my "higher power" was Jesus Christ. The room would get very quiet. At times, I would be asked not to speak in detail concerning my particular "higher power" and His identity. It was as if these so-called "brothers" hated me or my "higher power!" Maybe they did! The reason Jesus Christ is somewhat offensive to them is because they have fallen for the previously discussed lie that Jesus was just a good man.

If you are in such a program, let me remind you that how they react to and talk about Christians should be an underlying factor in your decision whether you should stay under their personal counsel. As discussed previously, our training should come from someone who is seeking advice from God. If they are criticizing Christians and showing a lack of compassion for others, the Bible says that they are liars. The Truth (Jesus) is not in them.

The truth is found in 1 John 4:21, 3:11 and 14 *And this commandment have we from him, That he who loveth God love his brother also... For this is the message that ye heard from the beginning, that we should love one another... We know that we have passed from death unto life, <u>because we love the brethren</u>. He that loveth not his brother <u>abideth in death</u>.*

Now I have taken a few things that I remember as being lies in society's programs and compared them to the truths I have since found in God's Word.

I know that good has come from these programs; the purpose of discussing these lies of society is not to criticize other programs. It is to analyze the truth. My main concern is for the eternal destiny of your soul, not your current battle with addiction! God can take that away in but a moment, but hell lasts forever! There is a better "way," and that's God's Truth—His Son, Jesus!

Now, I want to show you where all of these lies in society are coming from. They are not coming from the well-meaning people who are feeding them to you. They are coming from the devil himself.

Who makes a truth or a lie? There's a father for each—an origin, if you will. The devil is the father of all lies; and he has an intention for each one of those lies. His purpose is to keep us in the dark, to keep us from getting saved. And if we are already saved, his purpose is to keep us from growing in the grace of God and knowledge of Jesus Christ.

Once we receive Christ as our personal Savior, the devil can never get control of our eternal destiny. We are a child of God for all time. However, if he can keep our testimony (or, the story of our life) from affecting other people's lives, he then succeeds in making us a useless Christian.

John 8:44 says, *Ye are of your father the devil, and the lust of your father ye will do.* (Now he describes the devil) *He was a murderer from the beginning and abode not in the truth, because there is no truth in him. When he speaketh a lie, he speaketh of his own: for he is a liar and the father of it.* The devil is the father of all lies.

If the devil is the father of all lies, then it is equally easy to discover the origin of all truth. Let's see what the Bible teaches us about the father of truth.

Looking again at our key verse, John 14:6, *Jesus* (God's Son) *saith unto him, I am the way, the truth, and the life: no man cometh unto the Father, but by me.* We have already settled that Jesus is the Truth. If Jesus is Truth, and God is His Father (both physically and spiritually), that makes God the Father of the Truth. The devil is the father of all lies, and God is the Father of all Truth. God created what is right; the devil created what is wrong. These two facts are the basis for the battle within each of us. Who will control you? Right, or wrong? Truth, or lie? God, or the devil?

Thus, we can conclude that "the Truth," or Jesus, is our source of freedom from all sin. To fully comprehend this principle, let's look at John 8:31-32. These verses contain a formula for freedom. I believe that these two verses are the two most important verses in the Word of God on how to find freedom from the penalty and power of sin and its habitual hold on people! By dissecting and defining this verse, let's discover Christ's formula for freedom.

FORMULA FOR FREEDOM

> *Then said Jesus to those Jews which believed on him, If ye continue in my word, then are ye my disciples indeed; And ye shall know the truth, and the truth shall make you free..* —John 8:31-32

Step one of our formula for freedom is to believe on Jesus. (*Then said Jesus to those Jews which believed on him...*) The very first key to being set free from our addiction, and from the power and penalty of sin, set free from the control the devil has on us is to believe on Jesus!

- Mark 9:23 *Jesus said unto him, **if** thou canst believe, all things are possible to him that* *believeth.*

- John 3:16b *...that whosoever believeth in him should not perish, but have everlasting life.*

If you have not taken this first step, then stop taking your twelve steps! They are a waste of time! Step one is to believe on Jesus.

Step two of our formula for freedom is to continue in His Word. *(If ye continue in my word)* Jesus' Word is the Bible. John 15:7 says, *If ye abide in me, and <u>my word abide in you,</u> ye shall ask what ye will, and it shall be done unto you.* So many of us have gone to the Lord in prayer and said, "Oh, Lord, will You please remove this addiction, this stubborn habit, that I have? Could You please find it in Your heart, Lord, to help me?" But the Bible says that God's Word must abide in us to have our prayers answered. God will answer that prayer, but it requires that the Word of God abide in us.

God's Word cannot abide in us if we are not spending time in the Word of God. It's so easy to allow it to become a low priority in our lives. We will read for a period of time, then we go a few days without reading. The key is to <u>continue</u> in His Word. The fruit of daily persistence in reading, studying, memorizing, and meditation on the Bible will produce spiritual freedom. Our addictions and stubborn habits will eventually be overcome as God's Word abides in us and we abide in Him. This means that God's Word goes in and we yield to it. That is His Word abiding *in you* and you *in Him.* That brings victory!

Second Timothy 3:14-17 says, *But <u>continue</u> thou in the things which thou hast learned and hast been assured of, knowing of whom thou hast learned them. And that from a child thou hast known the holy scriptures, which are able to* *make thee wise unto salvation through faith which is in Christ Jesus. All scripture is given by inspiration of God, and is profitable* (or, the Bible's main purpose is) *for doctrine* (what is right), *for reproof* (what is not right), *for correction* (how to get right), *for instruction in righteousness* (how to stay right)*: That the man of God may be perfect, throughly furnished unto all good works.*

If we put those definitions together, we see that the main purpose for the Word of God is to teach a Christian what is right, what is not right (truth and lies), how to get right and how to stay right. Why does the Lord want to teach us what's right, what's not right, how to get right, and how to stay right? So *...that the man of God* (or, the Christian) *may be perfect, throughly furnished* (or, thoroughly equipped) *unto all good works.*

Step three of our formula for freedom is to be His disciple. *...then are ye my disciples indeed;* (John 8:31) A disciple is a student who follows His leader. This means that as we study under Him, we must also follow Him with our lives. Matthew 16:24-25 says, *Then said Jesus unto his disciples, If any man will come after me, let him deny himself, and take up his cross, and follow me. For whosoever will save his life shall lose it: and whosoever will lose his life for my sake shall find it.*

The cross that Jesus carried to Calvary and was hung upon was not His cross to bear; it was ours. He died for us! He died for you! He died in our place! That cross belonged to us. The cross was our burden to carry- not Jesus'; and He bore that burden for us. Matthew 16:24-25 is teaching us that if we want to follow Jesus, we must deny our own desires and pick up someone else's burdens. Pick up someone else's problems and carry them on our shoulders. We need to die to ourselves and follow Jesus' perfect example of meeting the needs of a dying world!

For whosoever will save his life shall lose it: We like to focus on our own problems and our prosperity. But if we do, we will lose it all. But ...*whosoever will lose his life for my sake shall find it.* Give your life to serving Jesus and you will find a life worth living, free from sin's power.

> The more we get to know Jesus, the more we will learn about Him and His freedom!

Step four of our formula for freedom found in John 8:32 is that we will know Truth. (*And ye shall know the Truth...*) Second Peter 3:18 says, *But grow in grace, and in the knowledge of our Lord and Saviour Jesus Christ.* That is the goal of a disciple (or, student follower) of Jesus. The more we get to know Jesus, the greater our level of freedom! John 8:32 tells us the result of our belief in Jesus and remaining under the influence of the Word—...*and the truth* (Jesus) *shall make you free.* A new child of God won't know Jesus very well. However, the more we get to know Jesus, the more we will learn about Him and His freedom!

Let's dissect and define Hebrews 5:13-14 to understand the growth process of a new Christian. *For every one that useth milk* (or, the simple things in the Bible) *is unskillful in the word of righteousness* (or, right living)*: for he is a babe* (or, new Christian). *But strong meat belongeth to them that are of full age* (or, grown up)*, even those who by reason of use* (or, repeated experiences) *have their senses* (or, thought processes) *exercised* (or, trained) *to discern* (or, consider) *both good and evil.*

This verse is teaching us that when we first come to Christ, we won't understand everything in the Bible; but don't get discouraged about that! God will help us understand little bits and pieces as we continue to be taught the Bible. So when you study the Bible, be patient with yourself! Be willing to learn a little at a time. The Lord is giving you just a little bit of "milk" because you are just a little baby. If He gave you strong truths, it would ruin your digestive system and stunt your spiritual growth!

Think about it this way. If we were to feed a baby a steak, it would destroy his digestive system; he isn't ready for the "strong meat" yet. Likewise, when the Bible feeds us milk, we grow spiritually and become strong. Then we can begin taking in "strong meat" as we develop. Strong meat is for those who are ...*of full age, even those who by reason of use have their senses exercised to discern both good and evil.* This means that they have used the Bible so much to discern what's right (doctrine), what's not right (reproof), how to get right (correction), and how to stay right (instruction in righteousness), that their thoughts are trained to consider both good and evil. They can continue in the Word because the Word continues in them.

All freedom is found in knowing Jesus and having a personal relationship with Him. That relationship comes from believing in Him and a willingness to be His student follower under the textbook of the Bible.

These four steps added together equal freedom. ...*And the Truth* (Jesus) *shall make you free.* (John 8:32b) Can you see how it all ties together? The more we know Jesus, the more freedom we gain! This takes the "us" right out of it. We're not the ones who make ourselves free. We are unable to do it. It's Jesus Christ alone that allows us to experience any kind of freedom, and it's only through His prerequisites of belief and discipleship.

Now remaining free from our addictions will require a yielding to His Spirit on our part; that's where "continuing in His Word" comes in. You see, we have a free will and a choice to return to this bondage. It's as if the prison doors are open and we choose to remain inside. Or, we come out of the prison doors, only to return when under pressure. We have a choice. Proverbs 26:11 says, *As a dog returneth to his vomit, so a fool returneth to his folly.* We are free; it is up to us to respond properly to our release from sin's custody and control!

If we stay busy serving the Lord and being His disciple (student follower), it will help us avoid temptation. Romans 6:18 says, *Being then made free from sin, ye became the servants of righteousness.* Because He's made us free, it is our duty to *become* a servant of righteousness. If we decide to use this freedom as opportunity to live our own life, you *will* fail. There's no option about it. His desire is that we serve Him because of what He has done for us. Service to others is an evidence of our appreciation for our salvation!

Finally, we need to remain unmovable in our beliefs. Galatians 5:1 says, *Stand fast* (or, unmovable) *therefore in the liberty* (or, freedom) *wherewith* **Christ** *hath made us free, and be not entangled again with the yoke of bondage.*

Jesus is the Truth. The more we know of Jesus the more freedom we will gain. And, friend, *If the Son therefore shall make you free, you* **shall be free indeed.** (John 8:38)

Jesus, the Life

Life is very important. We are only afforded one while here on earth. We all want a full and enjoyable life; but how do we attain that? And how do we gain this type of life while at the same time overcoming sin? Let's look at some of the world's philosophy on what makes a good life and compare it to Jesus, who is "the life."

THE ACCRUAL OF EARTHLY POSSESSIONS DEMONSTRATES A SUCCESSFUL LIFE.

While addicted to drugs, I realized that by dealing narcotics I could acquire many worldly possessions. I foolishly believed that once I received those possessions, I'd be a happy man. That definitely proved not to be true; it was a lie! Society will tell us that the accrual of earthly possessions demonstrates a successful life.

Luke 12:15 says, *And he* (Jesus) *said unto them, Take heed; and beware of covetousness* (or, the desire to have things that other people have): *for a man's life consisteth not in the abundance of the things which he possesseth.* I am so grateful that I discovered this truth! I'm not against having nice things; God isn't either. However, we err when our life is focused on the *abundance* of possessions. Life consists of so much more than the abundance of the things that we possess.

God has promised to meet our needs, but only if our life is focused on *His* heavenly possessions. Philippians 4:19 says, *But my God shall supply all your need according to his riches in glory by Christ Jesus.*

The Bible gives a parable (a story that tells of a lesson to be learned) of a rich man who made the mistake of believing that a successful life was dependent on his accrual of earthly possessions and enjoyable entertainment. Let us learn from his mistake.

Luke 12:16-23 *And he* (Jesus) *spake a parable unto them, saying, The ground of a certain rich man brought forth plentifully: And he thought within himself saying, What shall I do, because I have no room where to bestow* *my fruits? And he said, This will I do: I will pull down my barns, and build greater; and there will I bestow all my fruits and my goods. And I will say to my soul, Soul, thou hast much goods laid up for many years; take thine ease, eat, drink, and be merry. But God said unto him, Thou fool, this night thy soul shall be required of thee: then whose shall those things be, which thou hast provided? So is he that layeth up treasure for himself, and is not rich toward God. And he (Jesus) said unto his disciples, Therefore, I say unto you, Take no thought for <u>your life</u>, what ye shall eat; neither for the body, what ye shall put on. <u>The life</u> is more than meat, and the body is more than raiment.*

This rich man in Luke 12 had a bumper crop. He decided to build bigger and better barns for his abundant harvest. He was set for many years to come; life was good! What did he do then? He decided to just take life easy, to eat, drink, and be merry. Oh, how foolish! That night his life was required of him. He was a man who had been blessed, had more than he would ever need. But instead of focusing on how he could use his abundance for the Lord's work, or how he could better serve others; he decided to pool all that money into earthly possessions and to enjoy his life. He died that night, probably from drunkenness!

There is a moral to this story that will help us avoid this catastrophe in our life. Love God rather than life. This will result in a love of life. In this life, many are searching for happiness. All the years I struggled with my addiction, I was looking for love, enjoyment, happiness, contentment, financial prosperity; and these were the things that the Lord kept from me! Since my change of focus from self toward God, I have found a true joy and contentment in my life that only God could give. It is a joy and contentment that without Him, man could never attain.

To help us better understand this, let's dissect and define 1 John 2:15-17. *Love not the world, neither the things that are in the world. If any man love the world, the love of the Father is not in him. For all that is in the world, the lust of the flesh, and the lust of the eyes, and the pride of life, is not of the Father, but is of the world. And the world passeth away, and the lust thereof: but he that doeth the will of God abideth for ever.*

Love not the world. What is the "world?" God gives us a definition in the very next verse. *For all that is in the world,* **#1- *the lust of the flesh,*** *and* **#2- *the lust of the eyes,*** *and* **#3- *the pride of life…*** The world is made up of the lust of the flesh, the lust of the eyes, and the pride of life. You are probably asking right now, "What in the world does that mean?" Let's look at each one.

The lust of the flesh is a controlling desire to do.

The lust of the flesh is the controlling desire that tempts you to do anything you could ever want to do. If a man could *do* anything he ever wanted to do in his lifetime no matter what it was… go to a Chicago Bears game, fly the fastest jet around the world, talk with the President, go to Disneyland, anything he ever wanted to do… that would be a man who has gained one-third of the world. However, there's still two-thirds of the world yet to gain.

The lust of the eyes is a compulsive urge to have.

What you see, you want. If a man could *have* anything he ever wanted during his lifetime... a new car, nice big house, his very own island, his own country, anything he ever wanted... that would be a man who has gained the second third of the world. But there is still one-third left.

The pride of life is the consuming urge to be.

The pride of life is what you want to become. If I could be the president of my high school class... if I could be the president of a corporation... if I could be the President of the United States... if I could be a dictator of the world... If a man could *be* whatever he ever wanted to be during his lifetime, this would be a man who has gained the last third of the world.

So, if a man could *do* anything he ever wanted to do, *have* anything he ever wanted to have, or *be* anything he ever wanted to be during his lifetime, this would be a man who would have gained the entire world!

However, the Bible says that if you were to take that man who could *do, have,* or *be* it all and set him on one end of a scale with a new convert crippled with addiction on the other end of the scale, and ask the Lord to choose which one is of more value to him, He will choose the person with the addiction, the person crippled with the sin. Why? Because of Matthew 16:26 *For what is a man profited, if he shall gain the whole world, and lose his own soul?* What does it profit a man if he gains everything he ever wanted to do, be, or have, yet he loses his own soul? The verse in 1 John goes on to explain why it is futile to gain the whole world. *...the world passeth away, and the lust* (or, the desires to do, be and have) *thereof: but he that doeth the will of God abideth for ever.*

At the conclusion of the parable of the rich man recorded in

Luke 12:31 we are reminded, *But rather seek ye <u>first</u> the kingdom of God, and all these things* (that you want to be, do, or have) *shall be added unto you.*

What does it profit a man if he gains everything he ever wanted to do, be, or have, yet he loses his own soul?

THERE IS ONLY ONE LIFE; LIVE IT UP!

"You only live life once, so just live it up!" But Jesus taught that our life should be sacrificed so that He can bless us with a better life. Once again, we see in Luke 17:33 that, *Whosoever shall seek to save his life shall lose it; and whosoever shall lose his life shall preserve it.* Proverbs 8:35 also tells us, *For whoso findeth me* (Jesus) *findeth life, and shall obtain favor of the Lord.* There is an old saying that is so simple, but yet so true—'Tis one life will soon be past. Only what's done for Christ will last. Jesus wants us to sacrifice this life for His cause. There may be only one life here in this world, but there is good news, my friend. This life <u>can be better</u>, and there is another life after this one.

Luke 18:29-30 says, *And he* (Jesus) *said unto them, Verily I say unto you, there is no man that hath left house, or parents, or brethren, or wife, or children, for the kingdom of God's sake* (in other words, there's nothing we wouldn't give up for God) *who shall not receive manifold more <u>in this present time</u> and in the <u>world to come</u> life everlasting.* What a wonderful promise from God! There's nothing that we can give up, nothing that we can sacrifice, no matter what it is, that God will not give us much more in return in this life and in the life to come. He will not only give us more, but He will give us a life that lasts forever. Amen to that!

...Once to Die

Hebrews 9:27 *It is appointed unto men once to die, but after this the judgment:*

Unfortunately, for those of us who are not focused on giving to the Lord our lives, God reminds us that *this* life will end in His judgment.

- Romans 14:10b *...for we shall all stand before the judgment seat of Christ.*
- Second Corinthians 5:10 *For we must all appear before the judgment seat of Christ; that every one may receive the things done in his body, according to that he hath done, whether it be good or bad.*

Our entire lives we have heard lies about how we should live, for whom we should live, what is right and what is wrong, different ways to get to heaven... many lies, only one Truth. The Truth is free and obtainable through belief in God's Son, Jesus Christ. Remember God's plan?

- John 3:16 *For God so loved the world, that he gave his only begotten Son, that whosoever believeth in him should not perish, but have everlasting life.*
- Romans 10:9-10 *That if thou shalt confess with thy mouth the Lord Jesus, and shalt believe in thine heart that God hath raise him from the dead, thou shalt be saved. For with the heart man believeth unto righteousness; and with the mouth confession is made unto salvation.*

Do you believe in your heart that God sent Jesus to die for *your* sins, and three days later He rose from the grave, defeating death? You need only to accept Christ's payment of your sin debt by receiving His gift of eternal life. Faith in Jesus will save you from eternal life in Hell and replace it with eternal life in Heaven. First John 5:13 says, *These things have I written unto you that believe on the name of the Son of God; that ye may* **know** *that ye have eternal life and that ye may believe on the name of the Son of God.*

Freedom from addiction is <u>not</u> freedom from drugs and alcohol; it's not freedom from pornography; and it's not freedom from smoking, television, or the love of money. Freedom from addiction is being out from under the control of this world and under the control of Jesus. Freedom is control. It's not what controls you that separates freedom from bondage, it's *who* controls you that separates freedom from bondage. That's God's honest Truth!

Jesus *is* the only Way, the only Truth, and the only Life. Know Jesus and He *will* make you free… finally!

Chapter 2

𝕿𝖍𝖊 2 𝕮𝖔𝖒𝖒𝖆𝖓𝖉𝖒𝖊𝖓𝖙𝖘 𝖔𝖋 𝕮𝖍𝖗𝖎𝖘𝖙

Then one of them, which was a lawyer, asked him a question, tempting him, and saying, Master, which is the great commandment in the law? Jesus said unto him, Thou shalt love the Lord thy God with all thy heart, and with all thy soul, and with all thy mind. This is the first and great commandment. And the second is like unto it, Thou shalt love thy neighbor as thyself. On these two commandments hang all the law and the prophets.
–Matthew 22:35-40

As we saw in chapter one, Jesus is the source of our freedom from the penalty of sin. But did you know there is a second freedom that He provides to believers? It is a life free from not only the penalty of sin, but also the *power* of sin! But just like we chose to accept Christ's first gift of freedom, we must choose to accept this second freedom, as well.

You see, the cross represents our freedom from the penalty of sin by Christ's death, and the empty tomb represents our freedom from the power of sin by His resurrection. In Philippians 3:10, the Apostle Paul wrote longingly, *That I may know him, and the power of his resurrection.* By Christ's resurrection is how we can have the power of new life in Him, and that power is experienced by *knowing* Him. Learning how to know Jesus will be our focus from this point forward, as we delve into the way, truth, and life of living freely in a bound world.

As we look at our chapter key verse, have you ever wondered what it would be like to just sit down with Jesus and ask His advice on things? What would He say is the most important thing upon which to focus our lives? If He were to wrap up all His teachings into one truth, what would it be? Actually, the Bible answers these questions. Jesus summed up His entire ministry with two commandments on which everything in the Christian life will hinge.

Before we take a look at them, let's discuss the background of the above passage. Within these two verses are three lessons that are still applicable to our lives two thousand years later.

CHRISTIANS WILL ALWAYS BE QUESTIONED.
Then one of them, which was a lawyer, asked him a question...

Take time to imagine the scene here. Jesus is sitting in the temple, teaching a multitude of people. The people are fascinated with everything about Him! He can perform the impossible; He cares about the needs of the people; His knowledge and wisdom are superior to any other! The minds and hearts of some of them are beginning to believe that this is the Promised One–their Messiah!

Yet, there are negative elements in the crowd–the religious leaders of their city, the Pharisees and Sadducees. Jesus' teachings discredited the work to which their lives had been devoted! Jesus taught belief in Himself to be saved from the penalty of sin, while they looked for their salvation in the fulfillment of the Law. On several occasions they tried to trick Jesus into doing or saying something contrary to the Law. Such is the situation we have before us. But Jesus' response to their sinister, tempting questions always moved the people to love Him even more!

Now we hear from a lawyer, who was a Pharisee. We see in our text that he was coming for the purpose of tempting Jesus in order to publicly discredit Him.

Here is our first lesson. When you become a Christian, people in your life are going to question your beliefs. They will question three basic beliefs: *what* we believe, *why* we believe it, and *why they should* believe it. To be prepared for these types of questions, we must have our hearts yielded to God so that His Spirit might lead us in our response. First Peter 3:15 explains how we ought to prepare for these types of questions. *But sanctify* (or, make holy) *the Lord God in your hearts* (or, your thoughts and feelings): *and be ready always to give an answer to every man that asketh you a reason of the hope* (or, confidence) *that is in you with meekness and fear* (or, humility and reverence). Dissected and defined, this verse is saying, "Think holy thoughts so that we will be ready to give an answer to anyone that asks about the confident faith we now have. But do so with a humble attitude and an awe of appreciation for what God has done."

Colossians 4:5-6 reminds us to, *Walk in wisdom toward them that are without* (or, unsaved)*, redeeming* (or, valuing) *the time. Let your speech be alway with grace, seasoned with salt, that ye may know how ye ought to answer every man.* We ought to walk

> Think holy thoughts so that you will be ready to give an answer to anyone that asks about the confident faith you now have. But do so with a humble attitude and an awe of appreciation for what God has done.

wisely when we are around people that are without Christ! They are watching us! As they are watching us, they are formulating thoughts and opinions that may lend to questions. That is why it is so important that we know *why* we believe *what* we believe. *Redeeming the time* means to take advantage of every opportunity that God gives us to witness to them; make that question and answer time worth something.

Verse 6 gives us a guideline to follow when sharing the Gospel. *Let your speech be alway with grace, seasoned with salt...* When telling others about Jesus, be appropriate! What happens when we put salt on food? It tastes better; it goes down easier; it adds flavor. When we are explaining the Gospel to somebody, our speech should be appropriate–*seasoned with salt*–so that it is more "palatable" to the hearer. Good news, when presented properly, will always satisfy a hungry soul. When it is presented improperly, it can often destroy the appetite for it.

Another question of even greater importance is, *why should they* believe it? What's different from what we believe compared to what they believe? You see, we all believe in something–something we believe to be the truth. Second Timothy 3:5 defines the world's belief system as *Having a form of godliness, but denying the power thereof.*

In 2 Corinthians 5:9-12, Paul wrote to the church of Corinth regarding living a life that is acceptable to the Lord (vs. 9). Why? Because we will all have to give an account for everything we do (vs. 10). He pointed out that as a result of knowing that all men will have to give an account, *we persuade men* (vs. 11). He went on to say in verse 12, *we* (Paul and Timothy) *give you occasion to glory on our behalf, that ye may have somewhat to answer to them which glory in appearance, and not in heart.* What in the world does that mean? Let's dissect and define this verse.

We ...give you occasion to glory on our behalf... Paul is saying, "What God is doing through our ministry is an opportunity for you and your work to look good for God's benefit."

that ye may have somewhat to answer... "Because of what you have seen God do, you have a reason and an opportunity to share your answer with them which glory in appearance, and not in heart."

to them which glory in appearance, and not in heart. Who are they? These are the 2 Timothy 3:5 people. Their glory is in the outward man. They may look right, act right, and do right, but they are not right. Remember the religious crowd we were talking about in our key passage in Matthew 22? This would be them. The world has foolishly believed the lie that if the appearance is right, they're okay with God. But *the LORD seeth not as man seeth; for man looketh on the outward appearance, but the LORD looketh on the heart* (1 Samuel 16:7). In conjunction to this, Proverbs 23:7 says, *as* [a man] *thinketh in his heart, so is he.* The heart of the matter is a matter of the heart.

THE DEVIL WILL TEST OUR KNOWLEDGE OF GOD'S WORD.

Then one of them, which was a lawyer, asked him a question, tempting him…

This lawyer was actually trying to trick Jesus on His knowledge of the Scriptures! As we grow in our relationship with the Lord, the devil will constantly use others to tempt our knowledge of God's Word; his desire is to cast doubt in our mind. For instance, when you are in the midst of a trial, the Spirit reminds you that …*There hath no temptation taken you but such as is common to man: but God is faithful, who will not suffer you to be tempted above that ye are able; but will with the temptation also make a way to escape, that ye may be able to bear it* (1 Corinthians 10:13). But then Satan will whisper in your ear, "God doesn't really care about you. If He did, He wouldn't be allowing this to happen to you." Satan won't give up, either, friend. This is one of the many reasons why it is so important that you spend time daily growing in your knowledge of God's Word and rejecting anything or anyone that contradicts it.

Now, do not be so foolish as to believe that you will be an exception to this temptation. Satan is very skilled. The following are two Biblical examples that show Satan at work trying to cause someone to doubt God's Word.

The Garden of Eden–Genesis 3:1-5

Now the serpent (Satan) *was more subtle than any beast of the field which the LORD God had made. And he said unto the woman, Yea, hath God said* (Satan questioned God's Word and her knowledge of it)*, Ye shall not eat of every tree of the garden? And the woman said unto the serpent, We may eat of the fruit of the trees of the garden:*

But of the fruit of the tree which is in the midst of the garden, God hath said, Ye shall not eat of it, neither shall ye touch it (wrong–God had only said not to eat of it), *lest ye die. And the serpent said unto the woman, Ye shall not surely die* (Satan contradicted the Word of God): *For God doth know that in the day ye eat thereof, then your eyes shall be opened, and ye shall be as gods, knowing good and evil.*

The devil challenged Eve's knowledge of what God had said. He does the same with us. If he can get us to doubt what we know to be true in the Bible, he can then get us to doubt or fail to recollect God's goodness. You see, it wasn't that he was trying to trick Eve into believing that she could eat the fruit and get away with it. He attacked Eve's ability to trust God for what was good for her and her husband. He twisted the truth by saying, "If you eat of this tree, you will be just like Him. God knows that, and He doesn't want you to be like Him." He convinced Eve to doubt God's goodness to her.

I have counseled many students who fail in their walk with the Lord by indulging in stubborn habits. They inevitably ask, "Why doesn't God take this temptation away?" The problem is not that the temptation was there; the problem is that they did not take God's "way of escape." God's goodness leads to repentance (Romans 2:4). When we focus on God's goodness, then we will change our mind concerning our desire to indulge in a particular temptation. However, Adam and Eve chose to believe the lie of the devil as he tricked them into doubting God's goodness to them. Notice, as well, how the devil tempted them. He used an outside influence to stimulate the lust of the flesh, the lust of the eyes, and the pride of life. He showed them it was a tree that was good for food (lust of the flesh), and pleasant to the eyes (lust of the eyes), and a tree to be desired to make one wise (pride of life). This is how the devil works.

The Temptation of Christ–Luke 4:9-13

And he (Satan) *brought him* (Jesus) *to Jerusalem, and set him on a pinnacle of the temple, and said unto him, If thou be the Son of God, cast thyself down from hence: For it is written, He shall give his angels charge over thee, to keep thee: And in their hands they shall bear thee up, lest at any time thou dash thy foot against a stone. And Jesus answering said unto him, It is said, Thou shalt not tempt the Lord thy God. And when the devil had ended all the temptation, he departed from him for a season.*

The above passage is just the last part of the story of Jesus' temptation in the wilderness. He had been there forty days. Yet, in these verses we notice three truths: First, Satan's temptations came after a spiritual high-point of Jesus' ministry–His baptism. This happens so often! After you have experienced a great victory in your Christian life, watch out! Right around the corner is a trap of Satan awaiting you. New levels bring new devils. Second, Satan used Scripture for the purpose of temptation, and Jesus used Scripture to refute Satan. Third, once Jesus gained victory, Satan *departed* (but only)…*for a season*. Satan will usually return.

We have seen Satan tempting our knowledge of God's Word from the beginning of time and even during the ministry of Jesus. And, he is still doing it today. In fact, the Bible warns us to expect it: *Knowing this first, that there shall come in the last days scoffers, walking after their own lusts, And saying, Where is the promise of his coming? for since the fathers fell asleep, all things continue as they were from the beginning of the creation* (2 Peter 3:3-4).

THERE ARE THOSE WHO SAY THEY ARE FOLLOWERS OF CHRIST, BUT THEIR RESPONSES TO HIM SHOW THEY ARE NOT.

...a lawyer, asked him a question, tempting him, and saying, Master...

Scoffers will come in our life. They will test our faith and our knowledge of Scripture. Our next lesson from this passage deals with these scoffers and doubters who may even claim to be followers of Jesus! In our key verse, we see a well-educated man following Jesus from place to place. He eventually poses a question to Jesus, but introduces his question by first calling Jesus "Master." That is to say "teacher," or "leader."

If we were to meet this man, we would probably consider him a very godly man. He acted right, dressed right, and talked right, but he was dangerous. Was he dangerous to our Lord? Of course not. However, his questions had the potential to cast doubt in the hearts of the other followers who considered Jesus to actually be their teacher, their master. This man was dangerous to those who were just beginning to accept the message of Christ.

Herein lies our third lesson. All believers, especially new believers, must protect themselves from so-called followers of Christ who are not believers in Christ.

Friends should care about your spiritual condition. Enemies do not. If you have friends that do not care about your spiritual condition, you need to find new friends. Even when we think we have good friends, they can still do things to harm our spiritual development. Jesus, who was perfect, still had friends who brought him harm. Notice this truth concerning Jesus' friend Judas found in Matthew

26:48-50. *Now he that betrayed him gave them a sign, saying, Whomsoever I shall kiss, that same is he: hold him fast. And forthwith he came to Jesus, and said, Hail, <u>master</u>; and kissed him. And Jesus said unto him, <u>Friend</u>, wherefore art thou come? Then came they, and laid hands on Jesus, and took him.* Judas appeared to look to Jesus as his teacher, his master. They were friends, but still he doubted Christ's plan for him and did what he deemed was best for *himself*, not Jesus! Your friends need to believe the things you believe. If they doubt your doctrine, the devil might use them, like he did with Judas, to try to get you to doubt God's plan for you.

There are many who claim to follow Christ and may seek to befriend you. They may even have what appears to be great knowledge about God and power with God. Remember that having apparent spiritual gifts does not necessarily make someone the right type of person to befriend. Matthew 7:22-23 tells of people who had a great degree of spiritual power; I would imagine they would have appeared to be very good Christians, but they were not even saved. *Many will say to me in that day, Lord, Lord, have we not prophesied in thy name? and in thy name have cast out devils? and in thy name done many wonderful works? And then will I profess unto them, I never knew you: depart from me, ye that work iniquity.* Great power? Yes! But power with God? No! Wonderful works? No doubt! But wonderful relationship? Not even close! God says that He never even knew them. The word "knew" means "personal," such as personal property. In essence He is saying, "Depart from Me because you were not My personal property." They called him "Lord;" they preached and did miracles in His name, not the name of false gods; they performed *many* wonderful works. Good people? Maybe so. But *not* Christians; and they would be even worse friends! Make sure your friends believe what you believe and make sure they are followers of our Lord.

A key question to ask ourselves when picking our Christian friends is, what type of followers are they? The man in our key verse was a follower of Jesus, but he was also a tempter of Jesus. Judas was a follower of Jesus, but he was also a betrayer of Jesus. The false prophets and miracle workers in Matthew 7 were followers of Jesus but not believers in Jesus.

You see, a true follower is known by obedience. Jesus said in Luke 6:46, *And why call ye me, Lord, Lord, and do not the things which I say?* Wow! What a convicting verse! We call Him "Lord, Lord" (which is what the unsaved people called Him in Matthew 7) and yet we do not obey Him. Jesus told us that His sheep follow what He tells them. In John 10:26-27 He said, *But ye believe not, because ye are not of my sheep, as I said unto you. My sheep hear my voice, and I know them, and they follow me:* He not only speaks to His sheep, but His sheep follow His spoken word. What is the key ingredient to being

> A true follower is known by his obedience.

His sheep? Believing in Him. He goes on to say, "I know them." Oh, how glad I am that He will not say to me one day, "I never knew you," but rather will say, "I know him." Why? Because I believed. After that, I made a conscious choice to exercise my belief by following His word, spoken and written. I became obedient. You must do this to become victorious over stubborn habits; and you must surround yourself with others who will do this, as well.

Once you have accepted these truths–1. Christians will always be questioned; 2. The devil will tempt your knowledge of God's Word; and, 3. There are those who say they are followers of Christ, but their responses to Him show they are not–you may prepare yourself to do battle by taking the focus off of yourself and committing to follow the Two Commandments of Christ.

The Two Commandments of Christ

Here it is! Jesus' well thought-out response to those tempting His knowledge of God's Word. He chose to indulge the lawyer by answering him with the two responsibilities upon which your freedom in Christ will hinge. If you will live with a conscious effort to obey these two responsibilities, the first will remove your addiction, and the second will keep it from coming back.

Jesus said unto him, Thou shalt love the Lord thy God with all thy heart (or, your emotions)*, and with all thy soul* (or, your will)*, and with all thy mind* (or, your thoughts). *This is the first and great commandment* (Matthew 22:37-38).

LOVE THE LORD YOUR GOD

Our first responsibility is to God–to love *Him* with *all* our heart, with *all* our soul, and with *all* our mind. Our heart, soul, and mind are what I call our "outer man." It is who we are apart from God. The inner man, which is quickened (or, made alive) at salvation, is where the Spirit of God lives. This is the part of our being that died in the garden but was made alive upon the second birth. It is the part of us that communicates with God. The problem is that the outer man loves himself. Our love of self constrains the Spirit of God from flowing through us. The first and great commandment is telling us to love God with our outer man–our heart, soul, and mind. This is our responsibility to God. Meeting this responsibility will break the outer man, thus allowing the inner man to flow through us. *Meeting your responsibility to God will remove your addiction!* Let's look at each element of this responsibility.

All Your Heart

If we love God with all our heart, then we will love Him with our entire emotional being. The heart is the seat of emotions and passions. Emotional highs and emotional lows often lead to indulging in selfish sin. When we feel emotionally drained, we tend to get selfish. God's Spirit, who lives within us, cannot flow through us when our emotions are running or ruining our lives.

Sinful habits are often fueled by our unchecked emotions. But placing our emotions under the control of the Holy Spirit will allow God to defeat our outer man. Circumstances of life, which work together for our good, are allowed by God and are intended to break that outer man. Nevertheless, we get upset with these circumstances. We get emotionally upset or discouraged, and we fail to see that God is working on our behalf through our circumstances. If we would look at these circumstances as being helpful to our development, then His joy–which is a fruit (or, outcome) of His Spirit–would flow through us even during adversity.

If you will learn to not yield to your emotions, you will love God with your entire heart. But there is more. You must love God with...

All Your Soul

The soul is the human will–what we want to do, what we want to be, what we want to have. Love God with *all* your soul. This requires a complete, sacrificial surrender of our will to exercise and experience life as we would prefer. We all have plans for our lives–both day-to-day and long-term.

But do we consciously make these decisions in alignment with what we believe God would have us to do, be, or have?

What our souls want in life often conflicts with God's desires for our lives. We must force our desires (our human will) to yield to God's desires. We often think that if we were to get what we want out of life, it would bring contentment. When God gives us something different from what our souls desire, it is intended, once again, to work together for our good. Yet, many times, we get frustrated with this; our wish is not His command. We follow after the flesh and allow God's ways truly to bother us. But God's ways are not our ways. His will is intended to break our outer man so that the inner man can flow out of us.

If you will accept this truth, you will begin to love God with all your soul, because your soul will love what God wants you to be, do, and have. Your outer man will be broken and God's Spirit will have free course. He will guide your every decision. Should you indulge in your addiction? That's a hard question for the soul to determine, at times, but it's an easy question for the one who is led by the Holy Spirit, rather than the soul. Love God with all your soul. Yet there is more. You must love God with...

All Your Mind

Loving God with all our mind is the most difficult of these three disciplines. Our mind, of course, is the center of our thought processes. The sins of the mind are, for the most part, private. I have found while counseling that when one loses a battle to sin, that battle began and was lost in the mind. Reformers Unanimous principle #2 tells us that, we thought about it before we ever did it!

Our minds need to be under the influence of the inner man,

the Spirit of God. The hardest area of the outer man to control is the mind. It remains un-policed. Our emotions can show, our desires can be measured by our actions, but the mind is everyone's secret hiding place.

We are not just discussing sins that would be readily considered wicked, such as sins of immoral or dishonest thinking. We can have a mind free of wicked thoughts and still have a mind that is under our control and not the control of God. Often times, what we see with Christians is a mixture of the inner man with the outer man in the area of our thoughts. We take a Spirit-led thought and mix it with our flesh. We mix God's prompting with our own points of advantage. If we are not careful, it is possible to think within ourselves that our decisions are Spirit-led. However, after an honest examination we find that they are mixed: God's leading stirred with man's preferences.

Hebrews 4:12 says, *For the word of God is quick, and powerful, and sharper than any twoedged sword, piercing even to the <u>dividing asunder of soul and spirit</u>, and of the joints and marrow, and is a discerner of the thoughts and intents of the heart.* Let's dissect and define this verse. I believe it will help us to hand over the real estate of our minds to God.

The writer of Hebrews is describing the Bible as being sharp–so sharp that it is sharper than a two-edged sword. A two-edged sword can cut to the bone, no matter which direction it is applied. This "sword" can pierce the joints (which are attached to the bone) and it can pierce the marrow (which is located within the bone). This tells us that the inside and the outside of a bone can be pierced by a two-edged sword. This illustration is a description of God's Word. It can pierce both the inner man (your spirit) or the outer man (your soul–mind, will, and emotions). It goes on to say that the reason that this piercing is necessary is for ...*the dividing asunder* (apart) *of <u>soul</u>* (outer man) *and <u>spirit</u>* (inner man)! The verse then tells us that the Bible ... *is a discerner of the thoughts and intents of the heart.* We cannot discern our own hearts. Jeremiah 17:9 says that the heart is so wicked, we cannot even know it.

What can we do to see to it that our mind is submitted to the mind of Christ? We must allow our soul and spirit to be separated by the Word of God, regularly, in our life's decisions. The Word of God will show us when our thoughts are not lining up with His thoughts, but only if we will apply the Sword to our mind–our outer man. Second Corinthians 10:5c says...*bringing into captivity every thought to the obedience of Christ.* Bring your thought process into captivity. Take your thoughts captive–with God holding the key!

As mentioned before, God allows circumstances in our lives to lead to the breaking of this stubborn, selfish outer man. The outer man wants to *feel* what he wants (emotions). He wants to *do* what he wants (soul-will). He wants to *think* what he wants (mind). But if we will permit the circumstances God allows into our life to break the outer man, we will find that those wounds–which at one time were so hard to accept–are the very wounds that God will use to shine through to the world. Our shattered outer man obeys Christ, who dwells in our inner man. When circumstances are not what you would choose for yourself, accept God's truth that ...*all*

> God allows circumstances in our lives to lead to the breaking of our stubborn and selfish outer man.

things work together for good to them that love God, to them who are the called according to his purpose (Romans 8:28).

His purpose? The very next verse tells us what that is: ...*to be conformed to the image of his Son.* What image is that? The image of Jesus Christ–a Man who was tempted like us, but Whose outer man was submitted to His inner man, God's Spirit.

What does it mean to be conformed to the image of Christ and to take on the mind of Christ? Philippians 2:5-8 defines what the mind of Christ was. <u>*Let this mind be in you, which was also in Christ Jesus*</u>*: Who, being in the form of God, thought it not robbery to be equal with God: But made himself of no reputation, and <u>took upon him the form of a servant</u>, and was made in the likeness of men: And being found in fashion as a man, he humbled himself, and became obedient unto death, even the death of the cross.* I've heard it said before that the true test of a servant is if you act like one when you're being treated like one. If God is not treating you the way you want Him to, don't grumble in your mind. Do not complain. Do not let your thoughts run away with you. Accept your servant's role. You will then be conforming to His image by submitting to His mind, which is *in* you. Remember, you are not your own, so don't act as if you are. Give God the love of your mind. If you will do this, He will make you a servant–a servant of others.

Choose to love God with your heart, soul, and mind. Your outer man will then be broken (as well as your stubborn habits and addictions), and you will be free to be led by your inner man (God's Spirit). The inner man will lead you to others, and they are your second responsibility.

LOVE THY NEIGHBOR AS THYSELF

Jesus said our second responsibility is just like the first. *Love thy neighbor as thyself.* Our first responsibility is to God, and our second responsibility is to others. If our first responsibility of loving God will remove our addictions, then our second responsibility of loving others will keep our addictions from returning.

People are born selfish and self-centered. Every man since Adam was born with a dead spirit. When you were saved, that spirit came alive as the Holy Spirit came to dwell within you. Anything touched by God comes alive! Despite this glorious fact, we often find that we love ourselves very much. That's why our primary concern in life is for our *own* comforts, our *own* rights, what *we* want. But by shifting our focus off of ourselves and onto others, a specific change is inevitable. We will begin to see others as Jesus sees them.

God has clearly given the people within whom He dwells some *responsibilities to others*. His very purpose for dwelling within you is to flow through you and shine through your wounded and broken outer man. If we will accept these responsibilities as opportunities for Christ to shine, then the fruit of the Spirit will be evident in our lives. What a great life we can experience! It is the abundant Christian life!

Let's look at this responsibility to others as outlined in Romans 15:1-2 where we read, *We then that are strong* (or, capable) *ought* (or, are under obligation) *to bear the infirmities* (or, deterioration) *of the weak* (or, unstable)*, and not to please ourselves. Let every one of us please his neighbour for his good to edification.* This does not mean you have to be a spiritual giant to meet this responsibility–just capable. If you are a Christian, then the capability lies within you. [You] *can do all things through Christ which strengtheneth* [you] (Philippians 4:13).

Dissected and defined, we are being commanded to bear the deterioration of unstable people. This is more important than pleasing ourselves. Our selfish desire to please ourselves must go away. That doesn't mean that we are never able to be pleased. I think you will find that when you learn to focus on others, that is when you learn to experience pleasure that you never thought possible.

When I began Reformers Unanimous, my wife and I decided to hold the weekly class on Fridays. We figured that if we could have a Bible study for addicts and keep them sober on Friday night with an invitation to return on Sunday, they might be able to find the power to stay sober on Saturday night. Then, after attending church on Sunday, they would return to work on Monday having remained abstinent from their addictions for the whole weekend. They would be happy and convince themselves to try it again the next week. Seemed like a great idea.

I convinced a friend to share the responsibility. I would run the class one Friday and he would run it the next. I devoted every other Friday to addicts. After about two months, my assistant stepped down, requiring me to teach every Friday. I had a choice to make: a bi-weekly Bible study that left its students vulnerable every other week, or forsake my own pleasures and give up every Friday night. I took the easy way out and left the decision up to my wife. I'm glad that I did. She chose to give up *every* Friday night from that point forward. Praise God, what a difference it has made!

Shortly after we made that commitment, our Bible study for a half dozen addicts sprouted. Within a year it was up to thirty people and it doubled every year after that. Now our Rockford Reformers Unanimous reaches over three hundred addicts per week through the Bible study class and its local satellites. Since that time, that Bible study class model is now used in churches across America to reach the addicted.

Each one is led by people who are making that very same sacrifice–exchanging self–pleasure for bearing the deterioration of unstable people. Who are the beneficiaries of these sacrifices? The addicts, yes. But, these burden-bearers across America will tell you that it is *they* who have experienced the greater personal benefit. Such is true of all unselfish sacrifices. God rewards the sacrifice of your pleasures for the burden-bearing of the unstable with a freedom found only in Jesus.

Galatians 6:2 tells us to *Bear ye one another's burdens, and so fulfill the law of Christ.* We fulfill, or complete, the very teachings of Christ when we bear the burdens of others.

These are our two responsibilities: Love God with the outer man by yielding to the inner man, and love others by giving up our own pleasures for the benefit of those whose burdens are overbearing. If we will do this, we will experience the supernatural power of the Holy Spirit over the power of our addiction.

On these two commandments hang all the law and the prophets.

The Law and the Prophets are the summation of all the Old Testament Biblical teachings, God's written Word at the time of Christ. The Ten Commandments (Exodus 20:1-20) would be considered the Law. As you read the Ten Commandments, notice how each one can be traced back to either our responsibility to God or our responsibility to others.

Commandments 1-4: Our Responsibility to God

1. *Thou shalt have no other gods before me.*
2. *Thou shalt not make unto thee any graven image...*

3. *Thou shalt not take the name of the LORD thy God in vain...*
4. *Remember the sabbath day, to keep it holy...*

Commandments 5-10: Our Responsibility to Others

5. *Honour thy father and thy mother...*
6. *Thou shalt not kill.*
7. *Thou shalt not commit adultery.*
8. *Thou shalt not steal.*
9. *Thou shalt not bear false witness against thy neighbor.*
10. *Thou shalt not covet...*

...Fear not: for God is come <u>to prove you</u>, and that his fear may be before your faces, <u>that ye sin not.</u>

We know that it is not possible to live our lives without breaking commandments. Yet the Law was not designed to save from sin but to convict of sin. Remember the Pharisees and Sadducees in the crowd that we spoke of earlier? They saw their salvation in the fulfilling of the Law. But the purpose of the Law is twofold: 1. To purge sin out of our lives (...to prove you...); and, 2. To keep sin from ruling our lives (..that his fear [constant awareness of God's presence and my accountability to Him for my actions] may be before your faces, that ye sin not).

Notice the correlation between the twofold purpose of the Law and the Two Commandments of Christ: Love the Lord thy God with all thy heart, and with all thy soul, and with all thy mind... Meeting our first responsibility (to God) will remove our addiction, thus purging sin out of our life. And the second is like unto it, Thou shalt love thy neighbor as thyself... Meeting our second responsibility (to others) will keep our addiction from returning, thus fulfilling the second purpose of the Law–keeping sin from ruling our life.

It is when our outer man begins to yield to these two commandments that we begin to experience the victorious Christian life! I guess it was put best when it was said that the key to experiencing JOY in our Christian life is when we yield to our responsibilities in this order: Jesus, Others, and then You.

Chapter 3

Three Dedications for Discerning God's Direction

I beseech you therefore, brethren, by the mercies of God, that ye present your bodies a living sacrifice, holy, acceptable unto God, which is your reasonable service. And be not conformed to this world: but be ye transformed by the renewing of your mind, that ye may prove what is that good, and acceptable, and perfect, will of God.

Romans 12:1-2

Lots of D's for a title right? Well, don't get all tongue-tied! Let me first define the title so you will better understand where we are going in this chapter.

> **Dedications:** to set apart for sacred use
> **Discerning:** to come to know or to recognize.
> **Direction:** authoritative instruction and guidance.

So, the title of this chapter, <u>Three Dedications for Discerning God's Direction</u>, actually means the following phrase: Setting apart three definite areas of our lives so that through what we have learned as a way of life, we can come to know or recognize God's instruction and guidance for us. In other words, we will be discussing what we must do first in order to know God's will.

We have learned in order to live freely from this world of bondage that we must walk one way, believe one truth, and for one life—the way, truth, and life of our Lord Jesus Christ. That is God's plan for not only providing freedom from the penalty of sin, but His prerequisite for providing emancipation from the power of sin.

As we accept this relationship, we must develop it so that God's power will rest upon us. This development comes as we learn to love God and live for others. As you develop spiritually, God will lead you. This leading is not only year to year, but moment by moment. As you follow this leading, you will be submitting to what is referred to as the will of God.

For many, God's will seems to be something for which we tend to search, somehow expecting God to give us an A-B-C plan for us to follow. But it isn't something that we happen to find one day; it is something we *live* every day, doing what we know to be right for today while leaving tomorrow in God's hands. Waiting on God's timing and direction can be one of the hardest things to do, but Romans 12:1-2 gives us Three Dedications that *we* can make which will help us discern God's direction today.

Let's look at a dissected and defined explanation of our chapter key verse found in Romans 12:1-2. It reads,

> *I beseech you* (or, I beg you) *therefore, brethren* (Christians), *by the mercies of God, that ye present your bodies a <u>living</u> sacrifice, <u>holy</u>, <u>acceptable</u> unto God, which is your reasonable service* (or, the least that we can do).

And be not conformed to (or, molded like) *this world:
but be ye transformed by the renewing* (or, rearranging)
*of your mind, that ye may prove what is that good, and
acceptable, and perfect, will of God.*

Dedication One—Dedicate our Bodies to God
PRESENTATION

*I beseech you therefore, brethren, by the mercies of God, that
ye* <u>present your bodies</u>...

Presentation of our bodies (or, lives) is the foundational
dedication upon which the next two dedications will build.
It's the first step we can take. Paul, the writer of Romans,
calls the presentation of our bodies a "reasonable service."
Why do you suppose that it would be considered a
"reasonable service"? Because of the "mercies of God"! It
was God's mercy that allowed *His* Son to present *His own*
body as a sacrifice for us! The least we can do is give our
lives back to Him.

First Peter 1:3 says, *Blessed be the God and Father of our
Lord Jesus Christ, which* <u>according to his abundant mercy
hath begotten us again unto a lively hope by the resurrection
of Jesus Christ from the dead.</u> It is God's abundant mercy
that has given us new life and the hope of eternal life in
heaven.

Paul is simply saying in Romans, "I am begging you to do
what I am about to tell you to do, if for no other reason
than the fact that God has shown us so much mercy that it
is the least we can do for Him!"

So, what kind of a sacrifice should this be? Paul gives three
requirements for a proper sacrifice.

OUR PRESENTATION SHOULD BE A WILLING SACRIFICE.
I beseech you therefore, brethren, by the mercies of God, that ye present your bodies...

We must present ourselves willingly. God did not make us robots. We have the incredible tool of a free will. God in His omnipotence has all rights and ability to control our lives, but how much more precious it is to Him when we *willingly present* them to Him!

To better understand what a willing sacrifice is, let's look at the story of Abraham and Isaac. Isaac was Abraham's promised son for whom he had waited for many years. God gave Isaac to Abraham when Abraham was 100 years old!

Several years later, God told Abraham to go to a certain mountaintop, build an altar, and offer a sacrifice-the life of his son. The one thing that Abraham cherished above all, God was asking him to sacrifice! Remember that we are talking about a strong, teenage boy. His father is at least 115 years old now. Nevertheless, Abraham willingly rose up early the next morning with his son and headed toward the mountain to sacrifice Isaac to the Lord. The Bible tells us that Abraham believed God could raise Isaac from the dead (Hebrews 11:17-19). However, he was still willing to give that sacrifice with no guarantee of return.

Let's pick up the story here in Genesis 22:9-10. *And they came to the place which God had told him of; and Abraham built an altar there, and laid the wood in order, and bound Isaac his son, and laid him on the altar upon the wood. And Abraham stretched forth his hand, and took the knife to slay his son.* Think about what's happening here: We have a very old man telling his son that he is about to burn his body as a sacrifice unto God, and we have a strapping, strong teenage boy who could have *easily* overtaken his father in resistance. However, Isaac *willingly* allowed his father to bind him and place him on the altar. He was willing to be sacrificed without a struggle.

I have found, in my years of counseling struggling students, that we want God to free us from our addictions, but we are *unwilling* to sacrifice certain areas of our fleshly desires. I think we all fall into this trap sometimes. Are there things that you are struggling to do that you know are right, but it just seems there's always a good reason why you can't? Friend, it's not so much a *struggle* to do what's right; it's more of an *unwillingness* to make sacrifices for God. Are you *unwilling* to read your Bible? Are you *unwilling* to study your Bible? Are you *unwilling* to memorize your Bible? Are you *unwilling* to meditate on your Bible? Are you unwilling to hear the Bible taught? You will never do the things God wants you to do until you do the things God wants you to do even when you *don't* want to.

> Many times we are waiting for God to do what God is waiting for us to do. We want God to take away our addictions or temptations, but He wants us to forsake them. He wants us to say "no" to our flesh.

God will not force us to serve Him. However, God does allow us to go through incredible suffering to bring us to a point in our lives when we will finally say, "Okay, God! I'll stop fighting and I'll climb up on that altar." Many times we are waiting for God to do what God is waiting for us to do. We want God to take away our addictions or temptations, but He wants us to forsake them. He wants us to say "no" to our flesh. We have fed the flesh and its desires, so now we must willingly sacrifice our flesh by willingly starving it.

It is encouraging to me to know God recognizes that when we give our lives to Him, it *is* a sacrifice. When we give our entire beings to Him and say, "God, I want you to do with me whatever you please," He knows it's not going to be easy for us. But He faithfully rewards a life sacrificed to Him with a renewed life worth sacrificing for.

OUR PRESENTATION SHOULD BE HOLY.

I beseech you therefore, brethren, by the mercies of God, that ye present your bodies a living sacrifice, <u>holy</u>...

How can a life be a holy sacrifice? First Peter 1:15-16 says, *But as he which hath called you is holy, so be ye holy in all manner of conversation* (or, conduct); *Because it is written, Be ye holy; for I am holy.* Our lives should be holy, without evidence of a double standard. We represent Christ to the world. You may be the only Christian someone knows. Your conduct, or way of life, needs to exemplify Christ-likeness!

Romans 6:12-13 reads, *Let not sin therefore reign in your mortal body* (or, don't let sin control your life), *that ye should obey it in the lusts thereof. Neither yield ye your members* (your hands, eyes, tongue, feet) *as instruments of unrighteousness unto sin: but yield yourselves unto God as those that are alive from the dead, and your members as instruments of righteousness unto God.* In other words, when we die to ourselves, and sacrifice our lives to God, Christ will live through us! Now, each member of your body will be an instrument of righteousness. When our presentation is holy, that simply means that our *lifestyle* should show that we are making a *willing* sacrifice so that Christ may shine from within us.

OUR PRESENTATION SHOULD BE ACCEPTABLE UNTO GOD.

I beseech you therefore, brethren, by the mercies of God, that ye present your bodies a living sacrifice, holy, <u>acceptable unto</u>

God...

In Genesis 4, we see the account of Cain and Abel, two sons of Adam and Eve. *And in process of time it came to pass, that Cain brought of the fruit of the ground an offering unto the LORD. And Abel, he also brought of the firstlings of his flock and of the fat thereof. And the LORD had respect unto Abel and to his offering: But unto Cain and to his offering he had not respect...* (Genesis 4:3-5). Both sons brought an offering to God. Abel and his offering were accepted; Cain and his offering were not. Why? Attitude! The Bible tells us in 1 John 3:12 that Cain was a wicked man whose works were evil. By contrast, Abel was a righteous man, as evidenced by the description of his offering-he gave the best of the best of what he had. Cain's proud and arrogant self-righteousness negated any qualities his offering may have had. Abel's sacrifice was more excellent than Cain's in God's sight, and the difference was faith (Hebrews 11:4). *And Cain was very wroth, and his countenance fell. And the LORD said unto Cain, Why art thou wroth? and why is thy countenance fallen? If thou doest well, shalt thou not be accepted? and if thou doest not well, sin lieth at the door. And unto thee shall be his desire, and thou shalt rule over him* (Genesis 4:5-7). Although God encouraged him to do well, Cain allowed his selfish motives to lead him into an angry state of depression. The end result of his attitude was the murdering of his own brother! The consequence of presenting an unacceptable sacrifice to God is shown in verse 7, *sin lieth at the door.* Cain's life is a perfect example of that.

So, how can we make sure that our sacrifices are acceptable? It's this simple: an acceptable sacrifice requires that something must die. What is it that must die? Us! We must put to death our pride, our selfishness, and all of our motives for personal advancement. We must be willing to die to self on a daily basis. Are you willing to follow Abel's example of faith? Are you willing to give God the best of the best of your life? Are you willing to be proven as acceptable to God?

Our first dedication for discovering God's direction is to dedicate our lives as willing, holy, and acceptable sacrifices. If we will dedicate our lives to Him, God's power will change our stubborn wills, our unholy conduct, and our selfish possession-centeredness.

Dedication Two—Dedicate our Minds to Know God Personally *TRANSFORMATION*

…but be ye <u>transformed</u> by the renewing of your mind…

You'll notice that I am skipping a chunk of our key verse-*and be not conformed to this world*; but I believe that the second part of that phrase, *but be ye transformed by the renewing of your mind*, must come before the Conformation (Dedication Three). We cannot "un-conform" ourselves from the world until we are first transformed in our minds. Once God begins to transform our minds, then we can "un-conform" to the world. We will never change the way we act until we change the way we think. Therefore, Dedication Two is Transformation-the dedication of our minds to developing a dynamic relationship with God.

To better understand Dedication Two, allow me to define two of the words in this verse.

> **Transformed**: a change in form; a metamorphosis
> **Renewing**: to revive or reawaken

So, Romans 12:2 is saying that a change in our lives will

come by the reviving or reawakening of our minds. Therefore, our second dedication is to dedicate (or, set apart for sacred use) our minds toward God.

Why do you suppose that transformation (a change in form) deals with our minds rather than our actions? The reason is because the way we think defines what we do. Proverbs 23:7 says, *For as* [a man] *thinketh in his heart, so is he.*

God's way of thinking is often 180 degrees in opposition from the way man thinks. Isaiah 55:9 says, *For as the heavens are higher than the earth, so are my ways higher than your ways, and my thoughts than your thoughts.*

When I came back to the Lord after years of living in addiction, I got involved in my local church. I was doing the things I knew I should be doing-reading my Bible, memorizing Scripture, praying, going to church, etc. I soon gained the lofty title of Activities Director of my Single Adults Sunday School class. I was sure this was God's calling on my life. I had big dreams of serving the Lord in the singles ministry. However, something got in the way of this--I met my future wife. Obviously, this eventually put an end to my days of being the Activities Director of the Singles Department.

This is just a simple illustration of the omniscience of God's thinking versus our thinking. I was being obedient in the areas that God had shown me; and though I thought I could clearly see what God had called me to do, God had different plans. His ways were higher than mine. My thoughts were not His thoughts. His next opportunity for me was a Friday night Bible study for addicts that I called Reformers Unanimous. I'm glad my thinking was overruled by God's thinking.

God may have plans for you which are higher than you

could ever imagine possible. However, unless you are willing to give your thoughts over to God and trust Him to guide you, His direction for you will be limited. Proverbs 3:5-6 reminds us, *Trust in the LORD with <u>all thine heart</u>; and lean not unto thine own understanding. In all thy ways acknowledge him, and he shall direct thy paths.* His ways and thoughts are higher than yours. Trust that He knows what's best and be willing to submit whatever area in your life He may be asking you to give to Him.

Another reason it is so important to dedicate our thought process to God is because when God sees our sinful thought lives, it grieves Him. Our evil thoughts break His heart. During the days of Noah, Genesis 6:5-6 records that *God saw that the wickedness of man was great in the earth, and that <u>every imagination</u> of the thoughts of his heart was only evil continually. And it repented the LORD that he had made man on the earth.* Man's mind was so wicked that it repented God that He had created man!

You may be thinking right now, "My thought life isn't *that* bad. I'm okay." But Jeremiah 17:9 says *The heart is deceitful above all things, and desperately wicked: who can know it?* To put it very bluntly, our hearts are so wicked, we can't even know the full extent of that wickedness. If

> God's Word is what will keep our hearts tender to God and to His leadings. It will help us keep our minds pure.

we want to see our hearts' wickedness, we need to ask God to show it to us. Psalm 139:23-24 reads, *Search me, O God, and know my heart: try me, and know my thoughts: And see if there be any wicked way in me, and lead me in the way everlasting.* God's Word is what will reveal our true thoughts and intentions. Hebrews 4:12 says, *For the word of God... <u>is a discerner of the thoughts and intents of the</u>*

heart. God's Word! That is what will keep our hearts tender to God and to His leadings. It will help us keep our minds pure.

Our lives are wrecked by sin and we bear the scars from our past. But Isaiah 55:7 says, *Let the wicked forsake his way, and the unrighteous man his thoughts: and let him return unto the LORD, and he will have mercy upon him; and to our God, for he will abundantly pardon.* The cure given here for the unrighteous man forsaking his thoughts is returning to the Lord! That sounds like Dedication One-Presentation.

Proverbs 16:3 teaches an incredible principle regarding the sacrificing of our lives. This verse reads, *Commit thy works unto the LORD, and thy thoughts shall be established.* By committing our efforts (or, works) to the Lord, our thoughts will change. The previous verse in Proverbs 16 says, *All the ways of a man are clean in his own eyes; but the LORD weigheth the spirits.* We may think we are doing okay, or something may look "clean" in our eyes, but God looks from within at the inner man. He sees the heart. Therefore, we need to commit our works to God (i.e., be willing to do what God tells us to do, even if we don't understand why), and *after* we do our part, God will then establish our thoughts. We will never change the way we act until we let God change the way we think.

My first New Year's Eve after giving my life to God, I had an unforgettable experience. Though I was striving for victory over addictions, I still fell regularly. An announcement had been made in our church about an all-night activity to celebrate New Year's Eve. I made plans to attend. I was looking forward to a good, clean and sober New Year's Eve. However, when I arrived, I received a big shock-it was a teen activity! With utter embarrassment I began retreating from the gymnasium with every intention to go to a party at an old friend's house.

Just then, the church's youth pastor grabbed me and asked me to help with crowd control. "We've got more kids than we thought we were going to have," he said. I was thinking, *Crowd control... junior highers... New Year's Eve... they just don't go together.* But I agreed. We played volleyball, basketball, indoor mini-putt, and at 2 a.m., we watched <u>Dennis the Menace</u>. Only one person stayed up all night-me. I guess it was because I had a little more practice than those kids had at staying up all night! But what was unforgettable and unbelievable to me was I had the time of my life that evening with those kids!

As I was driving home from the activity that morning , my heart was overflowing with joy. I had a sober night *and* had a great time! As I pulled up to a stoplight, I saw some of my drug buddies on their way home from the party I almost went to. Unbeknownst to them, I was watching them; to my sorrow, I saw the shame, agony, and misery on their faces. I broke down and cried.

That day I saw the metamorphosis that was happening in my mind as I was committing my works to the Lord. My way of thinking was changing as I was doing what I knew to be right, as understood by reading God's Word and hearing it preached. This change in my mind was beginning to take the knowledge I had about God and was transforming it into a dynamic relationship with God. As a result of this relationship, I was able to recognize God's leading through dedication number three.

Dedication Three—Dedicate Ourselves to God's Standard CONFORMATION

And be not conformed to this world...

The very first Dedication is presenting ourselves to God as a sacrifice that is willing, holy, and acceptable-Presentation. Then, we dedicate our minds to God's Word by changing the way we think-Transformation. Our third Dedication is the devotion of ourselves to God's standard-Conformation. Our text verse says, *And be not conformed to this world.* What does "not being conformed to the world" mean? Unconformity to the world means that we should not be poured into the world's mold.

Why is this so dangerous? Think about it: The world's ways and philosophies are always changing. It wasn't that long ago when teenage pregnancy was nearly unheard of, much less, teenage abortions! Now, both are commonplace because society's standards of morality have changed. However, God's standard of morality never changes. As believers, we cannot afford to continue forming ourselves into the world's way of conducting our lives. Just because the world thinks it's okay to act one way doesn't mean God feels the same way. We are to be conformed to something completely different than the world's design, and that means being conformed to God's design.

The Bible's main purpose is to tell those of us who are believers what is right, what is not right, how to get right, and how to stay right.

We discussed the following passage in chapter one, but it bears re-stressing here. Second Timothy 3:16 reads, *All scripture is given by inspiration of God, and is profitable* (or, its main use is) *for doctrine* (what is right), *for reproof* (what's not right), *for correction* (how to get right), *for instruction in righteousness* (how to stay right). So the Bible's main purpose is to tell those of us who are believers what is right, what is not right, how to get right, and how to stay right. We use the Bible to determine what conduct is right and what conduct is wrong. The next verse goes on to say, *That the man of God* (Christian) *may be perfect* (or, maturing), *throughly furnished* (or, becoming "well-polished") *unto all good works.* That's exactly what conformation is-maturing our lives into God's design using God's Word as a road map and the Holy Spirit as our driver!

First John 2:15 further warns us against being conformed to the world's standards. *Love not the world, neither the things that are in the world. If any man love the world, the love of the Father is not in him.* In chapter one we learned that the world is made up of three things: the lust of the flesh, the lust of the eyes, and the pride of life. According to 1 John 2:15, if we love the things of this world, then the love of the Father is not in us. We cannot be conformed to the world and please God at the same time. It is impossible.

Romans 8:28-29 are two verses that almost everybody has memorized and, at times, have claimed. However, we rarely take note of its significance toward defining God's purpose for our lives. These verses tell us, *And we know that all things work together for good to them that love God, to them who are the called according to his purpose. For whom he did foreknow, he also did predestinate to be conformed to the image of his Son.*

Now, what does "all" mean? All means all, and that's all that it means. So, we know that *all* things in our lives work together for good if we are called to His purpose. In verse 29 is the explanation of the purpose for which God has called us-to be conformed to the image of His Son!

However, the flip side of this truth is that if we are *not* conforming to the image of God's Son, then we are not being called according to His purpose. Therefore we cannot claim the promise that all things will work together for good in our lives! When we turn our lives over to God (Presentation), God is able to work *all* things in our past, present, and future together for His good. Let me warn you, however, that if you are not willing to conform your life to Christ, don't expect everything to work together for good. Chances are, they will not.

Part of conforming to God's image means letting go of our past grievances. We often want to hang on to past hurts that God wants us to release and allow Him to work them out for His good! Ephesians 4:31 says, *Let all bitterness* (or, compressed feelings), *and wrath* (or, feelings of getting even), *and anger, and clamour* (or, arguing), *and evil speaking* (or, gossiping), *be put away from you, with all malice* (or, a desire for physical injury). If we allow these emotions to build up, they will slowly destroy us. The phrase "be put away from you" has behind it the idea of incarceration. Send them away and lock them up from ever returning again.

Verse 32 of Ephesians 4 holds the key to letting go of past grievances. *And be ye kind one to another* (outward expression of feelings), *tenderhearted* (inward expression), *forgiving one another* (upward expression), *even as God for Christ's sake hath forgiven you.* The phrase "even as God for Christ's sake hath forgiven you" is somewhat similar to the "reasonable service" we spoke of earlier. Surely if God can love us enough to give His own Son to pay our penalty for sin... if God can love us enough to give us freedom from the power of sin ... if God can love us enough to give us an eternal home in heaven... we can most certainly let go of past hurts and grievances and be *kind one to another* (on the outside), *tenderhearted* (on the inside), and *forgiving one another*!

Let go of past feelings that you may use to justify your wrongdoing. Incarcerate them! I know this is a touchy subject because we're talking about our emotional makeup. We learned in chapter two that this is something that the devil uses as a devastating weapon against many of us. If you will learn to harness your emotions for the glory of our Lord Jesus Christ and for *His* good, I promise you that freedom is inevitable! A life filled with joy is the end result, rather than these destructive feelings that we bottle up inside of ourselves. We must let God have control of our emotions. Let go, and let God be in control.

Properly controlled emotions show others that our strength is in Christ. Proverbs 16:32 says, *He that is slow to anger is better than the mighty; and he that ruleth his spirit* (or, temperament) *than he that taketh a city.* One who is slow to anger and controls his spirit is one who controls his emotions. But that control doesn't come from within one's self; it comes from God. Such a person practices Ephesians 4:31-32. According to Proverbs 16:32, this person is better than the mighty! He has more control than an army of soldiers!

Conversely, if we lose control of our emotions, we are vulnerable to Satan's attacks. Proverbs 25:28 says, *He that hath no rule over his own spirit* (or, temperament), *is like a city that is broken down, and without walls.* Old Testament cities had walls built around them to protect them from the enemy. Without the walls, these cities would have no protection from their enemies. When we don't control our emotions and we allow those Ephesians 4:31 feelings to creep into our lives, we are open to the attacks of the enemy, and so are those who depend on us for their own protection!

Of course, controlling our emotions will build a wall that will protect us from the influences and attacks of the enemy. Remember, though, once those walls come back down, we are immediately unprotected and vulnerable emotionally.

If we want to overcome attacks, and if we want to keep ourselves from being vulnerable, we must not lose control of our emotions. It's not the loss of control that conquers us; it is the loss of protection from the attacks of Satan that will conquer us. The world's mold is led by emotions. God's mold will control our emotions. Thus, to conform to the image of God we will be under the control of God's emotions, not our own.

Discerning God's Direction

Three Dedications-Presentation, Transformation, and Conformation. Now, how do these help us discern God's direction? Let's look at our verse again. Romans 12:1-2 says, *I beseech you therefore, brethren, by the mercies of God, that ye* (Dedication One) *present your bodies a living sacrifice, holy, acceptable unto God, which is your reasonable service.* (Dedication Three) *And be not conformed to this world: but* (Dedication Two) *be ye transformed by the renewing of your mind, that ye may prove what is that good, and acceptable, and perfect, will of God.* In other words, we will know God's perfect direction for our lives if these three areas are dedicated to God. Maintain these Three Dedications and God's direction will always remain clear. Though we may not see the future, we will know God's desire for the present.

A frequent question is, "How can I know God's will for my life?" It's really simple. God's will is a day-by-day process; these dedications are a day-by-day process. We do our part by committing to these Three Dedications, and God will do the rest by working His will out in our lives. Anytime you may struggle with foolishly thinking that God has forgotten about you, or He doesn't really care for you anymore, or you feel separated from or out of touch with God, investigate these three areas in your life. It may be that there is a Dedication missing on your part.

First Peter 4:1-2 reads, *Forasmuch then as Christ hath suffered for us in the flesh, arm yourselves likewise with the same mind: for he that hath suffered in the flesh hath ceased from sin; That he no longer should live the rest of his time in the flesh to the lusts of men, but to the will of God.* Because Jesus Christ suffered in the flesh for us (having no sin in His life), we should take upon ourselves the same mind of Christ! When we live in the mind of Christ, we will not live in the lusts of men, but in the center of God's will-the best place to be!

Devote yourself to these Three Dedications today! Present yourself to God as a living sacrifice. Commit yourself to the transforming of your mind to the mind of Christ. Determine that you will *not* be conformed to the mold of the world; rather, accept conformity to God's standard of living. When these Three Dedications are present in your life, you will never lack God's guidance for your life.

Chapter 4

The Four R's
of Reformers

I am crucified with Christ: nevertheless I live; yet not I, but Christ liveth in me: and the life which I now live in the flesh I live by the faith of the Son of God, who loved me, and gave himself for me. I do not frustrate the grace of God: for if righteousness come by the law, then Christ is dead in vain. **Galatians 2:20-21**

Knowing God is the absolute essential of the abundant Christian life. In this chapter, we will discover the key to understanding and applying this absolute to your walk with God. Galatians 2:20 is not only the key verse to this chapter, but it is the key verse to this book, as well. That is because I believe Galatians 2:20 is the key to your complete understanding, application, and experiencing the abundant Christian life. You see, we are dead. Nevertheless we live. So let us live freely in this bound world. Here is how it should be done.

As a result of our new birth, or what the Bible calls being "born again," we have a new existence that is being offered for our experience and enjoyment. Our key verses in Galatians teach us a few things about this new life in Christ. They first teach us that we are helpless. As a matter of fact, we have been put to death (*I am crucified with Christ*). Sometimes we may forget that we are dead. Dead people cannot help themselves. There will be times when we will have to **reaffirm our helplessness**. While teaching us to reaffirm our helplessness, these verses lead us to **realize our new identity in Christ** (*nevertheless I live; yet not I, but Christ liveth in me*). Our former helplessness is replaced with Christ who is limitless. To elevate our potential from helpless to limitless, we must **recognize the power of faith** (*...the life which I now live in the flesh I live by the faith of the Son of God*). Our final act of submission requires a willingness to **relinquish self-ownership** of our lives to the Christ who wants to live His life through us ([He] *who loved me, and gave himself for me*). Having been crucified yet living, we can now by faith submit to the inner man's leading.

In verse 21, Paul shows us that we are capable of slowing God's work in us; we can be guilty of putting on the brakes. We can throw a monkey wrench in the mix and mess up the Lord's work, effectively quenching the Holy Spirit. We can frustrate the grace of God by trying to obtain any level of righteousness by observing the Old Testament law (works) in order to obtain righteousness. Grace is in effect when God is doing the work; the law is in effect when man is doing the work. *Frustrate* means to violate or neutralize, rendering to a state of indifference. Paul is telling us that when we try to do the work of God in the power of our flesh, we violate God's grace. We neutralize it. God's grace in your life is dependent on you yielding your dead works to His living work within you. When you try to do good in the flesh, you set aside Christ's death and His continuing work. His sacrifice is in vain and His grace is frustrated. Your new life in Christ will suffer. Remember, God's power in your life is only limited by your fleshly efforts.

Do you find yourself in this position? You are not alone. The apostle Paul found himself in this position often. He had to reaffirm his helplessness regularly by dying not once, but daily (1 Corinthians 15:31). He had to realize his identity in Christ over and over again, as he considered himself the chief of sinners (1 Timothy 1:15). He struggled to recognize the power of faith, so God gave him a weakness that hampered him so much that he ...*besought the Lord...that it might depart from* [him] (2 Corinthians 12:8). But the Lord wanted him to see God's power and increase his faith. Paul's eventual conclusion was that ... *when I am weak, then am I strong* (2 Corinthians 12:10). He would once again relinquish self-ownership to God ... *that the power of Christ might rest upon* [him] (2 Corinthians 12:9).

Some say the Apostle Paul was the best Christian that ever lived, yet even he needed to be reminded of the Four R's of Reformers. Do not be discouraged if you need to be reminded once in a while. God understands that we are accustomed to doing our own work our own way. It began in the garden of Eden and will continue until He returns. Here are a few helpful hints that will aid you in avoiding the pitfalls that frustrate God's grace and His work on your behalf.

Reaffirm our Helplessness
I am crucified with Christ...

For dead people, we sure cause ourselves a lot of problems,

don't we? We would do ourselves well if we would remember our position in Christ. We died with Him. Romans 6:6-7 says, *Knowing this, that our old man is crucified with him, that the body of sin might be destroyed, that henceforth we should not serve sin. For he that is dead is freed from sin.* The "body of sin" is not a person; it is a ruling authority. We are born serving sin. When a person dies, his ability to serve is eliminated. God's purpose for our spiritual death (which precedes our spiritual re-birth) is that our ruler (sin) and its governing power might be taken away. This master within us must be subdued, weakened, and placed under the restraints of our new Ruler, Christ. The body of sin, like the body of Christ, has many members. Those members within us are naturally under the rule of sin. God's desire is for us to die like and with Christ so that sin's members and its deeds will be mortified, or put to death.

Our problem is not so much our continuing struggle with sin that slows our progress in the Christian walk. The real problem is that we fail to serve our new governing Authority. We tend to believe that we can do good without following our new Ruler. When we do this, we not only frustrate God's grace (God's great plan for us), but we also frustrate ourselves. We fail to achieve the progress in our Christian lives that we had hoped to achieve by our righteous living, and we become discouraged with ourselves. We forget that, being dead, we are helpless without this new and pure, living Authority ruling our lives. In Romans 7:24, Paul cries out in frustration, *O wretched man that I am! who shall deliver me from the body of this death?* Without God, we are nothing. Yet, we often foolishly attempt to accomplish our good works or make great feats of righteous living in our own strength. Before God can do anything with us, we must first come to the conclusion that without God's power on us, we are helpless. Without submission to His rule over our lives, we are helpless in overcoming the strongholds that sin (our former ruler) attempts to bring back into our lives. The power to gain such victories comes only through Christ living in us. His rule over us gives us the strength we need to resist the lure and allure of our former ruler. A verse so often quoted, Philippians 4:13, says *I can do all things through Christ which strengtheneth me.* Oh, how often we forget how helpless we are without the strength of Christ!

When I was running from the Lord and my addictions were crippling my life, I would cry out to God, "Why did You let this happen to me? Why won't You protect me from the devil? Can't You take away this temptation?" But, I had put myself in that position–not God. Galatians 6:7-8 says, *Be not deceived* (or, misled)*; God is not mocked* (or, imitated): *for whatsoever a man soweth* (or, scatters)*, that shall he also reap. For he that soweth to his flesh shall of the flesh reap corruption; but he that soweth to the Spirit shall of the Spirit reap life everlasting.* Let's dissect this verse and define the words so that we can have a greater understanding of what God is trying to teach us.

Be not deceived (or, misled); *God is not mocked* (or, imitated)

How do we imitate God? We imitate God when we live as if we control our own consequences for our wrongdoings. I made this mistake many times in my early flight to find freedom. I would go out for the evening, planning to enjoy myself. Yet I knew that if I allowed myself to walk out the door, I was going to do something before the night was over that was against the law and a sin against God. I knew that I would struggle with drugs and alcohol. However, I foolishly believed that if I controlled the atmosphere in which I indulged in these sinful things, somehow I could control the consequences of it. If I could keep myself from drinking too much, then I would not get a DUI. I could participate in drugs but hide it well enough so the cops would not find out. I was convinced that I could control the consequences of my choices. I mocked God. I imitated God by acting as if I had the power to control each and every circumstance. But, who truly is in control of everything? God is, of course. I lived as if I had no ruling Authority within me. I forgot I was helpless.

...*for whatsoever a man soweth* (or, scatters), *that shall he also reap* (or, receive in return).
Farming is exemplary for the Law of Sowing and Reaping. When a farmer goes to his field to plant his crop, he *sows* his seed. Figuratively speaking, that is what we do as we live out our lives. We leave distinctive paths behind us. Those paths are what we have sown. The seed will then ripen until harvest. It always does; it never fails. We will reap the fruit of whatever seed we sow. If a farmer plants corn, he will not reap green beans. So, the produce of whatever a man leaves scattered behind him is exactly what that man will eventually receive. Galatians 6:8 goes on to say, *For he that soweth to his flesh* (or, desires) *shall of the flesh reap corruption* (or, ruin); *but he that soweth to the Spirit shall of the Spirit reap life everlasting.* The man that lives for his own desires will reap ruin, but the man that lives under the control of the Holy Spirit (his new Ruler) will reap an abundant life.

We are responsible for where we are today. We are reaping what we have previously sown. Do not be misled. God is not going to be imitated. We can live neither righteously nor unrighteously without yielding our followship. We will either choose to follow our former ruler and reap ruin, or we will choose to follow the new Ruler within us and reap life. For whatever we leave behind in our lives, we will receive back the results of those same deeds. We are helpless. We cannot live righteously without yielding to our new Ruler, and we will not live sinfully without first submitting to our former ruler.

> The man that lives for his own desires will reap ruin, but the man that lives under the control of the Holy Spirit will reap an abundant life.

Our willingness to submit to the leading of our former ruler is what put us in this position of helplessness–not God; He is our helper. "Helper" is the definition of the Comforter (see John 14:16-18). He will help us reap life if we will sow submission to Him.

Let's take a look at the descending path of sowing to the flesh. First, we were deceived. You may ask, "How could I allow the devil to deceive me?" It's very simple. You see, Satan sows and reaps, too. When the devil plants a deceitful thought in your mind, you have the option to either accept it or reject it. *Be not deceived...* The choice is yours alone whether to be deceived or not.

Proverbs 3:5 says, *Trust in the LORD with all thine heart; and lean not unto thine own understanding.* When you give consideration to a deceitful thought and begin reasoning within yourself to justify it, you are handing the devil a building permit to start immediate construction of a stronghold in your mind. This will always lead to corruption in your heart. (Remember, the heart is the seat of belief.)

The Bible indicates that a stronghold in the mind exists when we choose to believe something to be true which contradicts the Word of God (see 2 Corinthians 10:3-5).

Hebrews 3:12 says *Take heed, brethren, lest there be in any of you an evil heart of unbelief, in departing from the living God.* It is very easy to be deceived when we stop believing the Truth. That is why we are so helpless without God.

After we were deceived, we then sowed our seed. Second Corinthians 9:6 says *...He which soweth sparingly shall reap also sparingly; and he which soweth bountifully shall reap also bountifully.* If we have bountifully scattered seeds of destruction behind us, we will reap that same destruction at some point in our lives.

I have made many bad decisions. These decisions were always the result of errors in my thinking. I was thinking with my deceived mind and it led me to yielding to the wrong authority. The key to sowing the right seed is yielding to the inner man rather than the outer man. By God's grace, I finally realized I needed to change my decision-making process. Seeing my need for guidance and direction, I began looking to God's Word to lead me in my decisions. Heeding the Bible helps us to avoid satanic deception.

As we discussed in chapter two, Hebrews 4:12 says *For the word of God is quick, and powerful, and sharper than any twoedged sword, piercing even to the dividing asunder of soul and spirit, and of the joints and marrow, and is a discerner of the thoughts and intents of the heart.* The key to the work of the Word in your life is the piercing and dividing of the soul (outer man) from the spirit (inner man). God's Word intends to separate your soul (mind, will, and emotions) and your spirit (God in you). Sometimes when God is giving us a leading, we begin to think about His direction. We begin to rationalize His will. Our emotions can begin to get involved and our stubborn wills react to His leading. Before we know it, our souls have cancelled out the Spirit's leading. We have taken God's thoughts or God's will or God's emotions and we have contaminated them with our selfish thoughts, desires, or feelings. When we are making decisions apart from His Word, we may be deceived by our own judgment. But if we run to God's Word for our answers, He will separate our deceived hearts from His clear direction. The Bible will point out areas in our lives that need to be changed. God's Word is *a discerner of the thoughts and intents of the heart.* Your heart may not always tell you the truth, but the Word will.

To protect yourself from being deceived, which leads to sowing the wrong seed, check your emotions, your thoughts, and your desires with the Bible. That's where your answers will be found. Remember 2 Timothy 3:16? *All scripture is given by inspiration of God, and is profitable for doctrine, for reproof, for correction, for instruction in righteousness:* The Bible's intention is to show us what is right (doctrine), what is not right (reproof), how to get right (correction), and how to stay right (instruction in righteousness).

So, the first "R" of Reformers is Reaffirm our Helplessness. Before God can do anything with our lives, we must reaffirm that without the help of God and His Word, we are helpless. But there is hope! Protect yourself from deception by seeking God's guidance.

Realize our New Identity in Christ
...nevertheless I live; yet not I, but Christ liveth in me.

When we were crucified with Christ, our subordinate members were no longer under obligation to submit to the ruling authority of sin. Rather, we are re-created in the image of Christ. Our members are now instructed by the Word of Truth and the Spirit of Truth to submit to our new ruling Authority. This is how God wants us to live. The Spirit of God that has quickened (made alive) your spirit will now guide you and direct you into all truth (Ps. 32:8). Submission to this inner Leader is referred to in our passage as Christ living in us. That is the manifestation of our new creation in Christ. We are no longer forced into submission to the body of sin. Instead, we are given the opportunity to yield in submission to the indwelling Holy Spirit. We do not have to work our way to righteousness in our own power. God is leading us into the paths of righteousness, and He is doing it for His name's sake (Ps. 23:3)!

In 2 Corinthians 5:17 Paul records this truth concerning the regime change within us: *Therefore if any man be in Christ, he is a new creature: old things are passed away; behold, all things are become new.* I have heard people argue that this verse is not referring to the "old man" passing away and a "new man" coming alive, but rather it is referring to the old covenant (the law) passing away and the new covenant (grace) replacing it. I would tend to agree that, in context, this is referring to the end of the law and the replacement of God's new covenant of grace. However, the truth of this passage is just as real as if the former view were being discussed here. Therefore, Paul is actually telling us that since we are in Christ, we are literally new creatures. The old covenant of man doing the work is passed away and has been replaced with the new covenant where God does the work. Amen!

I am so sick of this "try hard to do better" mentality that is permeating our churches and Christian schools. It is why Fundamentalist Christianity is so attacked by the seldom churched with charges of legalism. When it comes to justification, we all agree that Christ *did* the work, but when it comes to sanctification, we somehow believe that we must row our own canoe. We think the ability to live righteously is found in our effort and will power. This is not true. It is legalistic sanctification. Christ's substitionary death paid our penalty for sin and emancipated us from the power of sin. Christ's death paid our penalty; Christ's resurrection freed us from sin's power. A paid penalty is justification; emancipation is sanctification.

When we fail to understand our new identity in Christ, we lose focus on how to walk in victory. We are not so much required to do well as we are requested to yield to His leading. John 15:7 reads, *If ye abide in me...ye shall ask what ye will, and it shall be done unto you.* That's like saying, "If you cooperate with Me, things will happen for your benefit." He is willing to lead a cooperative subordinate. He will not force you to follow Him. If you know His voice is calling, you should follow.

It is a wonderful privilege to be a Christian! When we understand God's management systems, we will better understand who we are and how He intends to use us. In chapter three, we discussed this understanding process as the need to transform our minds. *Transform* means "to metamorphose; to change the character, nature, condition, etc., of something or someone."

"Don't make me angry. You wouldn't like me when I'm angry." In the early 1980's I enjoyed watching a television show called *The Incredible Hulk*. It was the comic book story of David Bruce Banner... "Physician... Scientist... searching for a way to tap into the hidden strength that all humans have, when an accidental overdose of gamma-radiation altered his body chemistry. And now, when David Banner becomes angry or outraged, a startling metamorphosis occurs..." They would then close the show's introduction with a view of David Banner becoming angry after injuring himself while changing a flat tire during a storm. Then, turning into a green, muscle-bound monster, he would beat up his car.

Though a silly story, there is a profound truth in this illustration. You see, when God transforms our minds, we begin to understand who we really are in Christ. Our identity in Christ is personally

> When God transforms our minds, we begin to understand who we really are in Christ. Our identity in Christ is personally experienced.

experienced. This position (in which we do not rule, but rather submit to Him) allows us to experience a startling metamorphosis during times of adversity when, in the past, we may have become frustrated or angry. Realizing our new identity, we may submit to a power greater than ours, one through which we will respond correctly to difficult circumstances. This metamorphosis is Christ in us, *the hope of glory* (Colossians 1:27). *Glory* means to bring the right opinion of. It literally means to make to look good. Christ living in us is our only hope of ever looking good when adversity strikes. God's purpose for us looking good is that we might make Him look good in the process. In other words, we glorify God (make Him look good) when others see this startling metamorphosis occur.

Society tells us that **behavior determines belief.** If you behave a certain way, you are providing insight into your belief system: If you are a drinker, then you believe that drinking is acceptable behavior; if you smoke dope, then you believe there is nothing wrong with drug use; if you live immorally, then you do not believe in the importance of moral purity; if you criticize others, then you are showing that you believe there is nothing wrong with giving evil reports. This is the system of the world–behavior determines belief.

God, however, has created a different management system. His system teaches us that **belief should determine behavior**. For example, if a young woman of the night–a harlot, if you will–were to be introduced to a king and fell in love with him, you might think it an odd thing. And if that king subsequently fell in love with this harlot, you might think it even more odd. But if these two unlikely candidates for love were to marry and move into his royal castle, do you think she would continue her trade of prostitution when darkness falls upon the city streets? No way! She would find her former behavior detestable. Why? Because she is no longer a prostitute. She is a queen! She is the wife of a king. How perverse and profane it would be if she ever went back to living like a harlot! She is going to behave differently because she rightly believes she has changed. No longer is she a "business" woman; she is a lady of the highest order.

It is the same for you and for me. We have been adopted. We are children of the King of Kings. That makes us royalty in His heavenly kingdom where Jesus is preparing a place for us. He has been working on it for over two thousand years. If He can create the splendor of the universe in six literal days, just think how marvelous our home in heaven must be by now. And because I *believe* this, I *behave* differently than I used to. You ought to as well.

Your identity is such that who you are in Christ determines how you behave. Often after conversion, new believers go from being ruled by the body of sin to trying to live righteously in their own power. The proper way to behave is predicated on understanding who you are in Christ–your new identity. You are His. He leads, you submit, and a supernatural power to face the circumstances of life is the guaranteed result. That is who we are in Christ. It is as simple as follow the leader. We followed the leader (our father, the devil) before our conversion. Now we must resist the temptation to self-rule. Spirit-rule is the key to the dynamic Christian walk.

Recognize the Power of Faith
…the life which I now live in the flesh I live by the faith of the Son of God.

Now, of course, understanding that Christ is in us and willing to lead us is not too difficult to accept. However, merely accepting this truth does not produce change. *Belief* is what produces change. Belief in God's substitutionary death of Christ on the cross is what grants us justification, and belief in God's substitutionary placement of Christ in us is what provides us with sanctification. Faith saves and faith produces change. We are so certain of the requirement of faith to produce a convert, but we often overlook the need for faith in Christ's leading in order to produce a changed life.

In our key verse, I am reminded that the life that I now live must be lived by faith–not faith in myself or in my church or in my works, but faith in the very same Son of God who saved my soul from hell. Praise God! His gift keeps giving!

What exactly is faith? I have heard it said that faith is a bold obedience to God's revealed will despite all circumstances. That may be the definition for a level of faith that changes you. But it is not the definition of the faith that saves you. Obedience doesn't produce regeneration. Yet faith does produce regeneration. Thus, faith has two definitions, or measurements. There is the faith that saves you and the faith that changes you. I define faith as, "the personal measurement of my level of confidence in what Christ can and will do in, through, and for us." When we exercise our faith, we are saying, "We are doing this because we believe the result will be exactly what God says it will be." This exercise produces a greater measure of faith.

As we saw in chapter three, God's will is revealed through our Presentation, Conformation, and Transformation (Romans 12:1-2). When His will is revealed, then real faith is measured by our willingness to step out in *bold* obedience and do as God directs, regardless of the circumstances.

It is important to understand this vital truth: God's acceptance of us cannot be acquired by what we have done for Him, nor can it be lost by what we have failed to do; we receive God's acceptance by having faith in His sacrifice for justification and faith in His guidance for sanctification.

There are three aspects of faith that we need to understand to properly exercise our faith:

FAITH DEPENDS ON ITS OBJECT.

Many people have faith in faith alone, rather than faith in an object. Your faith should be 100% dependent on the object in which you are placing that faith. If you have faith that a chair will hold your weight, then you have placed your faith in the object–the chair. You believe it will hold you so you exercise that belief by sitting in it. Many self-help programs in society will tell you to pick something or someone in which to place your faith. If you place your faith in something besides God's system of management, then you will have made the same mistake as those in society who are *Having a form of godliness, but denying the power thereof: from such turn away* (2 Timothy 3:5). Place your faith in Christ alone, both to save you and to lead you. Faith in Him is the *substance of things hoped for, the evidence of things not seen* (Hebrews 11:1).

THE DEPTH OF OUR FAITH IS DETERMINED BY THE DEPTH OF OUR KNOWLEDGE OF THE OBJECT IN WHICH WE PLACE OUR FAITH.

Do you need more faith? Gain more knowledge of your object of faith–God. Romans 10:17 says, *So then faith cometh by hearing, and hearing by the word of God.* Your faith and knowledge of God will grow as you are under the teaching and preaching of the Word of God.

I have two friends. Their names are John and Michael. John has been a friend for years. I just met Michael a few months ago. I have a lot of knowledge of John. However, I only know a little bit about Michael. If I needed to lend a one dollar bill to either of them, it would not take much effort on my part to exercise this measure of faith . I have little knowledge of Michael, but I am still willing to lend him something of so little value. However, if I had $100,000 in my pocket and I needed to find someone to entrust it with, I'm going to give it to John because I have more knowledge of him and can exercise my faith *in* him based on my knowledge *of* him.

Similarly, we only trust God based on how much knowledge we have of Him. If God asks us for a little, then we oblige Him. If God asks for much, then we hold back. Romans 12:1-2 begs us to give our lives to Him as a living sacrifice. We look at this life as being worth $100,000 and are unwilling to yield. God looks at this life as being worthless and the next life as being of great value. Luke 9:24 reminds us that, *whosoever will save his life shall lose it: but whosoever will lose his life for my sake, the same shall save it.* Because we do not know God well, we are unwilling to make a sacrifice above our current measure of confidence in

Him. Our sacrifice is limited, not by what He can do with us, but what we fail to believe. We do not recognize the power of faith.

> God's pleasure in us comes to a halt the moment we choose to follow our own will with disregard to His direction. At that moment, we cease from exercising faith.

Hebrews 11:6 says *But without faith it is impossible to please him: for he that cometh to God must believe that he is, and that he is a rewarder of them that diligently seek him.* Our ability to please God is directly related to our faith in Him. When we come to God, we must come *in faith* believing in who God is and believing that He will reward our diligence in seeking Him.

When we desire our will over God's will, we are not exercising faith in God. We have all been guilty of searching for God's direction and, having been shown His direction, we doubted our ability to follow it. Maybe God points out areas of our lives that need to change, or He may call us to the mission field or to change careers. God's pleasure in us comes to a halt the moment we choose to follow our own will with disregard to His direction. At that moment, we cease from exercising faith. We often want God's favor on our lives as a prerequisite to increasing our faith in Him. But it doesn't work that way. The step of faith comes first, then the reward.

FAITH IS AN ACTION WORD—NOT PASSIVE.

Faith says, "I am going to *do* right." James 2:17-18 says *Even so faith, if it hath not works, is dead, being alone. Yea, a man may say, Thou hast faith, and I have works: show me thy faith without thy works, and I will show thee my faith by my works.* Our outward actions reveal the inner condition of our faith. *Works* is an old English word for the Modern English word, effort. Our efforts do not save us, neither do they change us, but they are a by-product of our faith. Faith without works (effort) is dead. We need to recognize faith's power and then exercise that measure of faith.

Matthew 14:25-31 gives us the account of Peter walking on the water. The disciples were out to sea in the middle of the night when a strong storm came. In the midst of the storm, here comes Jesus walking on the water toward them. They thought it was a spirit! But in verse 27, *Jesus spake unto them, saying, Be of good cheer; it is I; be not afraid.* Peter's response was, *Lord, if it be thou, bid me come unto thee on the water. And* [Jesus] *said, Come. And when Peter was come down out of the ship, he walked on the water, to go to Jesus* (Matthew 14:28-29). Peter's faith was put in action by his immediate obedience to God's call, despite the potential consequences. The Bible goes on to say in verses 30 and 31, *But when he saw the wind boisterous, he was afraid; and beginning to sink, he cried, saying, Lord, save me. And immediately Jesus stretched forth his hand, and caught him, and said unto him, O thou of little faith, wherefore didst thou doubt?* When Peter's eyes were focused on Jesus, he was able to walk *in faith*. But as soon as he took his eyes off of Jesus and put them on the circumstances around him, he began to sink. When we take our eyes off of Jesus, our faith is going to waver. Friend, our faith is based on nothing less than Jesus' blood (for justification) and righteousness (for sanctification). You have died to the power of sin. You are now helpless to live righteously without your new identity, Christ in you. Recognize that these truths will change your life if you will only believe them. Once believed, simply exercise your faith by relinquishing self-ownership to God.

Relinquish Self-Ownership to God

...the Son of God, who loved me, and gave himself for me.

God gave Himself for me. Not for me to be me, but for me to be Him. If I give $10,000 for a car, I do not give it so the car can have some spending money. I give it so the car will belong to me and take me wherever I want to go. The same is true with Christ's gift. He gave it to take ownership of us. The last "R" of Re-borners is Relinquish Self-Ownership to God. We have given Him our hearts by being reborn, and now we must submit our lives to Him, also. As noted in Reaffirming our Helplessness, we know that without God's power, we cannot gain freedom in Christ. We have tried to work out our problems, but we just can't do it. The key is to overcome our sinful habits by the power that is within us–the power of the Holy Spirit. Remember, Philippians 4:13 says, *I can do all things through Christ which strengtheneth me.* We must yield our "rights" to Christ and let Him work through us to overcome our sinful habits.

A key verse that explains the truth of Relinquishing Self-ownership is found in 1 Corinthians 6:19-20, *What? know ye not that your body is the temple of the Holy Ghost which is in you, which ye have of God, and ye are not your own? For ye are bought with a price: therefore glorify God* (or, make Him look good) *in your body* (or, your outward actions), *and in your spirit* (or, your inner man), *which are God's.* The fourth R reminds us of who we are and why we are here. Jesus Christ gave His body to redeem us and His Spirit to guide us. We are His, inside and out! The impetus of this knowledge should be a constant motivation for us to continually make God look good.

Now, let me warn you that as we relinquish our lives to the Lord and begin to see victories, Satan is going to work that much harder to get us to doubt our abilities to serve God. The devil sees our spiritual growth, also. He is going to do everything he can to mess up the new path we are trodding–the new seeds we are sowing.

If the devil is not attacking us, then there is something wrong in our lives. Any growth on our part will attract the attention of the devil. He is the Great Deceiver, and he knows how to sneak into our lives. He knows our weak spots. Yet, we need to continually be relinquishing self-ownership to God to keep the devil from gaining any victory in our lives. If we make a mistake, we can remain confident that God is still going to finish what He started in us. Philippians 1:6 says, *Being confident of this very thing, that he which hath begun a good work in you will perform it until the day of Jesus Christ.* God is going to complete what He began in us!

The key to harmony with God is submission. It is the very basis of all four R's of Reformers. Don't try to make excuses for your struggles. Just determine that if God says something is wrong, it is wrong–submit to Him! That is why we were crucified with Christ. That is why He lives within us. That is why we must exercise our faith in willing submission to His leading. Making God look good makes us look good. You are dead. Nevertheless, you live! To live like Christ, you must act like a dead man.

Chapter 5

Forms for a
Firm Foundation

And he spake a parable unto them, Can the blind lead the blind? shall they not both fall into the ditch? The disciple is not above his master: but every one that is perfect shall be as his master. And why beholdest thou the mote that is in thy brother's eye, but perceivest not the beam that is in thine own eye? Either how canst thou say to thy brother, Brother, let me pull out the mote that is in thine eye, when thou thyself beholdest not the beam that is in thine own eye? Thou hypocrite, cast out first the beam out of thine own eye, and then shalt thou see clearly to pull out the mote that is in thy brother's eye. For a good tree bringeth not forth corrupt fruit; neither doth a corrupt tree bring forth good fruit. For every tree is known by his own fruit. For of thorns men do not gather figs, nor of a bramble bush gather they grapes. A good man out of the good treasure of his heart bringeth forth that which is good; and an evil man out of the evil treasure of his heart bringeth forth that which is evil: for of the abundance of the heart his mouth speaketh. And why call ye me, Lord,

Lord, and do not the things which I say? Whosoever cometh to me, and heareth my sayings, and doeth them, I will show you to whom he is like: He is like a man which built an house, and digged deep, and laid the foundation on a rock: and when the flood arose, the stream beat vehemently upon that house, and could not shake it: for it was founded upon a rock. But he that heareth, and doeth not, is like a man that without a foundation built an house upon the earth; against which the stream did beat vehemently, and immediately it fell; and the ruin of that house was great.

–Luke 6:39-49

We have explored many truths, or absolutes, that are foundational to our Christian life. The truth of the inner man and the outer man, the truth of freedom being found in submission to our authority, the truth of Jesus being the way, truth, and life worth walking, believing, and living, the truth of knowing and following God's will, and the truth of our death, burial and resurrection with Christ living in us... these are absolutes. They are foundations for justification and sanctification. With these foundations laid, it is imperative we build upon them things of value for our Lord. To do this we must understand the Five Forms for a Firm Foundation.

Everything in life depends upon foundations. Houses are built on solid foundations that support the structures we call "home." A business's success completely depends upon the foundation on which that company is built-its business plan. As adults, we are the product of the foundations we developed as children. Similarly, in the spiritual realm, the stability and growth of every Christian's life depends completely on the foundation on which it is built.

To understand what we will be discussing, let's dissect and define the title of this chapter, The Five Forms of a Firm

Foundation:

> **Form**: A mold or something that gives shape.
>
> **Firm**: established; unyielding to pressure.
>
> **Foundation**: a basis for supporting a structure.

Using these definitions, our title, Five Forms of a Firm Foundation, actually means the following phrase: Five molds that will shape an established and unyielding support for a structure known as the Christian life.

Just like our homes, the durability and growth of a spiritual life are entirely dependent on its foundation. Without a solid foundation it will crumble. Our key passage, Luke 6:39-49, gives us five forms for having this firm foundation.

Follow

The first Form of a Firm Foundation is to Follow. Whom we follow determines our destination. Luke 6:39-40 says, ...*Can the blind lead the blind?* (A rhetorical question that is setting the stage for Christ's teaching on follow-ship) *shall they not both fall into the ditch? The disciple* (or, student that follows) *is not above his master* (or, teacher): *but every one that is perfect* (or, properly trained) *shall be as his master* (teacher). So, we as the followers are not above our teachers. But, if we continue to be properly trained, we will be as our teachers. We will become like those whom we follow.

Choosing whom you will follow is very important. Following the wrong person will lead to destruction. Many times in secular programs, people are encouraged to "buddy up" with another person who has the same struggles and addictions. It is meant to be a support for both people. Yet for a Christian with addictions, there are two major flaws with that sort of a system. First, the other person may not have a love for the Lord Jesus Christ in his heart and life. He would not have the same goals, nor even be headed in the same direction, as the Christian should. Second, as our key verse asks, *Can the blind lead the blind? shall they not both fall into the ditch?* It is foolish to follow one who has the same "blindness" as one's self. No victory will be gained when following someone who is struggling in the same area. That person is just as blind. The result of a blind man leading the blind? They *both* will fall.

Psalm 1:1 describes for us the type of people after which we should not be following. *Blessed* (or, happy) *is the man that walketh not in the counsel of the ungodly* (does not get advice from those who do not love God), *nor standeth in the way of sinners* (does not engage in entertainment with those who do wrong), *nor sitteth in the seat of the scornful* (does not assume the position of critical people). We will be happy if we choose to *not* follow after the counsel of the ungodly, if we choose to *not* spend time around the worldly systems of entertainment, and if we choose to *not* be influenced by negative people.

Obviously, the best type of people to follow, the best teachers you could choose, are teachers who love God and give counsel as such, people who are not worldly in their lifestyles, and those who will encourage, build up, and edify you and others.

You see, everyone chooses teachers. You are a product of the teachers that you have chosen to follow. God has created a system and the world has created its own system. I call them both systems of management. God's system of management requires those whom He chooses for you to follow to help you make wise decisions. The world, under the authority of its prince, the devil, has a system of management which requires those whom you follow to help you make decisions in your life that *seem* right, but in reality are unwise. I call God's system of management, "The Umbrella of Protection." I call the world's system, "The Weathering of Destruction." God's system is intended to protect you from the elements of the world, and the world's system is intended to destroy you by slowly exposing you to its elements, thus weathering or wearing you down. God's umbrella of protection is His management system for the constant development of our lives. This umbrella consists of those whom He has placed in authority over us: our parents (especially as we are developing into young adults), our preachers, our teachers, our employers, and yes, even the government. These people are God-ordained authorities, designed by God to help us make the right decisions in the development of our lives. They are those God intends for us to follow. In short, they are what the Bible calls "teachers" (or, instructors).

> God's umbrella of protection is His management system for the constant development of our lives. This umbrella consists of those whom He has placed in authority over us: our parents, our preachers, our teachers, our employers, and the government.

Our key verse refers to them by using the Old English word "masters." In the Bible, the word "master" is used sometimes to define our employers, sometimes to define our Lord, and sometimes to define our government. In each case, it is referring to the primary function of teaching us. That is what our authorities do; they teach us. If you choose to follow God's ordained authorities, He can work through them to help you make the many wise decisions you will need to make in life. As a matter of fact, even if your authority is not godly, He will still use that person to help mold you. This is not true, however, if you are not under His umbrella of protection. If you choose teachers that are not God ordained, then you will be exposed to a system that will lead to your eventual destruction. Even if these authorities are good people, your development will be hindered because God has not chosen them to be the authorities through which He intends to work. Our key verse refers to them as being *blind*. It indicates lack of direction, especially in areas of spiritual direction. Good people without direction from God are blind. They cannot see afar off (2 Peter 1:9). Our verses tell us simply that if we follow those who do not have direction from God, both parties will fall.

What is God's purpose of ordained authority? Why do we need protection from the world's elements? Why is it so important to follow this authority? These are all very good questions. God designs His teachers to instruct us in principles that, when followed, will produce the structure necessary for us to make good decisions. There are four key decisions in life that God uses His teachers to guide us through:

- Choosing a mate and how to develop that relationship
- Choosing a career and how to develop that career
- Choosing and maximizing an income level
- Choosing to walk with God and how to develop that walk

In this life, God has a marital plan for you, and the devil has a marital plan for you. God has a career path, as does Satan. Both God and the devil have an income level for you. The devil even has a level for your walk with God that he will permit with little interference.

Now, what do you think are the chances that you will make

the right choice in each of these key areas without God's direction? No one wants the wrong spouse, the wrong career, the wrong income level, and if you are wrong in all these areas, you probably will not have a very strong walk with God. However, though we might never intentionally make the wrong choices, we often resist God as He tries to lead us in these areas through His teachers. We search for our own teachers who will allow us or encourage us to do what we want, feel what we want, or think what we want. These teachers are found in the world's system of management. They will lead you to make the wrong decisions in many, if not all, of these areas. As a result of these wrong decisions, you will be weathered and pressured throughout life. They will lead you toward your eventual fall.

No one ever taught me these things as I was growing up. I was raised under God-ordained leadership. They tried to lead me, but I refused their instruction as a teenager and searched for alternate teachers. All of God's teachers are on the same page, so I had to find teachers that would teach from a different book, so to speak. I found them in the world's system. Teachers who would promote my feelings over God's feelings, my desires over God's desires, my thinking over God's thinking. I found these teachers of ungodly counsel in worldly people, wrong entertainment (bad music and movies), and people who were critical of God's system in an effort to discount its importance to my life. These teachers led me into the ditch that I had to climb out of ten years later. (Truthfully, I had to go to the ditch to find them!) The result was ten years of loneliness, a horrible résumé, crippling debt, and a separated walk away from God.

But then, while still in that ditch, I came to the realization that in order to build a life that will withstand adversity, I needed to change my direction and stop following the teachers who were leading me. Praise God! He picked me up out of that horrible pit and placed my feet upon a solid foundation—the Rock, Christ Jesus-and He established my goings (Psalm 40:2). How did He establish my goings? He placed me back under God-ordained leadership: people who love God, avoid worldliness, and are positive and uplifting. These people-my preacher, teachers, my parents, my employer, and yes, even the government-began to lead my life. I followed my preacher's advice, I learned from my teachers, I began to develop my relationship with my parents again, and I worked hard for my employer (as unto Christ) while obeying the laws of the land.

Everything changed and, for me, it changed quickly. God gave me a beautiful wife within one year. By the second year, He granted me a great career, despite my poor résumé. This career position offered me a rather large income level, and He matched it with a heart to give to others. It wasn't long before I was debt free! Most importantly, He also taught me that I was created to walk with Him, and our relationship with each other began to grow again. What is the cost of following the blind? For me it was a decade of my life, and more.

Without a doubt, the best leader to follow is Jesus Christ. The best *forms* of Christ to follow are His God-ordained authorities.

Remember His encouragement in verse 40: *The disciple is not above his master: but every one that is perfect shall be as his master.* As students, we are not above our teachers. We are under them, which denotes protection. The word *perfect* here means fully informed. If we allow them to teach us, if we will submit to their leading and direction in life, then we will become fully informed. As a result, we will someday be teachers. Second Timothy 2:2 says *And the things that thou hast heard of me among many witnesses, the same commit thou to faithful men, who shall be able to teach others also.*

Focus

The second Form of a Firm Foundation is found in verses 41 and 42-Focus.

> *And why beholdest thou the mote that is in thy brother's eye, but perceivest not the beam that is in thine own eye? Either how canst thou say to thy brother, Brother, let me pull out the mote that is in thine eye, when thou thyself beholdest not the beam that is in thine own eye? Thou hypocrite, cast out first the beam out of thine own eye, and then shalt thou see clearly to pull out the mote that is in thy brother's eye.*

These verses are referring to our focus in life, what we are fixing our attention on. Jesus is explaining a flaw in focus that we all tend to have at times. We want to focus on the perceived spiritual needs and weaknesses of others rather than focusing on our own spiritual needs and weaknesses. A *mote* is defined as "a small particle." A *beam* is defined as "a large piece of lumber." Though it is somewhat humorous, this illustration is showing how flawed our focus can become. He indicates that a brother (a fellow Christian) is trying to assist another brother with a flaw. He says to his fellow Christian, "Let me, or, I want permission from you to help you. You have a small particle in your eye." However, he does not even perceive that his focus should be on the large obstruction that hinders his ability to help his brother. Jesus calls him a hypocrite. The word *hypocrite* is the word actor. He is saying, "You actor! You must first handle your large problems before you can even understand how to help others with their small problems."

Our Lord indicates that we cannot see clearly how to assist someone with a small problem until we first understand we have a large problem and then gain the assistance of someone to rectify it. Only then are we qualified to help our brothers. Our focus should always begin on our own personal weaknesses and flaws.

It is always easier to look at the flaws of others rather than our own. Romans 2:21 reads, *Thou therefore which teachest another, teachest thou not thyself? thou that preachest a man should not steal, dost thou steal?* These people mentioned here are teachers and preachers, yet they do not follow their own advice. I believe that this admonition to teachers and preachers is because they themselves sometimes focus on the needs of others, forgetting to focus on their own needs. If this can sometimes be true in the lives of our God-ordained authority figures, would it not be only natural to understand its relevance to us, the followers?

Verse 24 goes on to say, *For the name of God is blasphemed among the Gentiles through you, as it is written.* The word, *blasphemed* means "to speak evil of." The Bible is saying that unbelievers speak evil of God as a result of the hypocrisy of some teachers and preachers. When we have flaws that are obvious to those we are seeking to help, we cannot see clearly to help them, and those that are watching realize we are just actors. It makes God look bad.

Proverbs 20:6 reminds us that *Most men will proclaim every one his own goodness: but a faithful man who can find?* Most people are able to share how good they are to others (they are talkers), but to follow that proclamation with a faithfulness that proves it (a walker) is quite difficult. Verse 7 goes on to say, *The just man walketh in his integrity: his children are blessed after him.* There are lots of talkers, but very few walkers. I don't know about you, but I want to be a walker *and* a talker. I want God to develop my life so that I am qualified to teach others. As a matter of fact, if you are a walker and not merely a talker, your offspring (physical and spiritual) will be happy because of it. Your integrity directly affects the level of contentment of those following you. Wow, what an amazing truth!

In Luke 18:10-14 Jesus tells of *Two men [who]* went up into the temple to pray; the one a Pharisee (a law-abiding sect of the Jews), *and the other a publican* (a tax collector). *The Pharisee stood and prayed thus with himself, God, I thank thee, that I am not as other men are, extortioners, unjust, adulterers, or even as this publican. I fast twice in the week, I give tithes of all that I possess.* Notice that he lists to God what he doesn't do wrong and what he does do right; however, he makes no mention of what he *does do wrong!* However, *...the publican, standing afar off, would not lift up so much as his eyes unto heaven, but smote upon his breast, saying, God be merciful to me a sinner.* (Jesus said) *I tell you, this man went down to his house justified rather than the other.* The word *justify* here does not mean saved. It means "conformed to the law." This "sinner" was more conformed to the law than the "teacher" of the law because his focus was on what he did that was wrong, rather than on what he did that was right or what others did that was wrong. Jesus went on to teach, *for every one that exalteth himself shall be abased; and he that humbleth himself shall be exalted.* (Boy, ain't that the truth!)

Do your remember the Old Testament account of David and

Bathsheba? What a sad example of overlooking our flaws and judging the flaws of another. In 2 Samuel 12:1-7 we see that, *the LORD sent Nathan unto David...and said unto him, There were two men in one city; the one rich, and the other poor. The rich man had exceeding many flocks...the poor man had nothing, save one little ewe lamb, which he had bought and nourished up...and was unto him as a daughter. And there came a traveller unto the rich man, and he...took the poor man's lamb, and dressed it for the man that was come to him. And David's anger was greatly kindled against the man; and he said to Nathan, As the LORD liveth, the man that hath done this thing shall surely die...and Nathan said to David, Thou art the man.* David's beam was large, yet he didn't even notice it when faced with the flaw of another. David was a hypocrite. He was an actor. He believed that the rich man should die for his selfish act of theft, but he didn't see anything wrong with his own theft and murder of the person from whom he had stolen. David's focus was off. Way off. It cost him dearly. But to his credit, the lessons he learned from this failed focus changed his life for the better...forever (see Psalm 51).

Another illustration of focusing on the shortcomings of others is found in John 8:3-11.

And the scribes and Pharisees brought unto him (Jesus) *a woman taken in adultery; and when they had set her in the midst, They say unto him, Master, this woman was taken in adultery, in the very act. Now Moses in the law commanded us, that such should be stoned: but what sayest thou? ...he lifted up himself, and said unto them, He that is without sin among you, let him first cast a stone at her...And they which heard it, being convicted by their own conscience, went out one by one...and Jesus was left alone, and the woman standing in the midst. When Jesus had lifted up himself, and saw none but the woman, he said unto her, Woman, where are those thine accusers? hath no man condemned thee? She said, No man, Lord. And Jesus said unto her, Neither do I condemn thee: go, and sin no more.*

What hypocrisy! These scribes and Pharisees, the religious leaders and teachers, were ready to kill this woman who had sin in her life. Jesus simply reminded them of their own flaws. Anyone without a flaw could throw that first stone. Examining their own flaws led these men to be convicted (as well it should for any of us). They left, realizing they were no better than she. Then Jesus, the only flawless man in the crowd, decided rather than to condemn her, to encourage her ...*go, and sin no more.* She was fortunate to be alive, and rather than being placed in bondage and condemnation, He set her free with an opportunity to live independent of the power of sin.

What a beautiful picture of what Christ did for us at Calvary! Rather than condemn us, He provided Himself as a sacrifice. That sacrifice not only paid the penalty for our sin, saving us from certain condemnation, but it also provided us the emancipation from the power of sin, thus giving us freedom from the accuser!

> Before Christ, your spirit is dead; after Christ, your spirit is "made alive" and his Spirit comes to dwell within you.

We as Christians need to be more lenient toward those who are struggling. In Galatians 6:1 we are taught that what goes around comes around. *Brethren, if a man be overtaken in a fault, ye which are spiritual, restore such an one in the spirit of meekness; considering thyself, lest thou also be tempted.* Meekness is "getting along with others without causing friction." *Spiritual* means "consisting of a

Spirit." Before Christ, your spirit is dead; after Christ, your spirit is "made alive" and His Spirit comes to dwell within you. Though we may not act like it at times, we are referred to in the Bible as being spiritual or "consisting of a living Spirit."

Paul teaches us that if a brother in Christ has a flaw, fellow Christians should restore him. The word *restore* means "to return to [his] former place." It does not necessarily mean return to his former position, but he should be returned to his former place. It is referring to his relationship that was strained as a result of his flaw. He teaches us that the way this should be done is with fellow believers using a spirit of meekness, a temperament of cooperation. He warns us that if we fail to restore because we use the temperament of division or discord, we ourselves could be tempted. He tells us to consider ourselves, to look at our own flaws. Before we tackle another man's faults, we need to look at our own. We need to return ourselves to our former fellowship with Christ, then we will have the right temperament to help others.

If you are like me, you are more comfortable justifying your flaws by comparing them to the flaws of others. Second Corinthians 10:12 says, *For we dare not make ourselves of the number, or compare ourselves with some that commend themselves: but they measuring themselves by themselves, and comparing themselves among themselves, <u>are not wise</u>.* It is very foolish to compare ourselves with anyone other than our Lord Jesus Christ. If we stay focused on His example as our "measuring stick," we will be less inclined to turn a blind eye to our own flaws.

Fruitfulness

The third Form of a Firm Foundation is found in Luke 6:43-

45-Fruitfulness. *Fruit* means "outcome, or result." So, the Form of Fruitfulness would be the outcome, or result, of a life that has produced a firm foundation. These verses compare a good tree vs. a corrupt tree to a good man vs. an evil man. This comparison is based on their fruit, the outcome or result of their lives.

> *For a good tree bringeth not forth corrupt fruit; neither doth a corrupt tree bring forth good fruit. For every tree is known by his own fruit. For of thorns men do not gather figs, nor of a bramble bush gather they grapes. A good man out of the good treasure of his heart bringeth forth that which is good; and an evil man out of the evil treasure of his heart bringeth forth that which is evil: for of the abundance of the heart his mouth speaketh.*

A good man will bring forth that which is good from the good treasure of his heart. We are not talking about a physical heart, the organ that pumps blood and sustains life. We are referring to the seat of affections and passions. When your motive is good, your outcome will be good. Following the comparison of the man with the beam trying to help the man with the mote, we must understand that Jesus is teaching us that to help other people and to see positive results, we must have the right motives.

In our key verses for this point of being fruitful, Jesus speaks of *treasure*, which means "a great quantity of a thing that is collected for future use." The majority of the things we store in our seats of affections are for later use. They are saved for a rainy day, so to speak. That is, they are stored until our hearts feel they are needed. When we are faced with life's circumstances, our seats of affections and passions will respond. That is why they are there, to respond to stimuli. To this end, if we store in our seats of affections self-centered, possession-centered thoughts, and we store in our seats of passions thoughts of bitterness, resentment, anger, or malice, then when we are faced with adversity, these passions and affections will run rampant, feeling violated. This will be the outcome or result of "the great quantity that we collected for future use." The evil treasure of our hearts will bring forth (bear fruit) that which is evil. He goes on to say, ...*For of the abundance* (i.e., great quantity or overflow) *of the heart* [the] *mouth speaketh.*

Our verses remind us, however, that it works both ways. If we collect for future use an affection for things above (Colossians 3:2) and capture and collect our God-given passion for love, joy, peace and the other fruits of the Spirit, then when faced with a circumstance that violates those affections and passions, we will respond properly as a "result."

It is impossible for a good tree to bear bad fruit. So it is in us-we will bear fruit based on what we have collected as treasure in our hearts.

What does God really want to see by our being fruitful? What does God want the outcome, or result, of our lives to be? The answer is found in John 15:8. *Herein is my Father glorified, that ye bear much fruit; so shall ye be my disciples.* Whenever you see the word "herein," ask yourself, why is that word in here? Look closely at that verse. It gives us the formula for glorifying God with our lives. God is glorified (or, made to look good) when we bear much fruit. According to this verse, it is impossible to be a disciple, or student, who follows Christ, and not bear much fruit. If your "fruit inspection" is proving to be lacking, you are not the student that Christ wants you to be. Your fruit must not only be good, but it must be much, in great quantity. That is the only way to make God look good. He lists no other thing that glorifies him "in here." He indicates "herein" is how you make God look good-bearing much fruit. You will be one of His students who is truly following Him.

What is the fruit of a Christian? The first response to that question for a well-meaning Christian would probably be Galatians 5:22-23, ...*love, joy, peace, longsuffering, gentleness, goodness, faith, meekness, temperance*... But those are not the fruit of a Christian. Those are the fruit, or result, of the Holy Spirit indwelling you. I believe the outcome, or result, of a Christian is found in Proverbs 11:30, *The fruit of the righteous is a tree of life...*

Stored away in my parents' home is a photo album with a family tree drawn inside. That family tree represents the outcome, or result, of marriage unions from generation to generation. Similarly, what is the outcome, or result, of our marriage union with Jesus Christ? I believe the Bible indicates clearly that the outcome, or result, of our marriage union with Jesus Christ is baby Christians. The offspring of Christ, Who gave life, should direct that same opportunity of life to others. You will become fruitful when you begin to invest in the eternal destination of other people.

The formula for directing people to this opportunity of new life is found in Revelation 22:17. *And the Spirit* (the Holy Spirit) *and the bride* (the church) *say, Come. And let him that heareth* (that's you!) *say, Come. And let him that is athirst* (the lost) *come. And whosoever will, let him take the water of life freely.* I believe this verse is encouraging us to invite lost people to attend church with us. Let's follow this admonition in reverse order. It tells us that if we who have heard and taken of the water of life will invite those who are lost and without this life-giving water to "Come [to church]," then they will come. The bride (or, the church and its pastor) along with the Spirit of God[during the invitation], will then say, "Come." If the thirsty come, they will drink of this water and never thirst again (John 4:14). We have a responsibility to beckon others to come drink of the Water of Life. That is what glorifies God! That is the fruit which a follower of Jesus will bear-baby Christians!

Fulfilling God's Requests

Obedience to God is a prerequisite for success in supporting your structure of life. It is the fundamental element in living the victorious Christian life. Our next verse, Luke 6:46, says, *And why call ye me, Lord, Lord, and do not the things which I say?* How can we call Him our Master yet refuse to obey what He has told us to do?

God wants to communicate with us. He leads and instructs us through preachers/teachers. He gives wisdom through many counselors. He guides and directs through His Word. He communicates to us in prayer, and He leads and convicts us through His indwelling Spirit. These five forms of communication are intended to help us fulfill His will for our lives.

In John 16:7-14 we see an absolutely incredible truth being explained. Jesus is speaking to His disciples and He says, *Nevertheless I tell you the truth* (Usually, when someone prefaces a statement with "I am telling you the truth," it makes me wonder if they normally tell me lies. But that is not what Jesus is saying here. He is saying, "What I am about to tell you is going to be really hard to believe."); *It is expedient* (or, better) *for you that I go away: for if I go not away, the Comforter will not come unto you; but if I depart, I will send him unto you.* Now, I know why that would seem so hard to believe. I mean, if Jesus was living beside me and I was literally following Him for years, I would think I was better off with Him than without Him. As a matter of fact, if you look at the lives of the disciples, you would think that same thing. I mean, what a bunch of losers! They couldn't seem to do anything right. They questioned our Savior often and did not have the faith to trust Him in many areas. As a matter of fact, some of them were more concerned about who was going to be in charge and who was going to be considered the greatest in the kingdom that Christ was promising to them. These guys were doubtlessly doomed for failure if Christ left. Sure enough, when He was arrested and imprisoned (still here in bodily form, but taken from them in presence), they all took off like a bunch of yellow-bellies. Some went back to their old occupations, some even denied that they knew Him. Do you see why it would be so hard to believe that they are better off without Him?

> Obedience to God is a prerequisite for success in supporting your structure of life. It is the fundamental element in living the victorious Christian life.

However, a short time later He did leave this earth. And after His ascension He sent, as promised, His Comforter. What was the result? These eleven men went on to change the world. Ten of them died horrible, martyrs' deaths. History proves that each had been given an opportunity to recant his faith but refused.

Now, what in the world could have happened to these lovable losers that they would go from being scared of persecution while Jesus was here to changing the world and dying for His cause after He had gone? Only one thing changed about them-they were indwelt with the Holy Spirit. How did this help them? Let's look further into our verses in John 16. *Howbeit when he, the Spirit of truth, is come, he will guide you into all truth: for he shall not speak of himself; but whatsoever he shall hear, that shall he speak*: The Spirit of Truth (or, the Spirit of Jesus) will guide you into truth. He will not exalt Himself, He will simply share what He is instructed by Christ to share…*and he will show you things to come.* (That indicates an enlightenment of the hidden things.) *He shall glorify me* (He will make Jesus look good)*: for he shall receive of mine* (take what Jesus gives Him), *and shall show* (reveal) *it unto you.*

Here is the amazing part. We see in Act 1:8 that we *shall receive power, after that the Holy Ghost is come upon* [us]… What is this verse telling us in light of the verses we studied in John 16? It is showing us that the Holy Ghost comes into us and the Holy Ghost comes upon us. You may ask, "How does this help us to live a better life than if Jesus were still with us?" Well, it is simple to understand but hard-fought by the enemy to follow. Jesus will communicate the truth to us. This truth will be brought to us by one or more of those earlier-mentioned five forms of communication. When the truth is shared, it will bear witness with the Spirit within us. The Spirit will then guide and direct us in an area, often using conviction of that truth and our failure to *fulfill* it. When this happens, we will become *uncomfortable.* While in this uncomfortable position, we can ask God for His help to *fulfill* His request or truth, then He will send the Power of the Holy Ghost upon us and make us *comfortable* doing something that makes us *uncomfortable.* The primary function of the indwelling Holy Spirit is to make us uncomfortable with error in our lives. The primary function of the influence of the Holy Spirit *upon* us is to give us the power to be comfortable with His direction so that we may *fulfill* the leading of the indwelling Spirit in correcting that error.

However, when we say "no" to the conviction, "no" to positions of being uncomfortable, then we weaken the Spirit's influence over the soul. When we reject His leading, we will eventually reject His feeding. We will stave off the Spirit's ability to communicate to us. We will not listen to our preachers or teachers, we will not seek counsel, we will not read or try to understand what we read, and our prayers will be nothing more than grocery lists, if we pray at all.

Why does this happen? Because of our unwillingness to be uncomfortable. If God had intended for us to be comfortable, He would not have sent us a Comforter! You will not see God's power on your life or ministry until you allow His Spirit to communicate your error to you with that uncomfortable feeling of conviction, prodding you to turn to God with a desire to fulfill His every request. Upon doing this, He will step in with Holy Power from on High and make you comfortable again. Remember, if you are serving God and you are comfortable, then you do not need a Comforter. You are serving God in your power, not His. If you are doing anything in your power, then you are walking after the flesh, meaning your mind is in rebellion to the Spirit and in subjection to your own lustful desires. *For they that are after the flesh do mind the things of the flesh; but they that are after the Spirit the things of the Spirit* (Romans 8:5). Don't call Him Lord or Master or Teacher unless you are doing what He says, fulfilling His requests.

Founded

The previous four Forms of a Firm Foundation are really by-products of the fifth form. If we are **Founded** on the right foundation, then we will have a supernatural desire to **Follow** the right people, **Focus** on our own spiritual needs, bear **Fruit** that glorifies God, and to **Fulfill God's Requests** of obedience. Luke 6:47-48 tells us, *Whosoever <u>cometh</u> to me, and <u>heareth</u> my sayings, and <u>doeth</u> them, I will show you to whom he is like: He is like a man which built an house, and digged deep, and laid the foundation on a rock: and when the flood arose, the stream beat vehemently upon that house, and could not shake it: for it was founded upon a rock.* The foundation on which you place your forms will produce a structure that is capable of withstanding adversity. Of course, you should know by now there is only one foundation worth building the structure of your life upon. That foundation is a personal relationship with Jesus Christ. Being firmly founded on the solid Rock of Christ will guarantee our safety when the floods come and the stream beats vehemently upon our lives. We will still have troubles; we will still experience pain. It is inevitable; none of that will be removed. But our foundation will keep us safe from destruction.

In 1 Corinthians 3:11-17 Paul says, *For other foundation can no man lay than that is laid, which is Jesus Christ.* (There is no other foundation better than the foundation that was already laid) *Now if any man build upon this foundation gold, silver, precious stones,* (these represent the structures we place on our foundation that will last and be of great value) *wood, hay, stubble* (these represent the structures we place on our foundation that are temporal and of little value)... He goes on to say... *the fire shall try every man's work* (structure) *of what sort it is. If any man's work* (structure) *abide which he hath built thereupon, he shall receive a reward. If any man's work* (structure) *shall be burned, he shall suffer loss: but he himself shall be saved...* God's fire of judgement will determine whether you wasted the foundation that was given to you or whether you valued it enough to build something of value upon it.

Paul goes on to explain why this structure is so important. It is because the structure you are placing on this foundation of Jesus Christ is now going to be the dwelling place of God. Verse 16 reads, *Know ye not that ye are the temple of God, and that the Spirit of God dwelleth in you? If any man defile the temple of God, him shall God destroy; for the temple of God is holy, which temple ye are.* You don't want this to happen to you. You want to be a structure of value in which God may dwell.

Jesus tells us in our passage in Luke 6 how to make sure we are building such a structure. He compares the person who builds the proper structure on the proper foundation as being like someone who...*cometh to me, and heareth my sayings, and doeth them...* We have discussed coming to Christ, hearing His leadings, and doing them under His power. It is that person who will be founded firmly on Jesus Christ.

Verse 49 gives us the other side of the story, also. *But he that heareth, and doeth not* (notice he never came first, thus he has no real foundation), *is like a man that without a foundation built an house upon the earth; against which the stream did beat vehemently, and immediately it fell; and the ruin of that house was great.* The same trials and heartaches come to this individual. But notice what is different about his description compared to the first man-*he that heareth, and doeth not...* He heard about this awesome foundation, but he did not come to it to build his house. He did not follow the instructions (Christ's sayings) on how to build his structure and instead, built it upon the earth using the rudiments of this world. His life may seem glamorous, but it is built upon dirt. When those inevitable storms come and the rains do beat vehemently against that "house," it will immediately fall! Here is the saddest phrase of all-*and the ruin of that house was great.*

A house for our God must be a structure that is built within before it is ever built without. Within, by using the right foundation. Within, by fulfilling the requests of His Spirit. Within, by producing fruit. Within, by focusing on our own flaws. Within, by following the right people. This is where God wants to live-His Temple. These are the Five Forms of a Firm Foundation, the five molds that will be the basis for supporting your structure to house the Living God.

Chapter 6

6 Procedures
for Pleasing God

Furthermore then we beseech you, brethren, and exhort you by the Lord Jesus, that as ye have received of us how ye ought to walk and to please God, so ye would abound more and more. **1 Thessalonians 4:1**

I don't know about you, but if God is going to live inside of me, as we discussed at the conclusion of chapter five, then I want to get along with Him. I want to enjoy His presence. I don't want His presence within me to produce a convicting, guilty feeling as I act and react toward life and its circumstances.

In other words, I want to be at peace with God and I want God to be at peace with me. To do this I must be willing to please God. If I please God, I believe with my whole heart that He will please me and be pleased with me.

That brings us to a search, a search for pleasure. Pleasure that pleases God. I have found six of these pleasures. In this chapter we will talk about pleasure and how God intends for us to handle it.

You see, finding pleasure in life is an interesting search. If we live to obtain it, we may never get it. If we seek to give it, it will probably find us on its own.

At eighteen years of age, a young man had one ambition in life—to become rich and famous, gaining all that the world has to offer. That young man set out in a rock 'n roll career that within a few years had given him all that he could want. His fans numbered in the hundreds of thousands; there was no earthly pleasure that was withheld from him. While heading toward the peak of his fame and glory, when anything he desired was at his fingertips, he wrote the now-infamous self-portrait song, *(I Can't Get No) Satisfaction*. Though Mick Jagger had successfully gained all the fame and fortune that the world claims will bring satisfaction, he discovered that ultimately it will not bring a man lasting pleasure. To this day, I would probably safely assume that he has failed to find true satisfaction in life, though he has famously fed his every appetite.

Reformers Unanimous' Principle #4 of 10 reminds us that it is not possible to fight a fleshly appetite by indulging in it. We cannot feed selfish, fleshly appetites and find any level of satisfaction whatsoever. Ecclesiastes 5:10 teaches us that *He that loveth silver shall not be satisfied with silver; nor he that loveth abundance with increase: this is also vanity.* If you are looking for satisfaction from the accumulation of money or the accumulation of possessions, your search will be in vain; it will equal nothing. Solomon goes on to teach in verse eleven that *When goods increase, they are increased that eat them: and what good is there to the owners thereof, saving the beholding of them with their eyes?* The disappointment of having relatives, friends, enemies, and Uncle Sam seeking to take advantage of your fortune will outweigh the useful benefits of everything you have sought to gain.

> Bad things in life are enjoyed first and paid for later, but good things in life are paid for first and enjoyed later.

Of course, many of us have found this to be true. However, it is one of the most disregarded lessons in life. It just seems natural for us to believe that a focus on meeting our own selfish desires will improve our chances of providing ourselves pleasure.

Why is it so true that earthly possessions fail to provide lasting pleasure? Because of this very important principle: Bad things in life are enjoyed first and paid for later, but good things in life are paid for first and enjoyed later. I think most of us have seen this principle to be true in our own lives. Hebrews 11:25 tells us that sin *is* pleasurable, but only for a season. We have all made wrong choices that seemed to bring great pleasure at the time. But when the harvest came and we began reaping the consequences of our choices, we begged God for a crop failure! We enjoyed the wrong pleasures first and had to unwillingly pay for them later.

However, the opposite is true as well. The right pleasures are paid for first then enjoyed for the rest of our lives. It requires sowing the seeds of effort and righteousness. We will then reap a harvest of pleasure that can be enjoyed forever. The right pleasures do not consist of what pleases us but rather of whom we should be seeking to please. Pleasing God will bring us pleasure beyond compare-definitely far above the pleasures of this world.

Just as we like to experience pleasure, God also likes things to please Him. I have found in the Bible six ways that we can please God with our lives. Do you yearn to please the Lord? I know I do. In this chapter I will explain ways in which you can please God. I believe that if we seek to please God with our lives, He will reciprocate in bringing us great pleasure. Let me illustrate why it is so important to know what brings God pleasure and why it is equally important to understand what brings God displeasure.

God gave me a great dad. He taught me to have a good work ethic. He lived right, was faithful to my mother, raised my brothers and me in church, and provided us with a Christian education. I love to please my dad. But while I was growing up, he never actually told me whether I was pleasing him. I never really knew how to make my dad happy. We never talked about his likes or dislikes. I knew when I *dis*pleased him, but I never really knew for sure if I was pleasing him.

Years later, I became the supervisor of a chain of convenience stores. I had several employees whose main responsibility was to meet the standards set by our organization for sales, appearance, and quality of service. They worked hard to make me happy as their boss. One day while sitting in my office, a young lady (whom I had just given a poor review) came into my office with tears streaming down her face after viewing her report. She said to me, "I'm always trying to please you here at work, but you never tell me what it takes to please you." I immediately remembered the above description of my father. I remembered the frustration that comes when one is attempting to please but fails to understand the requirements necessary to make that happen. I had become like my father. I was convicted—as one in authority—that I had not properly communicated to those under me what it took to please me. Unless I changed, they would struggle to make me happy.

I was also convicted as I realized that as a teacher in the ministry of Reformers Unanimous, I had a responsibility to adequately inform my students as to the expected standard that would bring great pleasure to our Heavenly Father.

Fortunately, our Heavenly Father is not like I or my father was. He has told us in the Bible what pleases Him. We can know for sure if our actions and reactions are bringing Him pleasure or displeasure. Our key verse, 1 Thessalonians 4:1, reminds us that our teachers have a role in educating or at least informing us of this truth. *Furthermore then we beseech you, brethren, and exhort you by the Lord Jesus, that as ye have received of us how ye ought to walk and to please God, so ye would abound more and more.* The Apostle Paul wrote to the church at Thessalonica telling them, "We have shown you how to take steps repeatedly (walk) and what it will take for you to please God." He taught them these things so that they would grow and grow and grow.

WHOM ARE YOU SEEKING TO PLEASE?

Before we discuss pleasing and displeasing God, let me first ask you a question: Looking at the way you are living your life, are you currently seeking to please God, or do you appear to be seeking to please man? The Bible teaches that whom we serve indicates whom we please. Galatians 1:10 says, *For do I now persuade men, or God? or do I seek to please men? for if I yet pleased men, I should not be the servant of Christ.* Whom are you trying to persuade? Are you trying to persuade others that you are serving God, or are you trying to persuade God that you're living for Him? You can determine whom you are seeking to please by first determining whom you are serving with your life. If your focus is on pleasing man, you will not be a servant of Christ; you will seek to serve man. If you are seeking to please Christ, then you will focus your energies on serving Christ.

> Whom we serve indicates whom we please.

God created us for His pleasure, not for our pleasure, and not for the pleasure of our fellow man. Revelation 4:11 reads, *Thou art worthy, O Lord, to receive glory* (or, to look good) *and honour* (or, promotion) *and power* (or, authority): *for thou hast created all things, and for thy pleasure they are and were created.* We were created for His pleasure. Not only must we forsake our search for self-pleasure, but we need to cease our efforts to please everyone around us. We must have as our primary focus the desire to bring pleasure to our Maker!

So many of us have been a failure, to a degree, during periods of our life. During those periods, we have let many people down. We have brought them great displeasure with our lives, whether it was our parents (as it was in my case), or our preachers, our spouses, children, friends, employers, or all of the above. We often feel a debt to them to improve our lifestyles and, in doing so, to right the wrongs that we have committed against them. We begin to focus on improving our lives for their benefit. Often times, we feel the best way to benefit them is to serve them with our lives. But that will not bring them pleasure. If they love you and want God's best for you, then when you are focused on serving and pleasing Christ, you will bring them the pleasure they desire. That is for sure!

Let us begin our study in pleasing God by determining what the Bible teaches about *displeasing* God. He explains to us in His Word how we can avoid displeasing Him. Nobody who is trying to live for God wants to displease his Father—neither his earthly father nor his heavenly Father. It would be our pleasure to bring them pleasure. After a brief look at these forms of displeasure, we will discuss the ways in which our Father in heaven is looking for us to please Him.

WHAT DISPLEASES GOD?

Here are two areas of behavior that we must avoid if we are going to please our Heavenly Father. They are both self-centered. One shows our dependence on self, the other shows our reluctance to depend on Him. Let's take a look.

1. Flesh Displeases God.

The first thing that brings displeasure to God, or does not please God, is found in Romans 8:8-being in the flesh. Romans 8:8 says, *So then they that are in the flesh cannot please God.* If you are a Christian, then you cannot be "in the flesh" (Romans 8:9 *But ye are not in the flesh, but in the Spirit, if so be that the Spirit of God dwell in you*). If you are *not* saved, your life is lived "in the flesh." However, a Christian is "in Christ"—not in the flesh. Thus we are led of the Spirit, but if your soul (mind, will, and emotions) chooses to take repeated steps (or, walk) after the prompting of your body, you will find yourself walking "after the flesh." (Romans 8:1b *walk not after the flesh, but after the Spirit.*) This will not please God. Being in the flesh as a non-believer does not please God and walking after the flesh as a believer will displease Him, as well.

We have taught you in previous chapters that your flesh is defined as your soul (mind, will, and emotions) being in subjection to your body (or, your members). Living after the flesh is when what you want, feel, or think suppresses what God wants, feels, or thinks. When this takes place, your outer man (or, the flesh) is overruling your inner man (or, the Holy Spirit). You are in control of your life, rather than God.

There are many Christian people that think they are pleasing God with their lives. These are well meaning people. They read their Bibles, go to church, serve in ministries, give sacrificially and share their faith but they are walking after the flesh. They are "after the flesh" because they are doing these things the way they *want* to do them or the way they *think* they should do them or the way they *feel* that they should be done. Sure, they are doing good, but they are doing good "after the flesh." Their mind, will, and emotions are not in subjection to God's mind, will and emotions. The soul in us is not yielding to the Spirit. The inner man (or, the Holy Spirit) is not ruling the body. It is the lust of the flesh. That is oftentimes described as wicked behavior, but the truth of the matter is that the lust of the flesh is simply defined as the desire of your soul to follow your body's desires, albeit, in rebellion to your Spirit.

We that struggle with this are trying hard to do good, but we fail to please God and we do not experience the joy of the Christian life. Why? Because good flesh is just as bad as bad flesh and we cannot please God when we are walking after our flesh, no matter how much good we are doing.

Proverbs 14:12 teaches us that, *There is a way* (or, there is a course of life) *which seemeth right unto a man, but the end thereof are the ways of death.* This death is describing not only a potentially premature death, but primarily a spiritual death. This is so true. It is easy to understand how wrong behavior can lead to both of these outcomes. That is a

> Good flesh is just as bad as bad flesh and we cannot please God when we are walking after the flesh, no matter how much good we are doing.

presumption that needs no explanation. So what was Solomon trying to teach us? I believe he was trying to tell us that there are some behaviors that look right, act right, and feel right but yet are *deadly* wrong. This behavior kills us spiritually and possible puts unnecessary limits on our life. He is referring to doing what is right in our own eyes. That's right. Our focus is off again! We are not looking at things properly. Proverbs 30:12 reads...*There is a generation that are pure in their own eyes, and yet is not washed from their filthiness.* Our sins remain unconfessed because we don't even realize we are unclean. We are doing good in our own power and not the power of God. Doing good in our own power brings us pleasure temporarily. Sin is fun for a season, but it doesn't bring God pleasure. He wants us to depend on Him to do good. Paul, again reminds us in Romans 7:18, *For I know that in me (that is, in my flesh,) dwelleth no good thing...* When my body is ruling my outer man, I am walking "after the flesh." And that which dwells within my body is of no good. I have rebelled against God. He is displeased.

2. Our Lack of Faith Displeases God.

Hebrews 11:6 explains the second way in which we displease God—a lack of faith. *But without faith it is impossible to please him: for he that cometh to God must believe that he is, and that he is a rewarder of them that diligently seek him.* Once again, as in previous chapters, this is a review of truths that we have already explained, but I feel should be repeated again for the sake of learning. You cannot please God if your life does not show confidence in who He is and what He has promised to do. Within the context of this verse is a definition of what the author meant by faith that pleases God. <u>The first measure of faith is to simply come to God with your life</u>-to come to know and understand that the answer to life's problems is God. You are turning from yourself to an all-powerful God Who, by your faith, will save you.

The dictionary defines the word "come" as to advance near from any direction. No matter the distance we get from God, whether we have lagged behind or gone ahead of Him, our faith is shown by advancing nearer to Him. A step in the right direction is the beginning. James 4:8a tells us to ...*Draw nigh to God, and he will draw nigh to you.*

Does this mean that God turns in the direction of our sinful past as we turn away from it and toward our new direction? No. I believe that when we get involved in following after our flesh, we are getting ourselves ahead of God. Fruit follows, flesh leads! We are putting ourselves first. When we stop and say, "Wait a minute! I am away from God. I need to have more faith in Him to *lead* my life. I will turn around." Lo and behold, there God is, still going in the same direction as He always has been—not turning toward our bad behavior, but leading those who are not trying to get ahead of Him. As we turn around and draw nearer to God, He is then drawing nearer to us, and we can take our place in line. We can stop leading and start trusting. Hebrews 11:6 says in order to please God, we must take the first step. The first step of faith is to *come* to God.

<u>The second measure of faith is the one that saves us.</u> Hebrews 11:6 goes on to say, *for he that cometh to God must believe that he is* [God]... Our coming to Him will be devoid of benefit if it isn't accompanied by belief. We must *believe* that He is God! This, my friend, is the essence of

salvation-believing by faith in God's plan. His plan for your sinful condition is simple. He allowed the sacrifice of His only Son as the only acceptable terms of payment for your sin debt. We must accept this truth. We must accept His payment terms. We must believe in His plan. We must believe He is God. This is the faith that saves you. It pleases God for you to have this faith. Without this measure of faith, you will not only fail to please God, but you will spend an eternity in damnation to hell and its torments, separated from Him. That is hot displeasure! In Deuteronomy 9:18-29, Moses prayed diligently for the people of Israel and for his brother Aaron. They lacked faith in God and in their leader Moses. While He was away to receive our Lord's commands for His people, they exercised their lack of faith through idolatry and wicked behavior. They had not come to God; they had gone away and they did not believe in Him. They believed in pagan worship. In verse 19, Moses said, *I was afraid of the anger and hot displeasure, wherewith the LORD was wroth against you* (Israel) *to destroy you.*

This is how to begin the process of pleasing God—Step 1- coming to Him, and step 2- believing in Him. The rest of the definition of faith (which includes steps 3 and 4) will change how we live our lives. Steps three and four indicate a faith that, after coming to God and believing in Him, is willing to follow God (step 3) and expect things from Him (step 4). These are the manifestations of complete faith in God.

Let's look at our verse again. *But without faith it is impossible to please him: for he that cometh to God must believe that he is, and that he is a rewarder of them that diligently seek him.* Step three is to diligently seek Him and step four is to anticipate, by faith, a reward for that diligence. Of course, there are many earthly rewards for seeking God. They are the evidence of Christ living through His dedicated children: love, joy, peace, and the other fruits of the Spirit, which are no small reward. But what are the eternal rewards? As we saw in chapter five, I Corinthians 3:12-15 teaches us that *...if any man build upon this foundation* (the foundation of faith in Jesus) *gold, silver, precious stones* (things of precious or eternal value)*, wood, hay, stubble* (things of little or temporal value)*; Every man's work shall be made manifest: for the day shall declare it, because it shall be revealed by fire; and the fire shall try every man's work of what sort it is. If any man's work abide which he hath built thereupon, he shall receive a reward. If any man's work shall be burned, he shall suffer loss: but he himself shall be saved; yet so as by fire.* Now what is that telling us? It is simply reminding us that there is a faith that saves us, but there is also another measure of faith that changes us. God evaluates our measures of faith during our judgment. One measure of faith can bring us heaven as a reward; the higher measure of faith brings us the rewards of heaven.

I am grateful for the measure of faith that I have that saved me. But to increase my faith, I do not need to increase my belief in Jesus' sacrifice. I already believe! To increase my faith, I must believe more in God's ability to change me. This is a higher measure of faith. The simplest is a requirement for heaven; the higher measure of faith is a belief that He will use us for His glory.

The song title *Trust and Obey* tells us how to be happy in Jesus. There are many Christians who are not happy. I do not question unhappy Christian's faith in our Lord Jesus to save them. I would, however, question their faith in our Lord to change them. I want the heavenly rewards. If you read the parable of the talents in Matthew, you will see that

God gave one, two, and five talents to three respective individuals. Two of them increased His wealth; one simply protected His wealth. To each of the two who increased their talents, He said in Matthew 25:23, ...*Well done, good and faithful servant; thou hast been faithful over a few things, I will make thee ruler over many things: enter thou into the joy of thy lord.* They only had to be faithful in a few things—not in everything! Though one profited five talents when given five talents and the other profited only two when given two, they were both told they were faithful in a "few" things. These guys were not perfect in their faith. But they both received the same reward—ruler over much in the joy of the Lord (heaven). Why did they receive these rewards? For being faithful in a few things.

Strong faith only requires a few things: a belief that saves you and a diligent seeking that changes you. The man who had been given one talent (opportunity) did not believe in its value. He buried it and missed the reward of heaven. I do not want to have faith in nothing and be punished with hell. I do not want to have faith in one thing and get heaven, with little reward. I want to have faith in God to save me *and* to change me. I want to have faith in these few things and hear *Well done, good and faithful servant; thou hast been faithful over a few things*, and gain as a reward the opportunity to be a ruler over many things in heaven.

Well, how are we going to qualify for these earthly and heavenly rewards? What must be our measure of faith? Our level of faith must be measured by the level of our diligence with which we are seeking. Our verse tells us that He is a rewarder of them that diligently seek Him. "Diligence" is defined as a steady application; the word "seek" is defined as to go in search of. Dissected and defined, our next measure of faith that God is requesting of us is "a steady application of searching for Him." Simply put, it is a consistent effort of increasing our knowledge of and our fellowship with God. We are saved by believing in Him, and we are changed by knowing Him.

To please God, we must avoid displeasing God. He has told us in His Word that it is not possible to please Him if we are walking after our flesh and if we do not have faith. We can do good and believe in Him and still not please Him. It doesn't sound right, but it's true. Our good can be fleshly and our belief in Him, absent of diligent seeking, makes it impossible to please Him with our lives.

Now, let's look at some exciting things God requests of us that bring Him great pleasure. Remember, those who please God, God is sure to please in return. I consider these six procedures to be the way to "get satisfaction."

Six Procedures for Pleasing God

1a. GIVING PRAISE PLEASES GOD.

I will <u>praise the name of God</u> with a song, and will magnify him with thanksgiving. This also shall <u>please the LORD</u>... Psalm 69:30-31a

God lists two things in this verse that please Him. They are very similar in form. We will discuss them as one, though they can be two distinct forms of pleasing God. God is pleased when we praise Him, and God is pleased when we thank Him. We use those two words rather casually-praise and thanks-but what do these words actually mean?

The word praise defined in the dictionary means to give credit. When it comes to receiving credit for something there are three options: giving credit, taking credit, or withholding credit.

Here's a good example of praise, or properly giving credit: You are complimented on the successful completion of a task. But, behind the scenes there was someone else who did much of the legwork, someone who stood in the gap and benefited you in such a way that you looked good as a result of their help. The proper thing to do is to deflect the compliment back to the person who was a real benefit to you. You are giving credit rather than taking the credit for yourself.

When God does something for us, we oftentimes keep the credit that rightfully belongs to God. We should say when given a compliment, "Well, praise God!" While it may seem insincere to some, it should be our sincere attempt of reflecting credit that is given to us back toward the proper person—God. If we do not do this, then we are taking the credit that belongs to Him. Now, we may not be guilty of failing to do this, but that does not mean we are giving God all the credit that He deserves. You see, not only can we fail by taking credit, but we can also fail to please God by overlooking opportunities to give God credit or praise. God deserves the credit for everything! We please Him when we do this. It is simple to give God credit for good things. It is difficult and requires effort on our part to give God the credit that He deserves... the credit for all things. And this credit does not necessarily need to be declared in a public proclamation to others. It could be done in a private prayer to Him. Unless God is requiring of you a public praise, He is equally pleased with both.

Let's look at some examples from the book of Psalms to see how often we may overlook opportunities to give credit to God publicly and privately.

- Praising God for His willingness to overlook my injuries to Him

  Psalm 63:3 *Because thy lovingkindness is better than life, my lips shall praise thee.*

- Praising God collectively as a people

  Psalm 67:3 *Let the people praise thee, O God; let all the people praise thee.*

- Praising God throughout the day

  Psalm 71:8 *Let my mouth be filled with thy praise and with thy honour all the day.*

- Praising God for the span of our life

  Psalm 71:14-15 *But I will hope continually, and will yet praise thee more and more. My mouth shall shew forth thy righteousness and thy salvation all the day; for I know not the numbers thereof.*

- Praising God for our salvation

  Psalm 71:23 *My lips shall greatly rejoice when I sing unto thee; and my soul, which thou hast redeemed.*

- Praising God for His goodness and effort on our behalf

  Psalm 107:31 *Oh that men would praise the LORD for his goodness, and for his wonderful works to the children of men!*

- Praising God throughout the day for His right decisions on our behalf

  Psalm 119:164 *Seven times a day do I praise thee because of thy righteous judgments.*

- Praising God to our children for His efforts and actions on our behalf

  Psalm 145:4,10 *One generation shall praise thy works to another, and shall declare thy mighty acts. All thy works shall praise thee, O LORD; and thy saints shall bless thee.*

- Praising God for what He is going to do on our behalf

  Psalm 42:5 *Why art thou cast down, O my soul? and why art thou disquieted in me? hope thou in God: for I shall yet praise him for the help of his countenance.*

Jesus set the example for praising God in our prayer time.

In Luke 11, He begins His model prayer by praising His Father. *And he said unto them, When ye pray, say, Our Father which art in heaven, Hallowed be thy name. Thy kingdom come. Thy will be done, as in heaven, so in earth* (Luke 11:2).

Praising God pleases Him. We owe God the credit for every victory and for the lessons learned in every defeat; we ought to praise Him on our good days and on our bad days. That is why Reformers Unanimous International has prescribed a time in the *It's Personal* Daily Journal specifically to praise the Lord. It takes a conscious effort to praise the Lord throughout our day. It begins by praising Him and giving Him the credit He is due in the morning and continuing it throughout the day.

If God has given you victory over darkness, He deserves the praise for it! I have had old friends say to me, "Steve, I see that you've quit indulging in drugs and alcohol! Well that's great; I'm so proud of you!" It would be easy to just say something generic, such as, "Well, I've worked hard for my sobriety." But, that would be robbery! I owe God *all* the glory for my victories in life. I cannot take His glory; I must give Him the credit. It is only because of what God has done that I have attained any level of victory. I could instead say, "It's not me," but that would be falling short. I have not taken credit, but I have not given credit either. To please God, I cannot take credit, I cannot conceal credit, I must *give* credit. And so must you.

I have been to many churches. I have met leaders who take credit and I have seen people who give improper credit. When a pastor takes credit or someone credits a pastor as being a great "church builder," this is improper credit. There is only one Church Builder-Christ. He said, *I will build my church* (Matthew 16:18). "I" and "my" are possessional, not positional. If you are a church builder, then Christ is not the head of that church. The truth is that the pastor probably *is* the primary reason that God is building the church, because the pastor is willing to let God work through Him. However, God deserves the credit. In most cases it is not the pastor who tries to steal this credit. His members or other pastor friends, who mean well but overlook the importance of giving God *all* credit, usually improperly give it to the Pastor or church leadership.

The saddest experience of all, however, is that I have seen many members who fail to give credit or praise to God at all. In many churches today, testimony time or praise time is not nearly as vocal as the prayer time is. It seems easy for many to discuss publicly a perceived need but nearly impossible to get them to vocalize a victory on the part of our Lord. Why is that? I must assume it is because we love God but we don't appreciate Him. If we truly appreciated God, it would manifest itself in a desire to proclaim His goodness, a desire to give Him proper credit, a desire to praise Him. This is what it takes to please God. When we refuse to speak, whether publicly to others or privately in prayer, about the things that God deserves credit for, we are not pleasing God. We are, in fact, displeasing Him.

> If we truly appreciated God, it would manifest itself in a desire to proclaim His goodness, a desire to give Him proper credit, a desire to praise Him. That is what it takes to please God.

Reformers Unanimous International has, as its primary ministry, an addiction abstinence program. The format of our Friday evening class consists of three forms of talk. "Talking to God" in prayer and testimonies, "Talking to Each Other" in group counsel, and "God Talking to Us" through preaching. "Talking to God" is the first talk and lasts longer than all the rest. It is not intended to be that way; we often have to cut it off for the sake of remaining on schedule. Why? Because we teach our students to publicly express their extreme appreciation for who God is and what He has done for them. It is exciting to hear the dynamic praise reports of people pleasing God in praise and thanks. As a matter of fact, whenever I travel to churches that have chapters of Reformers Unanimous, I am amazed at the level of public praise I hear not only from the students, but from the church members as well. It seems as if the Friday first talk is spreading to the other services, and it is infecting the other members with a positive outlook toward God that is worth publicly commending. I believe God is very pleased with this. It is a procedure for pleasing God.

1b. GIVING THANKS PLEASES GOD.

I will praise the name of God with a song, and will __magnify him__ __with thanksgiving__. This also shall __please the LORD__... Psalm 69:30-31a

The next form by which we may please the Lord is similar to the first. The second part of Psalm 69:30 tells us to ... *magnify him with thanksgiving.* The word *magnify* defined means, "to make great or to enlarge," and *thanksgiving* means "expressing gratitude." So, we can please the Lord by enlarging Him or making Him look great with expressions of gratitude. Giving thanks is different than giving credit (or, praise). Credit is giving honor to whom honor is due. Thanks is a feeling of kindness that expresses itself in gratitude. It is the truest form of proving appreciation. When we appreciate something someone does for us, we usually respond with a "thank you." Does your thankfulness show through your actions toward others? It pleases God when we give Him the credit He is due and when we express to Him our gratitude for His behavior toward us.

Hebrews 13:15-16 says, *By him therefore let us offer the sacrifice of praise to God continually, that is, the fruit* (or, outcome) *of our lips giving thanks to his name. But to do good* (or, benevolence) *and to communicate* (or, participate) *forget not: for with such sacrifices God is well pleased.* Notice that God realizes that the giving of thanks is a sacrifice. It is not something that comes natural for us. He will be pleased if we will offer the sacrifice of praise to God *continually* and if we will respond with the giving of thanks. This, coupled with benevolence and service toward others, will bring God great pleasure. This pleasure will be a result of our actions to His opportunities.

What would your friends and family say about the outcome or fruit of your lips? Would it be continual praise or consistent negativity? I know I find this to be a convicting question for me and quite a challenge. I want to please God with what I say as well as with what I do. I am afraid that, although I am good about giving God credit, I fail to express gratitude with my lips.

We know that God's will for us includes things that are considered difficult to accept and often even more difficult to explain. These things we know and even believe will end up being for our good (Romans 8:28). But thanking Him for them is another thing. Are we willing to accept His will but not express gratitude for it? In 1 Thessalonians 5:18 we read, *In every thing give thanks: for this is the will of God in Christ Jesus concerning you.* This verse reminds us that for everything that God allows in our lives, we must give thanks. We must express gratitude. In other words, when bad things happen and since we know God's will is perfect, we accept them, persevere through them, and even go on to praise God both publicly and privately. That is when God's will is complete-when we learn to say "thank you." This is

God's will for everything concerning us.

Luke 6:45 tells us that ...*of the abundance of the heart* [the] *mouth speaketh.* So, if the fruit, or outcome, of your mouth is continual praise and thanksgiving toward God, your heart is in the right place.

2. OBEDIENCE PLEASES GOD.

Children, obey your parents in all things: for this is wellpleasing unto the Lord. Colossians 3:20

I realize this verse is speaking of the parent/child relationship, but let's look at the greater picture as it applies to obedience. God's intention for a child is to obey His parents. The parents also lend their authority to the child's teachers, their pastor, and other institutions for the benefit of the child. When the child disobeys any form of leadership that the parents have put over him, then he has disobeyed his own parents. This displeases God. He wants children to obey in *all* things.

Why is God concerned about a child's obedience to every form of authority? It is quite simple. God has ordained a system. In chapter five, I called it God's system of management. We explained this topic very briefly in chapter four, but I will repeat it as well as expound on it here. Remember, repetition is the key to learning.

God's system of management is made up of leadership that is intended to help us make good decisions. This leadership begins with our parents. God is pleased when we obey our parents because we are learning the importance of obedience as children. If this principle is learned, especially at a young age, we will develop properly under God's system of management because we will likely continue to follow God's ordained leadership throughout our lives. Most of us, of course, failed to learn this principle as children. We are learning it as adults. And it must be learned! We will never please God with our lives until we learn to obey.

God's Management System

Following God's management system pleases God. Let's look at the good decisions God intends to help us make using His ordained system of management—obeying authority:

Beginning in childhood, God uses authority to help us choose properly in these four key areas of our lives. Unfortunately, many of us did not follow God's system. As a result, our marriages are not what they should be, our careers are more like jobs, we can't seem to get ahead financially, and we have not placed any priority on our walk with God. Life seems to have no real meaning or purpose. Why has this happened? Because we did not please God with our lives. We cannot expect God to bless our lives if we are not pleasing Him. Obeying authority in *all forms* and in *all things* is what pleases God.

Important Decision	Young People Lean	Adults Learn
Your Life's Mate	Who it will be	How to develop that relationship
Your Life's Career	What it will be	How to develop that career
Your Income Level	What to do with it	How to grow that income God's way
Your Walk with God	How to have one	How to develop it for God's use.

So how do we correct our errors? It may be simple for me to explain, but make no mistake, it will be hard to follow. You see, God's intention for a child to obey his parents is so that the child may learn at a young age to submit to authority. God intends for this submission to be carried over to other forms of authority as the child grows and matures. If we did not learn to submit to authority early in life, then we have probably become somewhat resistant toward most authority. Our lifetime of resistance toward authority makes learning this lesson as an adult not only humbling, but difficult as well. However, if you will learn it, you can be sure that God can do for you the very same things that He intended to do for you since childhood. As you submit to God's ordained authority, you will learn *how* to develop your relationship with your mate. You will learn *how* to turn your job into a career that brings honor to our Lord. You will learn principles of submission that will have a positive effect on your income level. You will learn *how* to properly distribute that income in God's way, a definite strategy that will increase your income. You will learn *how* to have a dynamic love relationship with Jesus Christ! Why? Because you are following God's system of management. You are obeying authority. Obedience pleases God.

Let's look at the Bible to determine whom God has chosen to lead us from childhood through adulthood in His system of management.

1. Parents
   Ephesians 6:1 Children, obey your parents in the Lord: for this is right.
2. Pastors
   First Timothy 3:1-2, 4-5 This is a true saying, If a man desire the office of a bishop, he desireth a good work. A bishop then must be ... one that

ruleth well his own house, having his children in subjection with all gravity; (For if a man know not how to rule his own house, how shall he take care of the church of God?)

3. Teachers

    Second Timothy 2:2 And the things that thou hast heard of me among many witnesses, the same commit thou to faithful men, who shall be able to teach others also.

4.Employers

    Ephesians 6:5-8 Servants (employees), be obedient to them that are your masters (employers) according to the flesh, with fear and trembling, in singleness of your heart, as unto Christ; Not with eyeservice, as menpleasers (but rather as God-pleasers); but as the servants of Christ, doing the will of God from the heart; With good will doing service, as to the Lord, and not to men: Knowing that whatsoever good thing any man doeth, the same shall he receive of the Lord, whether he be bond or free.

5. Government

    Romans 13:1, 4 Let every soul be subject unto the higher powers. For there is no power but of God: the powers that be are ordained of God. For he is the minister of God to thee for good.

Although there are some who will argue against these positions of authority being God-ordained, I am sure that they are. The Bible says it, and my personal experience in submission proves it. I have learned, albeit the hard way, that God channels blessing through His authorities. When you are living in rebellion to any of the authorities God has put over you, you are out from under God's umbrella of protection. If there is going to be any benefit to your family, job, or income level, it is going to be because you did the work and God is being longsuffering toward you. It will *not* be because God is doing the work and blessing you.

The word *obedience* means to perform what is requested and abstain from what is forbidden. Based on this definition, are we performing and abstaining when it comes to God's ordained authority? We may think we are good employees because we show up and maybe even work hard. But look at your company's policy book. What does it say about attitudes toward one another? What does it say about your conversations between co-workers? If you say that their policy book does not cover those issues, then what does God's policy book say?

How about the government? How do you handle your tax burden? The speed limit? I have heard preachers talk with glee about their speeding habits. That does not please God. Obedience pleases God. We need to get serious about obeying authority if we expect God to get serious about blessing us. He will not bless a disobedient Christian. He only blesses people when He is pleased with them.

When my daughter Charity was about 4 years old, we established Daddy/Daughter date nights on Monday evenings. On one particular Monday, I called her a few times during the morning from work to remind her how excited I was about our date night and that I couldn't wait to see her. At the end of my workday, my wife came to pick me up. With frustration, Lori began to tell me that Charity had awakened from her nap very grumpy and had been disobedient. Although Lori had been consistent with her discipline, Charity had continued to misbehave throughout the day. My heart sank. As a father, I knew I could not reward the bad behavior of a disobedient child. Charity learned that night that disobedience hindered her from receiving something good from her father. Likewise, disobedience will hinder us from receiving something good from our heavenly Father, as well. I am praying that all my children learn this lesson earlier in life than I did. I want them to know that obeying their parents in *all* things will not only please Mom and Dad, but it will please God even more. We should focus less on "please, God!" and more on pleasing God.

3. BEARING FRUIT PLEASES GOD.

That ye might walk worthy of the Lord unto all pleasing, being fruitful in every good work, *and increasing in the knowledge of God;* Colossians 1:10

This is a great verse because it tells us how to live in such a way as to please God. That is the focus of this chapter—pleasing God with our lives. This verse gives us two more methods.

People often say that even on their best day, they still deserve hell. To be honest, that is not true. After all, as a blood-bought Christian, you no longer deserve hell. But I understand what they mean. Their best days probably seem to fall short of bringing glory to God. But do you know that your best days could be the days that the Lord is pleased with you? Deserving of Hell? Apart from Christ, yes. But still of great value to God. Our key verse tells us that we "might walk worthy." The word *walk* refers to repeated steps; the word *worthy* means deserving. Thus, this verse indicates that we can take repeated steps in our lives that are deserving of the Lord. We can deserve God. *Deserve* means to merit. We can merit God in our lives, but to do this we must take repeated steps that please Him. He then lists two things that please Him: being fruitful in good works, and increasing in the knowledge of God. Let's take a look at the first point.

Being fruitful in good works pleases God. The word *fruit* has been previously defined in other chapters as an outcome or result. We have also previously defined the word *work* as effort. So the definition of this admonition is "to have a positive outcome from our good efforts." God wants our work to produce positive outcome. Now, how could someone ever do a good work that does not produce a positive outcome? We don't have to think long before we realize there are unbelieving people who work hard to acquire a level of acceptance from God but will never receive it. These are good people who work hard at their jobs, do a good work rearing their children, do a good work in their communities, but in the end their good works will be burned in judgment by God. Why? Those works did not equal salvation. These types of people are unsaved in spite of their good works. They are on their way to hell. Realizing that God does not desire that any of them should perish (see 2 Peter 3:9), how displeased with us do you think He is if we are not doing the good work of leading them to a position of repentance? If we are not even attempting to lead the lost people in our lives to Christ, then we are not being fruitful in every good work. And they are all still on their way to hell, in spite of their good efforts! This greatly displeases God. And, if no one is accepting Christ as a result of your "lack of effort," this greatly displeases God even more!

Many argue, "I can have fruit other than converts and still please God with my efforts and works." And there may very well be truth to that statement. But how well will He be pleased? I am sure that He will not say that He is "well pleased." To prove this point, we must understand God's primary meaning of the word fruit.

Once again, what is the fruit of a Christian? Is it love, joy, peace, etc.? No. Those are the fruit of the Spirit. The outcome (or, fruit) of the Spirit of God living in us should be reactions of love, joy, peace, etc., in response to the actions of others. In review once again of chapter five, we see that the fruit or outcome of a Christian is given in Proverbs 11:30, *The fruit of the righteous is a tree of life; and he that winneth souls is wise.* This verse tells us that the fruit of a Christian is life. The tree bears the fruit of life. It is referring to not only this life (in Christ), but also the next life (as a result of Christ). It goes on to prove the point further by claiming that whoever wins souls is wise. It is clear to me that God intends our fruit to produce life. The outcome of our marriage (or, union) with Christ, like a family tree, ought to be new, baby Christians.

How might this apply to daily life? Not everyone can spend their days in full-time ministry, now can they? Actually, I believe we can. God's purpose for your life, upon conversion, is much different than your purpose for your life before conversion. For example, God's intention for you may be for you to be a good parent. Before conversion, you may have had that same desire. You wanted to be a good parent for the purpose of having good children. So what is the difference? After your conversion, God put it upon your heart to be a good parent, not only that you may have good children, but that your children might be saved. Once they are saved, God will develop them, through your leadership, to be good children. God will do the work in their lives, not you! Likewise, before conversion, you may have wanted to be a good employee for the purpose of advancement. Now, God would have you be good at work so you might win your co-workers to Christ. You are to be good to your neighbors. Not that there is peace in the neighborhood, but that they may know Christ. You are to be good to strangers. Not simply for the purpose of community outreach, but rather through the reaching out for their eternal souls. This is God's plan. To be a good parent, yes. To be a good employee, yes. To be a good neighbor, yes. To be a good citizen, yes. But all of these efforts (or, works) are for the primary purpose of bringing forth a good result—life that is everlasting. Bringing people to the Life is what pleases God. Parent, Employee, Neighbor, or Citizen... you are not pleasing God with your life if you are not a soulwinner, no matter how much good you are doing.

If it is possible for a Christian to merit God, to deserve God, I believe that possibility is only earned as we put forth the effort to please Him through the winning of souls. My good friend Jeremy Huglin once said, "There are those who are saved, and there are those who appreciate their salvation." If you appreciate your salvation, you will share it with others. You will not hoard the sacrifice of God's Son for yourself. Nothing would please God more, nothing would earn more merit with God, than for you to accept His sacrifice for yourself and share it for the benefit of others. Bearing fruit that remains pleases God.

> "There are those who are saved, and there are those who appreciate their salvation."   —Jeremy Huglin

4.   INCREASING KNOWLEDGE OF GOD PLEASES GOD.

That ye might walk worthy of the Lord unto all pleasing, being fruitful in every good work, and increasing in the knowledge of God; Colossians 1:10

I have explained in previous chapters the importance of knowing God. We will briefly revisit that subject here because knowing God and increasing our knowledge of God pleases Him.

Knowing God is the primary way in which we experience the benefit of sanctification. When we were first saved, we became justified and sanctified. *Sanctified* means "set apart." We are set apart for God's use. He dwells within us in the form of His Spirit, the Holy Ghost. We now have the Power within us to be used by Him in miraculous ways, as evidenced in the New Testament. This does not mean, however, that we automatically are enjoying the benefits of sanctification. Remember, the benefit of justification takes place because God knows you; the benefits of sanctification take place as you know God. You and I must grow in our knowledge of God to experience the benefits of His Power in our lives. Let me give you an analogy.

You do not need to know power to use power, but you need to know power to be USED by power. You see, power is *the ability to overcome by using a resource.* If you were to enter a dark room, your first reaction would be to reach for the power source—the light switch. The light would turn on and the darkness would be overcome by using the resource of the power supply from the electric company. You used the power; however, the power did not use you. But you must realize that the light switch was made available for your use because someone was used by that source of power for your benefit. Let me explain.

For the power to be available for you to use, someone had to be used by the power source. In order for that light switch to be there, an electrician was *used* to place it in that position. Thus, the electric company used him to channel the power into a position to overcome darkness. What was the prerequisite for that electrician to be used by the power source? Very simply, he had to understand this power. He had to know this power. He had to understand how this power of electricity works. He had to increase his knowledge of this power until he understood how to best use it for his own benefit and for the benefit of others who could then use it themselves. That is why you must be properly trained in electrical power before you work with it. It is that simple.

Second Peter 1:3 says, *According as his divine* <u>*power*</u> *hath given unto us all things that pertain unto life and godliness, through the* <u>*knowledge*</u> *of him that hath called us to glory and virtue:* The more we know Him, the more we will be able to be used by Him. That is why our verse in Colossians 1 offers two admonitions for pleasing God. He says that we will please Him if we are bearing fruit from our good efforts. Those good efforts *will* be fruitful if we increase our knowledge of Him, because He will be the One providing His power to our good efforts. Power with God brings power with man!

James speaks of faith and works (James 2:14-26). That is faith *plus* effort. In witnessing, it is our effort and others' faith leads them to Christ. And God does the work of saving. *It is the power of God unto salvation to everyone that believeth* (Romans 1:16). That power is given as a resource to overcome a sinful soul's destiny by someone who is being *used* by God, not someone who *uses* God. He wants to be used by us, but He wants to use us even more. To be used by God, we must know Him. To know Him is to be used by Him. Christians being used by God, rather than simply using God, will bring Him great pleasure. Others also will benefit from us being used by God because they will gain the great benefit of the Power that we supply to them-the benefit of our sanctification. In other words, if we are experiencing the benefits of sanctification, then as a result, others will experience the benefits of justification.

5. AVOIDING LIFE'S CONCERNS PLEASES GOD.

Thou therefore endure hardness, as a good soldier of Jesus Christ. No man that warreth entangleth himself with the affairs of this life; that he may please him who hath chosen him to be a soldier. 2 Timothy 2:3-4

Imagine this: a country has gone into war and a certain soldier is called into battle. During the battle, he goes to his commanding officer and asks permission to go home to take care of some personal affairs. "The rent is overdue and the wife needs me to work some overtime. The car hasn't been washed in weeks. She has the in-laws in town and they expect me to be there. She's tired and needs a short break from the kids."

Well, that would be ridiculous! A good soldier cannot be entangled with the affairs of this world. He has one goal in mind—to complete the orders given to him by the authorities that called him into the battle.

In 2 Timothy, Paul is telling one of his trained men to endure hardness as a good soldier. The word *soldier* means a person called into service. The word *hardness* is the same word translated in other passages to mean affliction. He is telling his trained man who has been called into service to put up with affliction and not be entangled with the concerns (affairs) of this world. Let's look at some other parts of the letter that Paul sent to soldier Timothy to encourage him in his battle with affliction:

- 2 Timothy 2:10 *Therefore I endure all things for the elect's sakes, that they may also obtain the salvation which is in Christ Jesus with eternal glory.*

- 2 Timothy 1:8 *Be not thou therefore ashamed of the testimony of our Lord, nor of me his prisoner: but be thou partaker of the afflictions of the gospel according to the power of God;*

- 2 Timothy 3:11 *Persecutions, afflictions, which came unto me at Antioch, at Iconium, at Lystra; what persecutions I endured: but out of them all the Lord delivered me.*

- 2 Timothy 4:5 *But watch thou in all things, endure afflictions, do the work of an evangelist, make full proof of thy ministry.*

It is clear to me that Paul was anticipating great affliction for young Timothy. He was warning him to not be distracted by the affairs or concerns of this life. I cannot imagine what the affairs of life were like back then. With the persecution of the church, it must have been very grave in comparison to the concerns of our lives today. These days, our main focus tends to be on paying bills, providing for and nurturing our families, personal time, and preparing for retirement. Although this list may not perfectly apply to all people, I have heard all of these "concerns" given as primary reasons why people fail to serve the God who has called them into service. When we focus on these concerns, we are bad soldiers.

Bad soldiers do not protect the investment of their leader and do not advance upon and free captives from the enemy. In battle, bad soldiers are easily wounded, adversely affecting the entire army. Other soldiers must be made available to meet the medical (or, in this case, the spiritual) needs of the wounded soldiers, slowing down the advance of that particular infantry division.

Paul is letting Timothy know that the afflictions that he will face as a servant of our Lord Jesus Christ will be manifested as attacks on his personal concerns in life. In other words, if we serve God the way He wants us to, then the enemy will attack our personal concerns in life. But, Paul explains, since we have been called into God's eternal service, we must not focus on temporal matters. Such concerns will certainly be attacked, and we must endure that affliction. If we do not entangle ourselves with those concerns during these attacks, then we will be good soldiers. We will protect our Leader's investments and advance upon the enemy's territory, taking captives for the cause of Christ.

You know, I have found this to be true: whenever my personal life is attacked and I keep my focus on the battle at hand while leaving my own needs in the hands of my Commanding Officer, victory is always just over the hilltop! Yes, we know that we must remain good stewards, and a degree of focus is necessary in our personal and professional lives to maintain good stewardship. However, there is a big difference between *focusing* on and *entangling* in the affairs of this life. Defined, we should have "times of concentration" but not "distract ourselves with the concerns of living."

We know God has promised to meet our needs. It pleases Him to meet our needs, especially if we are not distracting ourselves with concern for these needs. He is pleased when we focus on the battle of protecting His investment (*Bear ye one another's burdens* Galatians 6:2), advancing into enemy territory (*Let your light so shine before men* Matthew 5:16) and freeing captives for His cause (*And others save with fear, pulling them out of the fire* Jude 23).

6. FEAR OF THE LORD PLEASES GOD.
The LORD taketh pleasure in them that fear him, in those that hope in his mercy. Psalm 147:11

The "fear of the Lord" is an awe or respect of who God is and what He can do. It is respect for what God could do, what God would do, and what God should do. God alone is in control of what He does *to* us and what He does *for* us. When we walk with the Lord, He may do many things for us. He can increase our health, our wealth, our joy, our anointing, our livelihood, our productivity, our lifespan, and many, many other blessings to those whose hearts are stayed on Him. This ability of our God to bless our obedience should be of great importance to us. It should lead us to an awe and respect of *who* God is and *what* He is willing to do. To be able to do all of these few things I've listed is an impossibility for anyone other than God. That is how powerful He is.

Of course, when we walk in disobedience to God, He is equally capable and just to punish our wrong behavior, as well. When we are wrong, God has options to use for our benefit and to increase our fear of Him. He has the option of judgment. This is getting what we deserve, usually in the form of chastening. It is intended to bring about repentance. With repentance should come an increase in our fear of the Lord. He also has the option of mercy. *Mercy* is not getting what we deserve. God has often chosen to use mercy on His people for their benefit and to increase our fear of Him. Finally, He has the option for grace. *Grace* is getting what you do not deserve-God's unmerited favor. Grace, without question, will always create a personal benefit and should increase our fear of the Lord.

I believe God's most favorite way of increasing our fear of the Lord when we are engaged in wrongdoing is by granting mercy-not giving the wrongdoer what they deserved for doing wrong. This is so obvious in Scripture. The word *mercy* appears over three hundred times in the Bible, and nearly every time, it is referring to the mercy of

God toward a wrongdoer.

In our key verse, we see that *The* LORD *taketh pleasure in them that fear him, in those that* <u>*hope in his mercy*</u> (Psalm 147:11). It pleases God when we fear Him, and this fear makes itself evident in a hope for mercy. *Hope* means an expectation of obtaining a desire. In this case, the desire that we expect to obtain is mercy. Dissected and defined, the Lord is teaching us that our fear is proven with an expectation that God is capable of not giving us what we deserve. Now, of course, receiving that mercy is not dependent on our expectation but on God's goodness toward us. However, God is pleased when we realize our need and place our hope for mercy in Him.

God wants us to realize He is the Source of every good thing. When something goes right, respect God for what He has done. When something goes wrong, respect God for what He is doing (Romans 8:28). If you will do this, it will change the influence that sin has on your life. God's formula for removing us from evil behavior and influence is found in Proverbs 16:6, *By mercy and truth iniquity is purged: and by the fear of the* LORD *men depart from evil.* By God *not* giving us what we deserve and our willingness as a result of that mercy to conform to what is right, we will purge iniquity from our lives. This mercy should increase our fear of the Lord. If it does, then we will depart from evil. If His mercy does not increase our fear of the Lord, then we will not depart from evil and God will replace His mercy, in His time, with judgment!

Hope for His mercy. Conform to what is right and let the experience produce a respect and awe for our all-powerful God. You will depart from evil and bring great pleasure to God.

Does It Really Work?

Now that we have completed our examination of The Six Procedures that Please God, you may be wondering, do they really work? Do they really produce pleasure in your own life? There are Bible examples of people who pleased God and, as a result of pleasing Him, they found great pleasure in their own lives. Let's look at two of those people.

Enoch is a good example. Hebrews 11:5 says, *By faith Enoch was translated that he should not see death; and was not found, because God had translated him: for before his translation he had this testimony, that he pleased God.* Enoch's life was one that pleased God. He experienced a great benefit from God for doing this. He was ushered straight into heaven without the experience of physical death.

Jesus is another good example. John 8:29 says, *And he that sent me is with me: the Father hath not left me alone; for I do always those things that please him.* Matthew 3:17 says, *And lo a voice from heaven, saying, This is my beloved Son, in whom I am well pleased.* Jesus did those things which pleased His Father, and God's testimony was that He was very well pleased with the procedures that His Son used.

I am so thankful that God tells us in the Bible the things that do not please Him and the things that do please Him. It makes it possible to come to the end of life's journey and know that we brought our Savior great pleasure. How can it be done? By our willingness to yield our outer man to the inner man, and under the Spirit's leading, we:

- praised and thanked God
- obeyed God
- bore fruit for God

- increased our knowledge of God
- gave our life's concerns over to God
- increased our fear of God

Wouldn't it be great to get to heaven and have God say to you, "Well done. In you I am well pleased"?

Chapter 7

The steps of a good man are ordered by the LORD: and he delighteth in his way. Though he fall, he shall not be utterly cast down: for the LORD upholdeth him with his hand. I have been young, and now am old; yet have I not seen the righteous forsaken, nor his seed begging bread.
                                                              -Psalm 37:23-25

I am often asked if our program offers steps for sobriety. The answer is no, we do not. There is one step to get right with God (salvation) and we teach principles, or boundaries, to stay right with God. Steps are of great value. However, in your Christian walk, God talks about taking repeated steps (or, walking). He tells us how to walk and how not to walk. We have discussed many of these forms of walking in nearly ever chapter, especially in chapter six. Chapter seven will take you to another level in your walk with God and teach you some doctrines of the faith. These doctrines, if followed, will put you in a position where God's power can flow through you and benefit other lives. Each of these doctrines will be called "steps." As before, some are review of teaching found in previous chapters. I do not apologize for the repetition. It is simply to remind you for the sake of good learning. Let us discuss now how to be a good man. Is that possible?

The Hebrew word translated as "man" here is gender neutral, speaking of either a man or woman. In this chapter, we will examine seven habits, or steps, to becoming a good man or woman of God.

Let's first dissect and define verse 23. *The steps* (or, direction) *of a good man are ordered* (or, managed) *by the LORD* (or, the Holy Spirit): *and he delighteth in his way* (or, course of life). As we allow God to manage our direction through the influence of His Holy Spirit, our course of life will bring great delight to both Him and us.

I find it encouraging that in verse 24 we are reminded that good men still fall! Everyone makes mistakes. God is perfect, but we are not. There will be times of failure in each of these seven steps, but this verse promises us that we won't be *utterly cast down.* Why? [F]*or the LORD upholdeth* [us] *with his hand.* We have a God that is standing by to help us, to hold us up if necessary. In Isaiah 41:10, God tells us, ...*I will strengthen thee; yea, I will help thee; yea, I will uphold thee with the right hand of my righteousness.*

In verse 25 of our key passage, the Psalmist David concludes, ... *I have been young, and now am old; yet have I not seen the righteous forsaken, nor his seed begging bread.* He realized that God faithfully takes care of those who allow their direction to be managed by the Holy Spirit.

Let's look at a few other passages that give us examples of the Lord directing our way of life.

- Jeremiah 10:23 *O LORD, I know that the way* (or, course of life) *of man is not in himself: it is not in man that walketh to direct his steps.* Our steps are in God's control.

- Proverbs 4:10-12 *Hear, O my son, and receive my sayings; and the years of thy life shall be many. I have taught thee in the way* (or, course) *of wisdom; I have led thee in right paths. When thou goest, thy steps shall not be straitened; and when thou runnest, thou shalt not stumble.* God leads us in our paths!

- Proverbs 16:9 *A man's heart deviseth his way* (or, course of life)*: but the LORD directeth his steps.* We can try to figure it out ourselves, but God knows what we really need to be doing.

- First Peter 2:21-22 *For even hereunto were ye called: because Christ also suffered for us, leaving us an example, that ye should follow his steps: Who did no sin, neither was guile found in his mouth:* The Holy Spirit will guide us and direct us to live a Christ-like life.

Now, I want to be a good man whose steps are directed by the Holy Spirit. I want God to delight in my course of life. How do I achieve that? I believe there are seven steps to becoming that good man whom the Holy Spirit will influence and lead. We have learned and been reminded in almost every chapter that we are not going to be good in the power of the flesh. If we will implement these seven steps, or habits, then the Holy Spirit will have the free reign to lead, guide, and direct us. And though we may make mistakes and fall, we will not be utterly cast down. God will always prove Himself faithful and will never leave us. Let me explain how these steps have helped me:

In 1993 I had a near-fatal car wreck. My story is quite an amazing testimony of God's mercy toward a wayward child. While in the hospital bed, and after ten years of rebellion against God, I was searching for some answers. One of my former Christian schoolteachers visited me and encouraged me to read the Bible while in the hospital. I decided to take his advice and asked my nurse for a Bible. She reached into the dresser drawer and pulled out a King James Version Bible that had been placed there by an organization called "Gideons International." I appreciated their ministry that day, as I used that Bible to light my way (course of life) back to the local church of my youth.

After a few years of my spiritual development, I was invited to join Gideons International as a Bible distributing member, dispersing free Bibles to schools, colleges, hospitals, jails, and to military personnel. What a privilege! As a Gideon, I was first introduced to these seven steps. They call them "The Gideons' Spiritual Objectives." I will now add great detail and explanation to each of these Gideon International objectives that I focused on one "step" at a time, and I will explain what God showed me as I took these steps in my personal life.

Step 1 Men/ Women of the Book—the Bible

It is unfortunate, but to many, the Bible is God's unopened love letter. People often tell me, "Steve, I struggle to read my Bible. I struggle to get alone with God and to have devotions. I struggle to have a daily 'God and I' time." There are also people who don't think that it is necessary to read the Bible on a daily basis. But I want you to consider this: God's Word is like a roadmap, and He will direct your steps with it.

When you accepted Jesus as your personal Savior, His Holy Spirit took up residence within you. John 16:13 tells us that the Holy Spirit *will guide you into all truth.* However, He cannot guide you in your course of life if you are not reading the "roadmap." Your course of life is the way you choose to live your life moment by moment. Those choices need to be made by following your roadmap on a daily basis. There are basically four things that we should do every day with the Word of God:

READ THE BIBLE

Till I come, give attendance (or, attention) <u>*to reading,*</u> *to exhortation, to doctrine.* I Timothy 4:13

The first thing we need to do with the Word of God is to read it. Unfortunately, many people read the Bible and that is where they stop. In our above key verse Paul is giving Timothy direction for Timothy's ministry. His advice—... *give attendance* <u>*to reading,*</u> *to exhortation, to doctrine* (or, that which is strongly held to be right).

The phrase *give attendance to* means "to show up for, or to give attention to." When a school teacher takes attendance, she is accounting for each student's daily presence in that class. Similarly, you should show up every day for your appointment in the Word. And you are not the only person that will be attending this session; the Holy Spirit will be there, ready to give you direction.

There is a big misconception concerning reading the Bible. Many people believe that simply reading the Bible will develop a growing relationship that leads to prosperity. However, nowhere in Scripture do we see that God promises to prosper Bible-reading Christians. God's prosperity is given to Bible-*meditating* Christians! Simply put, we should read the Bible as a means toward meditation. Though reading without future meditating should not be considered a waste of time, reading for the purpose of meditation is the best way to develop a closer relationship with God. We cannot just start reading, however, and expect to immediately find ourselves in a position where we might maintain a spirit of meditation on what we have read. There is a method that should be followed in order to develop that spirit of meditation.

First, we must read the Bible with purpose. It is not merely the reading that will grow you, but rather the application of your reading. Keep in mind that this is a love letter from your Savior. When reading, look for principles, truths, stories and series of events that the Lord may use to speak to you. When God reveals something to you, there is your bonanza! It may be something you have seen before, but it caught your attention once again. Or, it could be something you have never seen before. Either way, who do you think it is that is revealing this truth to you? Do you think it is the devil? No? Well, then, by process of elimination, who pray tell do you think it is? Of course, it's the Spirit of God! The Holy Spirit is guiding you into a truth that He most certainly knows you need in your life *that day*. That is when you should *stop* reading for a few moments. Now, I know that if you are trying to finish a "Bible Reading in a Year" program that this will slow you down, but trust me. You do not need a large *quantity* of reading, but rather good *quality* in your reading. But when the Lord shows you something, it gives you an opportunity to take the next important step in your time in God's Word—studying.

STUDY THE BIBLE

Study to show thyself approved unto God, a workman that needeth not to be ashamed, rightly dividing the word of truth.
2 Timothy 2:15

When you find your bonanza, that gold nugget, it's time to study it out and determine how God may be ordering your steps. Take that little nugget and begin dissecting and defining it.

By dissecting and defining (as we have done throughout this book) we are simply taking apart a verse, defining the words, and putting it back together to better understand the insight, application, or conviction that the Lord is presenting to us. I would suggest two very helpful tools to assist you as you dissect and define Bible verses: a Strong's Concordance and an 1828 Webster's Dictionary. (I believe the 1828 edition of Webster's Dictionary is the closest version of the defined English language at the time the translators of the King James Version were choosing their Revised English words to represent the meanings of the Greek and Hebrew words of the ancient manuscripts.)

Most books are written for our information, but the Bible was written for our transformation. God's intention is for us to transform our minds through the Word of God. Our key verse for studying the Bible is 2 Timothy 2:15 which reads, *Study to show thyself approved unto God, a workman* (or, laborer) *that needeth not to be ashamed, rightly dividing* (or, dissecting and defining) *the word of truth.* Notice that "dividing the Word" is considered studying. This type of studying is approved by God.

The word *approved* means "accepted." God considers this an acceptable way of dividing His Word. We need

> Most books are written for our information, but the Bible was written for our transformation.

to *study* the Word of God.

Notice also that God considers this type of studying to be hard work. He calls the person who engages in dividing the Word a "workman," or, a laborer. God knows that this is harder work than just simply reading. That is why it is so acceptable to Him. He approves of this type of work, and it comes with great rewards. A better understanding of what we read will lead us toward a better preparation for that day's circumstances.

First, we must read God's Word. Second, we must study God's Word. Yet these exercises are not enough to help us prosper. We need to advance to the third purpose for God's Word—memorization.

MEMORIZE THE BIBLE
Thy word have I hid in mine heart, that I might not sin against thee. Psalm 119:11

What is the Bible referring to when it speaks of the "heart"? We have studied in previous chapters our inner man (God's mind, will, and emotions) and our outer man (our mind, will, and emotions). The heart is the trigger between these two entities, the spiritual and the carnal. It is what determines which switch will get tripped in a given circumstance. This trigger (the heart) should be protected at all times. *Keep thy heart with all diligence; for out of it are the issues of life* (Proverbs 4:23). When you protect your trigger and condition it with Scripture, then it will flip the switch to respond in the Spirit to life's trials. However, if you leave your heart unprotected and it becomes hardened by sin, then you will flip the switch toward your own thoughts, desires, and emotions rather than God's. The Bible memorized is thus "hidden" within this trigger and will help eliminate the problem of acting "after the flesh."

Deuteronomy 11:18 reminds us of the importance of this. *Therefore shall ye lay up these my words in your heart* (or, your inner trigger of passions) *and in your soul* (or, your mind, will, and emotions), *and bind them for a sign upon your hand, that they may be as frontlets between your eyes.* A little study of this custom teaches us that the Lord wants us to keep His words ever before us to remain focused on the path on which He has placed us.

Now, when God gives you a passage and you have studied it out or paraphrased it and understand its meaning, purpose to memorize it! I suggest using the RUI *It's Personal* Daily Journal, which has a section to help you with your Bible memorization. Here is what I do when God gives me a verse to memorize: I first will write it out in my *It's Personal* Daily Journal. I then read it three to five times.

Now remember, we do not have to memorize entire verses word for word and without error in order to meditate on God's Word. Often, I'll take the verse that sticks out during my reading and studying and paraphrase it in my journal, then memorize (by quoting it three to five times) either a portion of the verse or the paraphrased meaning.

By working in my journal and reading my Bible, God is preparing me for battle every day. He is giving me the truth I will need to be prepared for my spiritual battles that day (see Ephesians 6:14). My Bible memorization thus places this weapon into the memory of my inner man, effectively making it the Sword (or, offensive weapon) of the Spirit. With the truth sheathed within my inner man, I will be prepared to meditate on it throughout the day and pull it out for use (upon His prompting) to overcome a circumstance that would otherwise entice me to yield to my flesh. Such preparation leads to prosperity in the Christian life. But, we must read so that we can study; we must study so that we can memorize; and we must memorize so that we can engage in the final and most important purpose of the Word of God—meditation!

MEDITATE ON GOD'S WORD

But his delight (or, enjoyment) *is in the law of the LORD; and* <u>*in his law doth he meditate*</u> (or, think upon) *day and night. And he shall be like a tree planted by the rivers of water, that bringeth forth his fruit in his season; his leaf also shall not wither; and* <u>*whatsoever he doeth shall prosper.*</u> Psalm 1:2-3

This book of the law shall not depart out of thy mouth; <u>*but thou shalt meditate therein day and night,*</u> *that thou mayest observe to do according to all that is written therein:* <u>*for then thou shalt make thy way prosperous,*</u> *and then thou shalt have good success.* Joshua 1:8

The first time I ever flew in an airplane was on my honeymoon to Cozumel, Mexico, with my wife Lori. My face was pressed against the airplane window throughout the flight as I watched the beautiful landscape below. At one point, we came over what looked to be a stream or river of water. As my eyes traced that stream, I noticed that all the trees on its banks were much larger, greener, and taller than those growing on the outskirts. I immediately thought of Psalm 1:3. A man who meditates on the Bible will be like those trees. His "branches" will extend farther and higher; his growth will be much faster and deeper than those outside the reach of the life-giving water of the river. Fruit-bearing and beautiful, any righteous thing such a man (or woman) does will thrive.

A man who meditates on God's Word delights in God's Word, meaning that he enjoys this meditation. You will too, once you begin seeing the result of your own meditation, that is prosperity in your course of life. The sad truth is, many of us find reading the Word of God something of a chore or minimum requirement for pleasing God. That is not how it should be! It ought to be a delight! God wants to guide and direct us through His Word that we might make wise decisions leading to prosperity in specific areas of our lives. He wants to order our steps. He wants us to be grounded, fruitful, and prosperous. But it will require a delight in God's Law that manifests itself through meditation on this Law, beginning every morning and continuing right through the night. God will indeed prosper a Bible-meditating Christian!

Enjoyment is simply a matter of appetite. To enjoy something, an appetite for it needs to be created and fed. When I was younger, I hated stuffing. My mother could not get me to eat it, and after many attempts, she finally stopped trying to make me. However, after I got married, Lori consistently tried to get me to eat her stuffing. She made it regularly and was quite persuasive in her attempts to get me to try it—and like it. Not wanting to upset my new bride, I decided to try her stuffing. It was the first time I could remember actually even tasting stuffing. After all those years, I came to realize that I had never really tried to like it. I simply rejected it and, as a result, I had no appetite for it. Well, as you probably guessed, I really liked it. (Sorry, Mom! Nothing personal.) As a result, she increased the frequency at which she served stuffing, and I developed an appetite for it that often leads me to be, well…quite stuffed!

Reading the Bible is the same way. We don't have a strong appetite for it, but we have never really tasted it. Oh, we read it, skimming through it like we are picking at it with a fork. But we fail to really take the time to try it and like it.

If we will take the time to read, study, memorize, and meditate on God's Word, we will see Him at work in our lives. We will be able to see that God is directing our steps as we exercise the four-fold purpose of His Word. This will excite us! We will become delighted in the way in which He is leading us. It will lead to prosperity and our "God and I" time will, as a result, become intensely personal and intimate. This exercise in God's Word is sure to increase our appetite for God's Word and we *will* be delighted in it.

Read so you may study what God shows you. Study so you may understand its meaning. Memorize so you can remember what God has shown you. Meditate so you will be prepared to apply the two-edged Sword in the time of adversity. Doing these four things is the first step of a good man, a man of the Book—the Bible.

Step 2   Men/Women of Prayer

God will order our steps through the prompting and leading of the Holy Spirit as He speaks to us in prayer. Prayer is supposed to be two-way communication with God. Your personal prayer time is a time in which we not only talk to God, but God talks to us, as well. However, we often treat prayer as our chance to bring God His "to do" list for the day, expecting Him to have it all completed when we "check back in" with Him later. How sad it is that we are missing out on the opportunity of communicating with God during prayer! Let's look at what the Bible teaches regarding prayer.

In the Sermon on the Mount recorded in Matthew 5-7, Jesus taught the multitudes how to pray:

> *But when ye pray, use not vain repetitions, as the heathen do: for they think that they shall be heard for their much*

speaking. Be not ye therefore like unto them: for your Father knoweth what things ye have need of, before ye ask him. After this manner therefore pray ye: Our Father which art in heaven, Hallowed be thy name. Thy kingdom come. Thy will be done in earth, as it is in heaven. Give us this day our daily bread. And forgive us our debts, as we forgive our debtors. And lead us not into temptation, but deliver us from evil: For thine is the kingdom, and the power, and the glory, for ever. Amen. Matthew 6:7-13

Our Father which art in heaven, Hallowed be thy name. Thy kingdom come, Thy will be done in earth, as it is in heaven. This is a time of appreciation for who God is and what He is doing in our lives.

Give us this day our daily bread. Jesus teaches us to ask God for our personal provisions.

And forgive us our debts, as we forgive our debtors. We learn that we must forgive and request forgiveness.

And lead us not into temptation, but deliver us from evil: A personal prayer of protection for others and ourselves. This plea focuses on God's decisions to lead us into temptation and a special request of deliverance from evil when God does lead us into temptation. God's determination to lead us into a position of temptation, while not personally tempting us Himself (James 1:13-14), is a strange decision for us to understand. However, we know it is something that happens. We first see it in Matthew 4:1, *Then was Jesus led up of the Spirit into the wilderness to be tempted of the devil.* God's purpose for this adversity is seldom known in advance of the temptation, but it is usually understood upon our proper response to that temptation. Requesting God to reprieve us from this temptation is something Jesus considered an important part of His (and thus, our) prayers. Realizing the prerogative belongs to Him, we need to leave no stone unturned, requesting God to deliver us from the evil that comes with any such temptation.

Now, how does this "model prayer" apply to our special time communicating with God? I can explain it best by using our "system of prayer," as depicted in the RUI *It's Personal* Daily Journal, the 365-day Planning Journal, and the Kids and pre-teen Walkie/Talkie Journal. This is how we teach the four categories for our prayer time, as outlined in the Lord's prayer. Let's take a look at each of these categories. The blanks at right are for you to fill in as you try this method of personal communication with God.

Praises (Pause)	Needs (Pause)
Forgiveness (Pause)	**Protection (Pause)**
Things I Said	
Things others have said	
Things I thought	
Things I did	
Things others did	

1. **Praise** is "asking God and pausing" to show us which things to praise Him for.
2. **Needs** is "asking God and pausing" to show us which

needs to pray for.

3. **Forgiveness** is "asking God and pausing" to prompt us about things that need forgiveness.

4. **Protection** is "asking God and pausing" to determine whom we should pray for protection.

Notice the phrase "Asking God and Pausing" in each of those categories. This type of praying, where we ask the Lord what we ought to praise Him for and then pause for His leading in our praises, is a unique way in which we may experience two-way communication with God.

When I first began to live for God in the mid-1990's, my prayer life was a struggle. I would merely quote my list of requests, which amounted to nothing more than a shopping list and errands that I wanted God to run for me. Seldom did I experience what seemed to be an answered prayer request. And if I did, it was never on my time table, leading me to believe it was just a coincidence. As a result, I began to conclude that prayer was an exercise that I needed to perform to prove my faith in God. This led me to being discouraged and to pray less. One evening, during our church's mid-week service, we had an elder missionary in town who was preaching on prayer. He explained that prayer was intended to be two-way communication with our Savior. Well, that was frustrating to hear, for surely I did not experience this in my life. I spoke to this senior saint after the service and told him just that. I did not even feel God's presence in my prayer time. Much less did I feel that He was actually listening or responding in any way. This kind missionary asked me one question: "Do you think the reason that you do not hear God talking to you when you pray might be because you are too busy talking and not listening?" Wow! That made sense. I did not know how to fix it, but I knew it sounded like it could be fixed. That night, I began to study the Lord's prayer model given to His disciples in Matthew six.

The first thing I noticed was His reminder, *But when ye pray, use not vain repetitions, as the heathen do.* Well, I did not know what that meant, so I dissected and defined it. The phrase *vain repetitions* literally means "speaking without thinking." Unbelievable! That's exactly what I was doing with my grocery list of prayers that I had practically memorized and could quote without emotion or petition. God did not appreciate my grocery lists! (By the way, I would assume He does not appreciate any prayer that is spoken without a meaningful thought process. I would think that this would include our quick prayers before meals and even those prayers during our church services that oftentimes seem more of a curtain close to allow singers or piano players a chance to get in place for the next event on the service itinerary.) We get so wrapped up in our "to do" list for God that we don't even give the Holy Spirit an opportunity to speak to us!

After continuing my study on prayer that evening, I came up with this simple chart that I might journalize God's communication to me. I began with my prayer for praise and asked God what I should praise Him for, and then I shut up! I paused. Within a couple of moments, God prompted me on four or five things that I would never have praised Him for on my "grocery list." It was unique and felt real. My excitement grew. I knew I could have quickly come up with a few dozen more praises, but I would have been doing it at my prompting, rather than God's. So I concluded my praises by thanking God for these things. It seemed so very real—so very personal.

I continued by asking the Lord what needs I should petition Him for, and I paused. Within a few moments, He brought to my mind some things that would never have made my list in the past, simply because they were really needs for others and brought little benefit to me. But that is what God prompted, so I wrote it down. It may seem odd, but within days, each of those requests had been answered. Since that time, I have seen multiplied hundreds of requests answered rather quickly. I feel it's as if God is prompting me to pray for the needs that He is getting ready to answer so that when He answers them, my faith will grow and so will our personal relationship. It may seem hard to believe, but I am convinced it is true.

Continuing, I began to ask the Lord for things I had said, thought, or done that were wrong and may be hindering my relationship with Him. I was amazed as certain things that I had said and done and even thought the day before began to rush back into my memory. I began to deal with them one at a time. I was even convicted to go back and apologize to people that I had wronged.

I concluded with a prayer of protection for those whom the Lord prompted me to pray for. It was, of course, for people who meant a lot to me. I prayed for protection for my family, my students, my pastor, R/U leaders, and others. As I prayed for their protection, I found myself realizing how important these people are to me and how thankful I am to God for their roles in my life.

Yes, indeed, it may sound simple. But I am being honest with you when I tell you that my prayer life has literally come alive! It is personal and definitely two-way communication with God. I am so thankful that we have a God who wants our relationship with Him to be

> If you want your steps ordered by the Lord, become a man or woman of prayer. God will lead you, and you will be delighted in His way.

personal. If you want your steps ordered by the Lord, become a man or woman of prayer. God will lead you, and you will be delighted in His way.

If you would like help with these first two steps, I would strongly encourage you to purchase our *It's Personal* Daily Journal for adults and/or the *Walkie/Talkie Journal* for pre-teens and kids. It has helped others and I'm sure it can help you, too!

Step 3   Men/Women of Faith

God's definition of faith is found in Hebrews11:1- *Now faith is the substance* (or, made up) *of things hoped for, the evidence of things not seen.* In other words, faith is made up of things we confidently hope to be right, though we have no visible evidence. It is simply what we believe to be true! We have discussed faith in deep detail in chapters four and six. We will not repeat these many details again, but if you are teaching this point in your R/U class, I would encourage you to teach it using those details again. We will however brush on those details in this chapter. Thus, as a point of reminder, there are three things I want you to notice about faith.

OUR FAITH SAVES US

For by grace are ye saved through faith; and that not of yourselves: it is the gift of God: Ephesians 2:8

It takes *things hoped for* to save us. Works will not save us; giving will not save us; praying will not save us. Salvation is a free gift from God to those who receive it through faith. Faith is what it takes to be saved. *For by grace are ye saved through faith* (a belief in things hoped for). We are saved through our hope in the unseen, believing it to be true. We believe, hope, and put our trust in Jesus Christ's sacrificial blood, His substitionary death, His subsequent burial, and His sanctifying resurrection for our eternal security. The cross provides our justification, and the resurrection provides our sanctification.

You see, the world says, "Show me and I will believe you." Christ says, "Believe me and I will show you." There was a time in my life when I placed my faith in Jesus Christ's payment for my sin. As a result of my faith, God saved me and then began to show me supernatural things by the leading of His Holy Spirit. I am led through life by exercising that same faith. It is "evidence" that I believe in the things that I have not yet seen.

OUR FAITH PLEASES GOD.

But without faith it is impossible to please him: for he that cometh to God must believe that he is, and that he is a rewarder of them that diligently seek him. Hebrews 11:6

Not only does faith save us, but it also pleases God. Our key verse tells us that without faith it is impossible to please God. This verse also tells us how to determine if we have faith that is pleasing to God—whether we are showing an "evidence of hope for the things not yet seen." Here is our test of faith: 1. Approach God; 2. Believe that He *is* God; 3. Believe that He is a rewarder; and, 4. Diligently seek Him. We must come to God, believe that He *is* God and, as proof of our belief, diligently seek Him, confident that we will be rewarded. As we saw in chapter six, God rewards those with whom He is pleased, and He is pleased with those who have faith in *Him*!

OUR FAITH DETERMINES OUR DIRECTION (OR, WALK).

For we walk by faith, not by sight: 2 Corinthians 5:7

Not only does our faith save us and not only does our faith please God, but our faith also determines our direction in life. Faith is not something that talks; faith is something that walks. I have heard it best said that faith is to believe what we do not see, and the reward is to someday see the things that we believe. We can't talk faith without walking faith. A lot of people saw Christ crucified, but that did not save them. Sight never saves. Faith saves us, faith pleases God, and faith journeys with God.

Step 4 Men/Women with a Separated Walk

If our steps are going to be ordered by the Lord, we must walk a separated walk. We must first walk a separated walk from the world. We are going to have to separate from certain people if we want to be influenced by the Holy Spirit. R/U Principle #6 of 10 says, "Those who do not love the Lord will not help us serve the Lord." If they don't love God, how in the world are they going to help us serve God? In chapter five we have taught you that it is true that God intends for us to play a key role in the lives of people who need the Lord. Of course, this would be very difficult to do if we separate ourselves from involvement with the people of the world. Though it is true that God wants us to impact the lives of the lost for Christ, He likewise requires that we not allow the lost to impact our lives away from Christ. If our friends do not love God, they simply will not help us serve God. If our friends are not helping us serve God, then maybe they are not the type of friends our Lord would lead us to spend large amounts of time with.

Don't get me wrong. I have some friends that, despite my efforts to persuade them otherwise, remain unconvinced that Jesus paid it all. These people are long term projects.

> If our friends do not love God, they simply will not help us serve God. If our friends are not helping us serve God, then maybe they are not the type of friends our Lord would lead us to spend large amounts of time with.

I am very careful to not alienate them or to eliminate our relationship, but I wisely limit my time and, without question, limit my activities with them. Let me explain.

In chapter one, we discussed those who love the things of the world. Since they love these things, the love of the Father is not in them. The things of the world (found in 1 John 2:6) are listed as the lust of the flesh, the lust of the eyes, and the pride of life. We defined them in order as a controlling desire to do, a compulsive demand to have, and a consuming drive to be. If these people could do, have, or be whatever they wanted to do, have, or be, they would gain all of the world. However, the love of God would not be in them. It does not profit a man to gain the whole world and then lose his own soul (Mark 8:36). Such people are spending the majority of their lives attempting to do, have, and be all they want.

However, I personally want to spend my time yielding to what God wants me to do, have, and be. But, I have found that when I spend too much time with people of selfish motives, I tend to become somewhat fleshly led to do what I want, to have what I want, and to be what I want. I eventually end up in a very disconcerting position. I do what God wants, but I do it my way; I have what God wants, but I have it my way; I am what God wants, but I am in my own way. I begin to focus on living God's life for me, my way. That is a completely frustrating position to be in, and it comes complete with a loss of joy. Therefore, without isolating myself from my old friends, I am careful to limit my fellowship with them, knowing that "bad company corrupts good morals."

Some may say that I am wrong for keeping in contact with old friends or for building friendships with people who are not saved. Please realize that the reason I keep a short distance from them is not because I do not love them; rather, it is because I do love them. For surely, when they realize their personal lives need repair, I am often the fortunate one to re-introduce them to Christ at just the right time.

I would ask those who stay closely involved with their unsaved friends, how many have you been able to lead to the Lord? Probably not too many. I have personally experienced the privilege of leading dozens of my old friends to Christ *after* separating my walk from them, in love. Through diligent prayer, occasional phone calls, letters, cards, and even a few cups of coffee coupled with God's basic law of sowing and reaping, they have returned my outreach by reaching out to me during their times of urgent need. Without fail, each of those friends told me that when they reached their breaking point, I was the only one that they thought could help me. I now enjoy close friendships again with Jeff, Todd, Tom, Tim, Ron, Mike, Darren, Rick, Craig and even my own brother, Barry!

In my early walk with the Lord, when I tried to balance my relationships with these very same people and others who, at the time, loved the things of the world, their influence on me derailed the Lord's work in my life. He could not clearly direct me because I was directing myself. As I separated from them, God led me on the right path to be what He wanted, to do what He wanted, and to have what He wanted. It has been an incredible joy to experience His desires for my life over my own desires. I dare say that my old friends, who are now my new friends in Christ are thankful that I made this decision. If you love your friends who do not love God or serve Him, then you will separate—not sever—from them and let the Lord lead them to you when their hearts are the most tender to His call.

Additionally, the Holy Spirit will influence us and order our steps through our good Christian friends. Many tend to think that the primary function of Christian friends is merely for socializing or "fellowship." But Christian friends are also intended by God to be Spirit-led counselors in our lives. Not all Christians will fit into this category. Proverbs 11:14 says, *in the multitude of counsellors there is safety.* Our multitude of counselors ought to consist of spiritually discerning Christians. Many consider only their pastors as effective counselors for the Lord, but that is not necessarily true. God did not intend for us each to have a multitude of pastors, but He does instruct us to value a multitude of wise counsel. Good Christian friends may help us understand things about God that we do not understand. They may know God better than we know Him in one or more areas. I think having Christian friends is a must to give the Lord every option in ordering our steps. He wants to work through clean vessels—wise counsel from godly friends. However, if we do not separate from our friends who love the things of this world, we will not have time nor even see the need to make Christian friends. This will hinder God's direction in our lives. Bad friends will consume the time that God intends for us and our good friends to enjoy. Without good Christian friends, we close off one clear channel of communication with the Lord.

We see this explained in part in 2 Corinthians 6:14, 17-18 where we read, *Be ye not unequally yoked together with unbelievers: for what fellowship hath righteousness with unrighteousness? and what communion hath light with darkness? Wherefore come out from among them, and be ye separate, saith the Lord, and touch not the unclean thing; and I will receive you. And will be a Father unto you, and ye shall be my sons and daughters, saith the Lord Almighty.* The picture being drawn here in verse 14 is like that of yoked oxen. Two yoked oxen going in the same direction will produce a desired effect. However, yoking an ox with a horse, or an ox with a lion, would be an unequal yoke. Similarly, we cannot yoke a believer with an unbeliever. Why? They are going in two separate directions.

As believers, we are yoked with Christ. The word *yoke* literally means "to partner." The verse also uses the synonyms *fellowship* and *communion*, which mean the

> We should not partner with anyone who has not partnered with Christ. Jesus partners with those whom He lives in and through, and He begins that partnership at the moment they believe.

same thing—to partner. Paul is telling us that we should not partner with anyone who has not partnered with Christ. Jesus partners with those whom He lives in and through, and He begins that partnership at the moment they believe. His only *partnership* is with those who believe! If He will not yoke with an unbeliever, then neither should we.

Make no mistake, Paul is not saying that unsaved people are "second class," nor that they should be avoided. A basic study of the definitions of *friend* and *yoke* will explain the boundaries of our relationship with unbelievers. Truly, there are many options for developing relationships with people that do not require us to yoke with them, or to become partners with them. What God is requesting of us is a separation which is intended to *improve* His work through us that we might reach our lost friends for Him. To be effective for God requires a separated walk. If we want to walk with God, we cannot walk with the world.

An equally explosive topic within the body of Christ is our friendships with other believers. Sometimes these friendships can also greatly hinder our walk with God. We see this admonition found in Romans 16:17-18 which says, *Now I beseech* (or, beg) *you, brethren* (or, fellow Christians), *mark* (or, make note of) *them which cause divisions and offences contrary to the doctrine* (or, right teaching) *which ye have learned; and avoid them. For they that are such serve not our Lord Jesus Christ, but their own belly* (or, fleshly appetites); *and by good words and fair speeches* (or, creative methods) *deceive the hearts of the simple* (or, naive).

In these verses, we see some direction given by Paul that is often misunderstood. He is referring to people who claim to love God but do not serve God. Notice, I did not call them Christians. They could be, but they might not be, as well. As Paul tells us, they serve something other than Jesus and they cause divisions and offenses among Christians, especially new believers. Now, I understand that we do not have to see eye to eye on every doctrine to be Christians. However, don't forget which book of the Bible this verse is found—Romans, the book that contains the "road map" to heaven. There are many other doctrines found in Romans besides the doctrine of salvation (by grace, through faith), but it is the primary doctrine that is being taught throughout the book of Romans. Obviously, those who reject and cause divisions among people in the doctrine of salvation are unbelievers and must be avoided.

These verses are often interpreted to mean that we cannot associate with Christians who do not believe exactly the same way we do. And the truth is we cannot associate with *some* Christians who do not believe exactly the same way we do, but some we can. Paul is not telling us to avoid believers whose doctrines are different. He indicated we should avoid people who create divisions and offenses in our doctrinal differences. Not every Christian who believes differently than I do on some doctrines is looking for a fight or trying to divide me from God or other good Christians.

Paul goes on to say these same divisive people are self-serving and try to persuade naive people. How could anyone think they could grow closer to God if they allow close association with self-serving, deceitful people who are always divisive and offensive? Note them and avoid them. They will hinder God's direction in your life.

We need God to lead us for any lasting good to come out of our lives. He clearly shows us that He will lead through people in whom He lives (believers), especially through believers who are not divisive, offensive, and self-centered.

Step 5 Men/Women with Compassionate Hearts

God, in the form of the Holy Spirit, directs His people through their hearts. As I have said before, the heart is the trigger of the soul. The soul comprises our mind, will and emotions. The heart is the trigger that causes the mind to think, the will to want and the emotions to feel. To be under the influence of the Holy Spirit, the soul (what we want, think and feel) must submit to the spirit (where God places what He thinks, wants, and feels). When we do this, we are walking in the Spirit. As a result, God will lead us by first stimulating that leading in the heart, the trigger of the soul.

Having a hard heart, not feeling compassion for others, and focusing on our own problems will limit God's leading in our lives. He will not force me to do what my soul is not willing to do. My soul will not do what my heart will not convince it to do. My heart cannot be influenced to negotiate with my soul if it is not sensitive to the leading of God's Spirit. The steps of a good man are ordered by the Lord, not ordered by himself!

Throughout the Bible, we see that when struggling with a hard heart, man will always do what he thinks, feels, or wants. We see that to be especially true in the book of Exodus. When Moses and Aaron approached Pharoah for the release of the children of Israel, God hardened Pharoah's heart. With his hardened heart, he constantly made selfish decisions that proved to be extremely foolish and damaging to those under his rule (the people of Egypt). It is understood that God had a purpose for Pharoah's hard heart, but that doesn't change the fact that people with hard hearts don't yield to what God thinks, feels, or wants; they follow what they think, feel, and want! By contrast, a person with a compassionate heart has a heart that is yielded to God's mind, God's will and God's emotions.

One of God's many potential emotional responses to our actions is compassion. Compassion is defined as "willing to suffer with another." Compassion is actually passion that is **com**pounded. Compassion is two passions **com**bined, thus the word **com**passion. The two **passions** that are **com**bined to show **compassion** are love and sorrow. It indicates that we will love someone, even if something has been done that makes us or them sorrowful.

Notice the attributes of God that we enjoy as a result of His compassion for us when we make mistakes:

♦ Psalm 86:15 *But thou, O Lord, art a God full of compassion, and <u>gracious</u>, <u>longsuffering</u>, and <u>plenteous in mercy and truth</u>.*

♦ Psalm 111:4 *He hath made his <u>wonderful works to be remembered</u>: the* LORD *is gracious and full of compassion.*

♦ Psalm 112:4 *<u>Unto the upright there ariseth light in the darkness</u>* (or, spiritual direction)*: he is gracious, and full of compassion, and righteous.*

♦ Psalm 145:8 *The* LORD *is gracious, and full of compassion; <u>slow to anger, and of great mercy.</u>*

Surely since God is full of compassion, He wants us to be compassionate as well. It simply proves that when we yield to having our steps ordered by the Lord, we will find ourselves exercising the very same attributes—graciousness, longsuffering, mercy, truth, good works, giving spiritual direction, and being slow to anger. Sounds like a very compassionate person to me! Outward demonstrations of love, even in times of sorrow! God's compassion can flow through us and influence others as well, if we would only allow God's heart of compassion to influence our sometimes self-centered hearts.

> The two **passions** that are **c o m** bi n e d to s h o w **compassion** are love and sorrow.

The earthly ministry of Jesus was filled with outward expressions of His inward compassion. Scripture teaches us that He had compassion on people who were lonely, hungry, mourning, tired, and sick. In other words, Christ had a lot of compassion for hurting, helpless people who had no idea how to help themselves.

In Mathew 9:36-38 we see the compassion of Christ demonstrated. *But when he saw the multitudes, he was moved with compassion on them, because they fainted, and were scattered abroad, as sheep having no shepherd. Then saith he unto his disciples, The harvest truly is plenteous, but the labourers are few; Pray ye therefore the Lord of the harvest, that he will send forth labourers into his harvest.*

Here are some things to notice about the compassion of Christ:

- He had compassion on many people, not just a few.
- He had compassion because they were weak.
- He had compassion because they were separated—having gone astray.
- He had compassion because they had no leader .
- His compassion caused Him to try to motivate others to help Him reach out.
- His compassion led Him to solicit God's help in His endeavor.

God is teaching us here that He has never had a problem generating a harvest. His problem has always been His workforce. We, as God's people, often claim to be His workforce. And we are. So why is He looking for more laborers? I think it might not be that He is in need of more laborers as much as He is in need of laborers like Jesus Who will look on people and have compassion. I think God has a lot of people who labor, but their efforts do not come from a heart of compassion. Rather, we find ourselves laboring for Christ out of a heart of duty. Duty is often given begrudgingly and immediately ceased when the debt is perceived to be paid. However, in laboring with a heart of compassion, the laborer will with great care and concern continue to labor until the sorrow is gone. In the case of the multitudes, the sorrow will remain until their needs are met.

How can we demonstrate God's compassion toward these scattered multitudes of sheep that have no shepherd to lead them? By bringing them into a relationship with *our* Shepherd! They will not be scattered if they leave the wandering multitude and join the flock of God. Let's look at the familiar passage of Psalm 23.

> *The LORD is my shepherd; I shall not want. He maketh me to lie down in green pastures: he leadeth me beside the still waters. He restoreth my soul: he leadeth me in the paths of righteousness for his name's sake. Yea, though I walk through the valley of the shadow of death, I will fear no evil: for thou art with me; thy rod and thy staff they comfort me. Thou preparest a table before me in the presence of mine enemies: thou anointest my head with oil; my cup runneth over. Surely goodness and mercy shall follow me all the days of my life: and I will dwell in the house of the LORD for ever.*

If the Lord is your Shepherd, than you are a very blessed person. This wonderful Psalm is a list of the many benefits of His compassion toward His sheep.

God will use you to make a difference in the lives of multitudes of people if you will become a laborer who, with a heart of love, will sorrow with others. Men and women with compassionate hearts are men and women whose steps will be ordered by the Lord. You will be led to many people so you may bring them to our Shepherd. And, you will delight in the way in which He does this.

Jude 22 says, *And of some have compassion, making a difference:* Do you know what that means? It means that some don't have compassion. And because they don't have compassion they don't make a difference. People who are led of the Lord will be people who make a difference. To make a difference, you must have a compassionate heart.

Step 6   *Men/ Women Who Witness*

The word *witness* is often misunderstood. By definition it simply means "to testify." *Testify* means "to communicate to others knowledge of something not known by them." It is simply sharing with others the Good News (the Gospel) of Jesus Christ. If you are going to be a good man or woman whose steps are ordered by the Lord, then you will, under the influence of the Holy Spirit, be a man or woman who witnesses. It is the natural outgrowth of the Spirit's work in a believer's life. Let's take a look at one of the primary roles of the Spirit of God—bearing witness, or "producing knowledge of something not known by someone."

In John 16:7, Jesus is speaking to His disciples about His impending betrayal and departure from this world. He said, *Nevertheless I tell you the truth; It is expedient for you that I go away: for if I go not away, the Comforter will not come unto you; but if I depart, I will send him unto you.* I realize that I expounded at length on this passage of Scripture in chapter five, but I want to revisit it here because it is so applicable to this subject of witnessing. And once again, repetition *is* the key to learning.

As you will recall, Jesus was telling His disciples that they would be better off with Him absent than with Him present. He was saying they would be better off with God *in* them, rather than God *with* them.

Now, I can understand why this would have been hard for the disciples to believe. Certainly, it would seem to be easier for me to live the Christian life if Christ were *with* me versus *in* me. I would like to think that if Christ were standing beside me, walking with me, watching me, and advising me, I would be a better Christian and respond better to life's adversities. To understand the basis of the disciples' concern, let's look again at how they responded when Jesus did leave.

It began in the garden when the guards took Him. Their first response to Jesus not being with them was to run and hide. During His incarceration, they all hid out of fear of physical harm. Only one had the boldness to show up at the Crucifixion. (That was John, the only one who did not die a martyr's death. Think about that!) After His resurrection their belief grew, and after His ascension we see them gathered (in secret) in the upper room. It is there that we see Jesus's promise of the Comforter fulfilled. The account in Acts 2:1-4 reads like this:

> *And when the day of Pentecost was fully come, they were all with one accord in one place. And suddenly there came a sound from heaven as of a rushing mighty wind, and it filled all the house where they were sitting. And there appeared unto them cloven tongues like as of fire, and it sat upon each of them. And they were all <u>filled with the Holy Ghost</u>...*

The Holy Spirit arrived on the scene and indwelt these men. The Comforter had come! In John 16:13-14, Jesus explained to His disciples the purpose of the Comforter. *Howbeit when he, the Spirit of truth* (that is, the Spirit of Jesus), *is come, he will guide you into all truth: for he shall not speak of himself; but whatsoever he shall hear, that shall he speak: and he will show you things to come. He shall glorify me* (or, He will make Jesus look good): *for he shall receive of mine* (or, from Jesus), *and shall show it unto you* (that is, personal revelation). Jesus taught His disciples that when the Comforter arrived, He would be the very

Spirit of Jesus living within them. His Spirit would guide them into what is true. He would not exalt Himself, but rather He would exalt Jesus. Jesus then explained that He would communicate to them through the leading of His Holy Spirit. Is this what happened? Let's take a look:

We see in Acts 2 that within moments of being filled with the Spirit, the disciples came out of their hiding place and were thronged by a multitude of people who were at first perplexed by their behavior. Then Peter, who had been one of the spiritually weakest and least productive of His disciples, stepped before the crowd under the influence of the indwelling Holy Spirit and did something that, before, would have made Peter very *uncomfortable*. Therein, in that one word—"uncomfortable," lies a primary role of the Holy Spirit. Allow me to explain it to you again as we did in chapter five.

GOD COMMANDS US TO WITNESS

Before Jesus ascended, He proclaimed that we would receive a special kind of power. The verses are found in Acts 1:8-9 *But ye shall receive power, after that the Holy Ghost is come upon you: and ye shall be witnesses unto me both in Jerusalem, and in all Judaea, and in Samaria, and unto the uttermost part of the earth.* In these verses, we see a different role of the Holy Spirit than Jesus was speaking about in John 16. We see the Holy Spirit not as a form of leading, but as a form of power. This power would manifest itself in a boldness to testify to those without the knowledge of the things which we have come to know. This is another function of the Holy Spirit. Not to come *in* us (He is already there at salvation), but to come *upon* us. Now, we must understand how Jesus uses these two functions in conjunction with one another to bring about

His will in our lives.

When I first got saved, my pastor told me that I needed to get baptized. I was very *uncomfortable* with that. He then taught me that I needed to read, study, memorize, and meditate on God's Word every day.

> The power of the Holy Spirit will manifest itself in a boldness to testify to those without the knowledge of the things which we have come to know.

"Every day?" I thought. "Surely I cannot be that faithful!" The thought of being able to commit portions of God's Word to meditation every day was a very *uncomfortable* thought to me. One Sunday, he encouraged me to get involved serving in our local church. Serving myself had been my forte. Serving others made me very *uncomfortable*. Later, he taught tithing and financial giving. That made me very *uncomfortable*. Then, he taught me that I needed to be sharing my testimony and reaching others with the Good News of salvation. Now *that* made me *extremely uncomfortable*. In other words, just about everything my pastor taught me to do made me feel *uncomfortable*. However, at the same time that I felt *uncomfortable* from my pastor's *outside pressure*, I felt an *inward persuasion* to commit to what he was teaching, and that was *written proof*. While teaching it, my pastor would use Bible verses that backed up what he was saying. He was applying an outward pressure and producing a written proof that was "bearing witness" with an inward persuasion that what he was saying was true and was God's divine direction for me. Under the influence of my preacher's outside pressure, God's written proof, and the Spirit's inner persuasion, I would step out on faith and do something that I found to be very *uncomfortable*.

In a very short amount of time, something absolutely amazing took place. As I would obey God's leading within and engage in His will (while very *uncomfortable* in the role), the Spirit of God would come *upon* me and give me the power to do the work. All of a sudden, I became very *comfortable* doing what was asked of me. That's right, getting baptized in public, committing key Scriptures to meditation, attending services regularly, serving others, giving of my income, and yes, even boldly proclaiming the Gospel to strangers and friends alike became very *comfortable* things to do, as God's power rested *upon* me.

I believe our biggest problem with sharing the gospel is we are *uncomfortable* with the thought of talking to others who may or may not be interested. The truth is that we *should not* be comfortable doing it, and we *will not* be comfortable doing it until we do it with God's power upon us! If we were *comfortable*, we would not need God's help or His Helper—we would not need the *Comforter*. Consider, if God had intended His children to remain *comfortable*, then why, pray tell, would He have sent us a *Comforter*?

Below is an equation that I believe is the biblical method for experiencing that "deeper anointing" that everyone is always asking God to give to them.

<u>Outside Pressure</u> + <u>Inside Persuasion</u> = <u>Uncomfortable Opportunities</u>
(God's leaders/His Word) + (from the Holy Spirit) = (that we may experience God's power)

Then, as a result

<u>Uncomfortable Opportunities</u> + <u>My Submissive Yielding</u> = <u>His Power on us</u>
(for us to experience God's power) (to God's inner persuasion) (to do His will with joy)

GOD REWARDS OUR WITNESS

Throughout the Bible, we see that God rewards those who obey Him. There are many passages of Scripture that prove this to be true. We saw this in one such passage we dissected and defined in other chapters, including chapter six—Proverbs 11:30 *The fruit* (or, outcome) *of the righteous* (or, one who has been made right in God's eyes) *is a tree of life* (or, eternal life)*; and he that winneth souls is wise.* This verse is telling us that the outcome of God's people under God's control will bring forth eternal life. The outcome of the righteous and our marriage, or union, with Christ is spiritual offspring. To those of us who witness He has promised to grant wisdom. *Wisdom* is "skill in living." There is no greater skill to be gleaned than the skill of being obedient to God—no matter how uncomfortable we might be doing so—by His power coming upon us, that we may do it well.

GOD DESIGNS OUR WITNESS

God will not ask us to do what He will not give us the power to do, along with the understanding of how it should be done properly. This truth is exemplified in the story of the Gadarene demoniac. The account is recorded in the fifth chapter of the book of Mark. We will look at this story in greater detail in chapter eight, but let's glance at it here for just a moment so I may explain what I believe is the best way to witness to other people.

In this story, Jesus encountered a man who had many demons living within him. Many people had tried to help this man, but the demons so controlled him that he rejected their help in violent ways, bringing himself great harm and emotional sadness. Jesus had compassion on the man and cast out the "legion" of demons, and the man became right-minded. Seeing this, the people of the city, out of fear and frustration, begged Jesus to leave. He complied with their request, and the former demoniac sought permission from Jesus to go along with Him.

Howbeit Jesus suffered him not, but saith unto him, Go home to thy friends, and tell them how great things the

Lord hath done for thee, and hath had compassion on thee. And he departed, and began to publish in Decapolis how great things Jesus had done for him: and all men did marvel. Mark 8:19-20

Jesus refused the man's request to spend more time with Him. Instead, He instructed him to go tell his friends what the Lord had done for him and how the Lord had shown Him great compassion.

Now let's stop there for just a minute. God does not ask us to witness by only warning people about hell. Doing so doesn't properly lift up Christ. That's the Bad News, not the Good News! And if you do that as your only form of witness, I believe you will do it without the power of the Holy Spirit coming upon you. No, I believe Christ wants us to witness to friends and to strangers in the same way He asked the former demoniac from Gadara to witness: go and tell about the great things that God has done and of His great compassion. If we were to go to our friends, our family, our neighbors, and our co-workers and share with them God's great goodness and compassion in our lives, we might be amazed at how many would be interested enough to ask questions or even consider getting saved. That doesn't mean we should never share the "bad news," but remember, it's God's goodness that leads a man to repentance.

Looking further into the story, we see the result of Christ's unique design for this man's witness: he departed and began to declare in Decapolis (a ten-city region around Gadara) what great things Christ had done for him. I am sure that he was very uncomfortable telling these people about Jesus after they had just asked Him to leave, but he did what Jesus wanted him to do. He allowed God to order his steps. He did that which was uncomfortable, and the Bible says, *all men did marvel.* Later, we see that when Christ returned to the region, many people thronged Him with hopes of being healed. Included in these miracles was the healing of Jarius's twelve-year-old daughter and the woman who had an issue of blood for twelve years. How did all these people go from despising Jesus off their coast to welcoming Him with a great crowd of believers? Very simple, one man told what great things Jesus had done for Him and the compassion that Jesus had on him.

That is God's simple design for witnessing—telling others the great things God has done for us. In Colossians 4:3-6, we see the apostle Paul explaining how he felt was the best way to witness to others.

> *Withal praying also for us, that God would open unto us a door of utterance, to speak the mystery of Christ, for which I am also in bonds: That I may make it manifest, as I ought to speak. Walk in wisdom toward them that are without, redeeming the time. Let your speech be always with grace, seasoned with salt, that ye may know how ye ought to answer every man.*

This, too, is an amazing story. The Apostle Paul was in prison in Rome when he wrote this epistle to the church at Colosse. What was his charge? He was imprisoned for preaching the Gospel. And in the face of it all, he was asking the church to pray for him, that an opportunity would be made available to him to preach the Gospel while incarcerated. What an unbelievable witness! Talk about doing something that was uncomfortable and having God make it comfortable! He then defines how to witness to others. He tells us to walk with skill toward them that are without Christ and to value every opportunity. Don't lose the opportunity by being unwise or by procrastinating away the opportunity.

When we begin to share this mystery of the Gospel we must make sure to do it with grace (where God is doing the work) and that our language is seasoned as with salt. Salt preserves from corruption and adds flavor. In other words, it keeps things alive and tasting good. As we have discussed previously, when we present a witness to others, we should let God do the work, not our own fleshly method. God's grace will promote the witness. He will see to it that it administers life to the dying and comes across appetizing rather than bland. That, Paul goes on to say, is how we ought to answer every man.

Paul's design was simple. We must be willing, even in uncomfortable settings, to take advantage of our opportunities to witness. And when the opportunity presents itself, let God do the work. It will come across much more appealing and save that individual from their corruption.

God wants us to be men and women who witness. All we must do is follow His steps. When God is leading you to witness and you submit, even though you are uncomfortable, God's power will come upon you. Your steps will be ordered by the Lord and you will be delighted in His Way.

Step 7   *Men and Women Who Are Giving*

God will lead good people to give. We ought to always be willing to give of what God gives to us. First Chronicles 29:12-14 says, *Both riches* (or, wealth) *and honour* (or, promotion) *come of thee* (of God)*, and thou reignest* (or, are in charge) *over all; and in thine hand is power* (or, authority) *and might* (or, physical strength); *and in thine hand it is to make great, and to give strength* (or, ability) *unto all. Now therefore, our God, we thank thee, and praise thy glorious name. But who am I, and what is my people, that we should be able to offer so willingly after this sort? for all things come of thee, and of thine own have we given thee.*

The phrase *in thine hand* means "within one's possession and control." These verses are telling us that God is in possession of all these listed things that are of such great value. Whether it be riches or promotion, powers or might, greatness or strength. These are God's resources that are within His possession and control, and as He provides these things for us, we should be able to offer the same things to others, willingly. If we are given riches, they come from Him. If we are given honor (or, promotion), it comes from Him. Power (or, His authority) and might (or, physical strength) are gifts of God. Greatness (or, esteem among men) and strength (or, ability) are commodities that are given to us by God. The verses in 1 Chronicles go on to say, *and... we should be able to offer so willingly after this sort* Realizing that these things come from God, we can now willingly offer them back to Him by, under the influence of the Holy Spirit, giving a portion of these resources for the benefit of others. Let's look at each commodity that God makes available to His people for further distribution to others.

GETTING AND GIVING RICHES

Getting money is often the beginning of materialism. However, giving away our money will cure any struggle with materialism we may have. Giving is the sure cure for selfishness. A true giver realizes that God ultimately owns everything. Givers find great joy in being trusted by God to distribute His money for the needs of others.

Most people are not satisfied with what God has given to them in the way of money. Have you ever stopped to ask yourself this question, "I wonder if God is satisfied with the money that I have given to others?" Let's not forget God's biblical method for obtaining. It is found in Luke 6:38. *Give, and it shall be given unto you.* Before God could commit what we think is a "monetary injustice" to us, we will first commit a monetary injustice to others. It is that simple. We are the first piece of the equation that unlocks God's treasure chest of riches. If we will show God we are not materialistic but, rather, opportunistic with what we have been given, then what we are given will be increased. It is not a principle—it is a promise! Those who say it is a principle that cannot be counted on are probably poor givers, justifying their self-centered or possession-centered lifestyles. Christ went on to teach in verse 38 that what is given to us will be given in ...*good measure, pressed down, and shaken together, and running over* (now that's prosperity!), *shall men give into your bosom. For with the same measure* (or, determined length) *that ye mete* (or, limit) *withal it shall be measured to you again.* These verses remind us of some basic principles:

This verse does not mention money. It is a promise for any given commodity, including money.

- Our giving precedes our getting.
- Our getting is more abundant than our giving—running over (we cannot out-give God).
- Men will be returning your investment—it may not appear to be coming from God.
- The measuring stick that limits our giving will also limit our receiving.

I find one of the best principles that I have learned concerning creating wealth is taught by Jesus in Luke 16:10-14.

> *He that is faithful in that which is least is faithful also in much: and he that is unjust in the least is unjust also in much. If therefore ye have not been faithful in the unrighteous mammon, who will commit to your trust the true riches? And if ye have not been faithful in that which is another man's, who shall give you that which is your own? No servant can serve two masters: for either he will hate the one, and love the other; or else he will hold to the one, and despise the other. Ye cannot serve God and mammon. And the Pharisees also, who were covetous, heard all these things: and they derided him.*

Mammon is a Babylonian term for "money." Jesus is giving us a lesson in stewardship. *Steward* is an old English word for the modern English word "manager." Thus, Jesus was referring to money management! He told His disciples that if we are unfaithful in the little things, we will be unfaithful concerning larger matters. He then specified one of the little things that people can be unfaithful in stewarding, or managing—money. If we fail to be faithful in managing what is entrusted to us by another, why would that person ever give us anything to keep? Similarly, if we are not giving what we are supposed to be giving, we are not going to be keeping what we hope to be keeping. Jesus then explained what makes us unfaithful in the distribution of the financial resources that He has given to us to manage. He called it "serving money." *No servant can serve two masters…Ye cannot serve God and mammon* (money). Serving is not the same as slavery. Serving means "to work for." In today's vernacular, the word *servant* means "employee" (whether paid or volunteer service). So, He is teaching us that we cannot be employees of God and employees of our money. Some wealthy people advise, "Don't work for your money, let your money work for you." Jesus is teaching this same financial principle. Don't be an employee of your money. Don't let it dictate what you do and how much you get paid for what you do. Rather, serve God. Be an employee of God and let Him determine what you do and how much you get paid for doing it.

> Don't be an employee of your money. Don't let it dictate what you do and how much you get paid for what you do. Rather, serve God. Be an employee of God and let Him determine what you do and how much you get paid for doing it.

Another part of Christ's teaching on money should be noted. Concerning service to two masters, He points out, *for either he will hate the one, and love the other; or else he will hold to the one, and despise the other. Ye cannot serve God and mammon.* Based on the order that He listed the two masters (God first and then money), He is teaching us that if we love money, we will hate God. But, if we cling to God, we will despise money. *Despise* simply means "to have a low opinion of." In other words, loving money will replace our love for God with hatred toward Him. However, if we cling to God as our source of life and prosperity, then we will have a low opinion of money. I have found that when one's opinion of money is in the proper perspective, that person is a giver of it and not a keeper of it. Givers are receivers! God never gives the gift of giving without giving the gift of earning!

Now for those who may disagree, I offer the final phrase of this passage that Jesus taught His disciples: *And the Pharisees also, who were covetous, heard all these things: and they derided him.* The Bible says that those who disagree with this teaching will laugh at it and ridicule it because they are covetous people.

I certainly do not know whom God intends to be people of wealth, but I do know this one thing: they will obtain it because they are givers of what He gives them. He will bless their giving with more things to manage as they remain givers. This is the best way to compound wealth.

GETTING AND GIVING HONOR

We see in our key verses in 1 Chronicles that God also bestows honor upon us that we might willingly offer it to others. *Honor* is "the promotion of another." It is within God's power to give to us promotion among others. Of course, the pattern for obtaining honor is the same as the pattern for obtaining riches. *Give and it shall be given unto you*. However, as is the case for wealth, we are tempted to try to obtain our own esteem without first esteeming others. We want to receive without first giving.

As with money, we say, "I would value and respect others if more people would value and respect me!" That's like saying, "I would give more money, if I could get more money first." It doesn't work that way. We must first give in order to receive. The reason we don't like to give in order to receive is because we are not naturally "other people-centered." We tend, in the natural man, to be "self-centered." Our pride stops us from valuing and respecting others without first being valued and respected. The word honor (spelled *honour* in the King James Version) is found over 135 times in the Bible, and every time it is used, it denotes a submission of some sort. The Bible is clear on this: we will not receive honor from others if we do not give honor. Furthermore, we cannot give honor if we are struggling with self-centered pride. Let's look at a few verses that point this out.

- Proverbs 15:33 *The fear of the LORD is the instruction of wisdom; and before honour is humility.*
- Proverbs 18:12 *Before destruction the heart of man is haughty, and before honour is humility.*
- Proverbs 22:4 *By humility and the fear of the LORD are riches, and honour, and life.*
- Proverbs 29:23 *A man's pride shall bring him low: but honour shall uphold the humble in spirit.*

Scripture clearly presents to us that we must humble ourselves before we will be honored. God holds back promotion, or respect and value, from those who are struggling with pride. The Bible cites two things that destroy a man. One makes him fall repeatedly, and the other turns those repeated falls into permanent destruction. They are revealed in Proverbs 16:18. *Pride goeth before destruction, and an haughty spirit before a fall.* Pride is "undue esteem; respect or value of oneself." A *haughty spirit* (otherwise known as arrogance) is "undue contempt for others." In other words, having a low opinion of others will cause a man to fall, and that low opinion of others will eventually lead him to have an undue high opinion of himself. When that takes place, he will experience destruction in his life. Before we will ever think too highly of ourselves, we will *first* begin thinking lowly, or less, of others. Consistent falling precedes destruction and arrogance toward others precedes pride in oneself!

We need to be humble. If we don't do it to ourselves, God will do it for us. If we will take our focus and place it upon those who are in need of value and respect, we will find ourselves thinking more of them and less of ourselves. Our focus is everything. When it is on us, it leads to pride; when it is on others, it leads to humility that manifests itself in the giving of honor to them.

> *But now hath God set the members every one of them in the body, as it hath pleased him. And if they were all one member, where were the body? But now are they many members, yet but one body. And the eye cannot say unto the hand, I have no need of thee: nor again the head to the feet, I have no need of you. Nay, much more those members of the body, which seem to be more feeble, are necessary: And those members of the body, which we think to be less honourable, <u>upon these we bestow more abundant honour</u>; and our uncomely parts have more abundant comeliness. For our comely parts have no need: but God hath tempered the body together, <u>having given more abundant honour to that part which lacked</u>: That there should be no schism in the body; but that the members should have the same care one for another. And whether one member suffer, all the members suffer with it; or one member be honoured, all the members rejoice with it. Now ye are the body of Christ, and members in particular.*
> 1 Corinthians 12:18-27

Here we see God giving honor to someone who lacked

honor. He tells us to do likewise. Those who lack honor, or respect, esteem, and value, are the people who are less comely or less desirable. He says that we will *think* that such people are less honorable, yet these are the people that God gives honor to. He tells us to not only give them honor, but also to give them "abundant honor." The need for honor is among those that are less desirable. This is so against our human nature, yet it is God's nature. In His power, under His influence, we will give honor to whom honor is due.

This type of honoring of others will produce humility. God will unleash His honor upon the humble. He promises. *Give and it shall be given unto you.* It is in God's hand to give honor and He gives it to those who willingly give it to others.

GETTING AND GIVING POWER

Power is defined as "authority." God is the giver of this commodity. He wants us to *offer willingly after this sort*, as well. Authority is given by God to those who can handle authority. We call them "leaders." Leaders are usually leaders because they are good followers. The same principle of giving and getting applies to this gift from God, too. As we yield (which is a form of giving that is within our power) to our God-ordained authority, God will cause others to yield to our ordained leadership.

> The best people to advance within my organization have been people that will yield to authority.

As an employer, I have found over the years that the best people to advance within my organization, both in the secular world and in ministry, have been people that will yield to authority. Those who yielded to authority usually ended up in authority. Quite simply, give ground and you will get ground. No one wants employees that resist direction from those in authority over them. As a result, those who resist authority are seldom allowed to rise up the chain of command because of their resistance. Have you ever wondered why those with less talent than you were able to rise higher in the company than you? Wonder no more! They gave respect to their authorities, and their authorities gave it back to them. To get power, we must yield to those in power. It is that simple. It may sound wrong, but it is right. Let's see what Scripture has to say about how God distributes His mighty power:

2. All power belongs to God. *God hath spoken once; twice have I heard this; that <u>power belongeth unto God</u>.* Psalm 62:11

3. God alone can give power. *...the God of Israel <u>is</u> <u>he that giveth...power</u> unto his people. Blessed be God.* Psalm 68:35

4. God chose to give all His power to His submitted Son. *And Jesus came and spake unto them, saying, All <u>power is given unto me</u> in heaven and in earth.* Matthew 28:18

5. God gave us the power to become sons of God if we have received Him. *But as many as received him, <u>to them gave he power to become the sons of God</u>, even to them that believe on his name:;* John 1:12

6. This power is made available through God in us. *But <u>ye shall receive power</u>, after that the Holy Ghost is come upon you...* Acts 1:8

7. We are powerless without God. *I am the vine, ye are the branches: He that abideth in me, and I in him, the same bringeth forth much fruit: for <u>without me ye can do nothing</u>.* John 15:5

These verses simply remind us that all power belongs to God; we are powerless. He can give us power, but it is based on our willingness to submit to Him. Jesus proved this through His own submission. He was given all the power that belonged to God. This same power is available to the submitted believer. The power available to us is not only the power to become a child of God, but to have access to the power given to Christ as we submit to Him Who is in us—the Holy Ghost. What an amazing truth!

You are under the power of someone. Everyone is. No one is a power unto himself. You are under someone. As a matter of fact, if it is not God, it is the devil. We read in Acts 26:18 the very reason why God sent His only begotten Son: *To open their eyes, and to <u>turn them</u> from darkness to light, and <u>from the power of Satan unto God,</u> that they may receive forgiveness of sins, and inheritance among them which are sanctified by faith that is in me.* God's plan has always been to redeem man from the power of Satan unto the Power of God. God has all authority; He gave it to His Son, Jesus. It is available for our use, as children of God, submitted to the One who now holds that power, that authority. Psalm 106:8 reads, *Nevertheless he saved them for his name's sake, that he <u>might make his mighty power to be known</u>.*

God gives us power as we give, or, yield, to those in power: Ephesians 3:20-21 *Now unto him that is able to do exceeding abundantly above all that we ask or think, according to the <u>power that worketh in us,</u> Unto him be glory in the church by Christ Jesus throughout all ages, world without end. Amen.*

GETTING AND GIVING MIGHT

Many of the words found in our key verses in 1 Chronicles 29 seem synonymous. In some ways they are—power, might, strength. But there are some basic differences. Not so much in the getting of the commodity, but definitely in the giving of the commodity. *Might* is defined as "physical strength," the physical strength necessary to perform a function. God gives this and we are in a position to give *willingly after this sort.* Again, the same principle as before applies. To get strength, we must give strength. *Give, and it shall be given unto you.*

Have you ever been low on physical strength? It is times like that when we are incredibly dependent on God. We need God to increase our strength when we are faint. In Isaiah 40:29 we read, *He giveth power to the faint; and to them that have no might he increaseth strength.* He goes on to say that even young men will faint and fall as a result of their lack of physical strength. In verse 28 we read that God is the Creator of the ends of the earth and He doesn't faint, nor is He ever weary. Then, in verse 31, He goes on to tell us how to gain this physical strength from our Lord at our times of urgent need: *But they that wait upon the LORD shall renew their strength; they shall mount up with wings as eagles; they shall run, and not be weary; and they shall walk, and not faint.*

This is a very popular verse, but I believe it is often misunderstood. I have heard people explain this verse to mean that we must sit patiently and "wait," and then God will give us what we need so that we may mount up, walk, and run without a loss of physical strength or might. But that interpretation would be against God's nature. Not that God doesn't tell us to "wait" at times, because He does. Rather, God does not give anything, including physical strength, unless we first give it ourselves. (*Give, and it shall be given unto you.*)

Realizing this truth, I interpret this verse just a bit

differently. We see that the person that is waiting on the Lord is already walking and running, albeit wearily and fainting. I highly doubt God is talking about someone who is sitting and "waiting." Instead, I believe that God gives physical strength to those who "wait" on Him like a waiter waits on us at a restaurant. Have you experienced a bad waiter before? Of course you have. He is not waiting on you; you're waiting on him. He is not serving. He is not there to please. He is focused on too many things. He is slow and impatient with you. That is a poor waiter. God is looking for a good waiter. One that does not make Him wait to place an order. A waiter that quickly runs to His side, taking His order and filling it. He serves—with a smile! He realizes that if he "waits" on the Customer properly, he will receive a good tip. That motivates his good service to the Customer.

> If we want strength, we must give our strength to God. We must wait *upon* Him rather than waiting *for* Him

If we want strength (or might), we must give our strength to God. We must wait *upon* Him rather than waiting *for* Him.

I found this truth to be evident in my life. As a younger Christian, I struggled to give God enough time. I would get up for work without giving Him any time in my morning. I would work hard all day and come home dog-tired. I would try to take care of a few things around the house. I then would spend time with my wife and kids, and by the time I wound down from the day, I was too tired to do anything for others or even catch up on my "God and I" time that I had skipped that morning. I always seemed sapped of my energy to do anything with God or for God, much less for others. I found this a frustrating way to live. It did not seem to be the *abundant* Christian life, it was more like the *redundant* Christian life.

God was not giving me any might or strength, as I was not giving Him, or others for that matter, any of my might or strength.

I decided to make a change. Reading our verse that states, *Give, and it shall be given unto you,* I came to suspect it had to do with more than just monetary resources. Maybe it could include physical resources like strength and time. If I gave God more of my energy and time, maybe God would give me more energy or time, at least make me more productive and happy with my productivity.

To this end, I began to study my Bible and found that God has given the following admonitions in Scripture:

1. Ten percent of what God gives (first fruits, or gross amount) should be given back to Him. I decided to give God the first ten percent of my time per week. That would be seventeen hours. I did that by making the following commitments that no other opportunity would take priority over:

   - One hour of "God and I" time every morning—first thing in the morning. This equaled seven hours of my time. (The *RUI It's Personal Daily Journal* was designed to help me meet this commitment. As a result, I have never struggled to fill a full hour.)
   - Church Services. I would attend Sunday School, AM, PM service, Mid-week service, and RU class on Friday. This equaled ten hours of time. Worship would be the "fuel" that my service to others would burn! (7+10=17 hrs. given to God)

2. *Six days shall a man work.* I decided I would work no more than six days per week for no more than

fifty hours in a week.

- That's five days for "the man" and one for the "wo-man," so to speak.
- I would work for my employer during the week and around the house on weekends no more than fifty hours total in a week.

3. Family time and time invested in others. I could not find anywhere in the Bible that discussed time commitments to family, but I saw indications such as "we should love our neighbors as ourselves" and we must "hate [family] and serve God and others" (See Luke 14:26). If this latter admonition is not to be taken literally, then at least we can be sure that it means that family should not overrule our commitment to God and others.

- I would spend twenty hours with my wife and children, uninterrupted, every week.
- I would spend twenty hours serving others. This would show God that I love others as much as I love my family.
- I would serve others and attend services *with* my family so that I could add extra time to the twenty hours I was spending with them and teach them the value of worship and service, as well.

4. That would leave about sixty hours a week to do with as I pleased. I decided I would try my best to get eight hours of sleep per night (fifty-six hours) and spend the rest of the time in preparation and transportation. Thus, if I needed to adjust anything, I would do it in this order:

- I would never steal time from God for work, family, others, or sleep

- I would never steal time from work for family, others, or sleep
- I would never steal time from family for others, or sleep
- I would never steal time from others for sleep.
- To spend more time on any of the above, I would have to steal time from my sleep.

My life changed dramatically. From that point on, I found I had the strength to carry out my responsibilities to God, my employer, my family, and to others that I had never had. It was incredible! It was like I was a new man. Before, I would retire to bed feeling half-dead and wake up (running late for work) frustrated and discouraged in my Christian life. After these commitments kicked in (and after much attack from the enemy to get me to compromise), I found myself going to bed feeling half-dead and waking up rested and excited for the day. But best of all, from that day forward I have experienced a productivity in my personal and professional life that I never thought possible.

I had never been an incredibly productive person, but I must say, it is the one thing I receive more compliments on than anything else. God did that! Why? Because I first gave to Him *willingly after this sort* of my strength, and He returned to me renewed strength. God is the One who led me to do this. My soul would not want to give first. It wants, thinks, and feels it should receive before giving. God is not this way. He wants, thinks, and feels that we should give first. He promises to give us the strength to do this. I remind you that He says in 2 Corinthians 4:16, *For which cause we faint not; but though our outward man perish, yet the inward man is renewed day by day.* If you serve in your own power, you will be faint and feel frustrated and fleshly every new day. If you serve in God's power, His Spirit will do the work—renewed, every day, brand new!

GETTING AND GIVING GREATNESS

In our key verses in 1 Chronicles, we are told, [it is] *in thine hand...to make great.* The phrase *to make great* means "to bring an advance upon one." Literally, it means to advance someone in life. As with all the other commodities that God is able to offer, the power of advancement is not found in getting, but in giving. Yes, we are *able to offer willingly after this sort*, as well.

> To get ahead in life, we need to look out for Number One and Number Two.

Society has taught us that to get ahead in life, we have to look out for number one. Actually, biblically speaking, we need to look out for Number One and Number Two to get ahead in life. The problem is that most people fail to understand whom God considers to be Number One and Number Two. I am sure you will remember this from chapter two. Number One is to love God with all your heart, soul, and mind; and Number Two is to love others as yourself. These two commandments are the cornerstone of Christian behavior. Under our own influence, we will struggle to meet either command. Under the influence of the Spirit, we will fulfill them both. Esteeming others is the best way to get ahead in life—to advance.

I think the verses in the Bible that best define the pathway to personal and professional success are found in Philippians 2:3-11.

> *Let nothing be done through strife or vainglory; but in lowliness of mind let each esteem other better than*

themselves. Look not every man on his own things, but every man also on the things of others. Let this mind be in you, which was also in Christ Jesus: Who, being in the form of God, thought it not robbery to be equal with God: But made himself of no reputation, and took upon him the form of a servant, and was made in the likeness of men: And being found in fashion as a man, he humbled himself, and became obedient unto death, even the death of the cross. Wherefore God also hath highly exalted him, and given him a name which is above every name: That at the name of Jesus every knee should bow, of things in heaven, and things in earth, and things under the earth; And that every tongue should confess that Jesus Christ is Lord, to the glory of God the Father.

Now that's a success story! From a servant to being highly exalted with a name that would cause people to bow! Let's look at the key ingredients of Christ's success:

1. He did not seek to cause contention among others.
2. He realized it was a waste of time (vain) to make Himself look good (glory).
3. He was humble (lowly) and considered (esteemed) the needs of others.
4. He did not focus on His reputation as God, but on His opportunity to serve as a man.
5. He sacrificed His life to meet the needs of others.

As a result, the Bible tells us that God exalted Him. It is within His power to "make great." And He did! He made Jesus the greatest name in all the earth! He made Him King of kings and Lord of lords! The day will come when every knee will bow at the feet of this great God who became a Servant. Jesus loved God enough to serve others. He became the two commandments personified.

I was never a leader in life. I was always a follower. If you were to see a story of my life, you would see a young man overshadowed by his much more talented siblings. You would see a boy who struggled to get through school, being held back a year once and almost twice. I was a boy that was "void of understanding." I knew everything there was to know *about* God, but I did not *know* God. He knew me and I was going to heaven, but my relationship with Him as a young, Christian school graduate was weak. As a result, I was vulnerable to the tempter. I found myself getting farther and farther from God. As a follower, I strayed from my good friends and found more "exciting" bad friends. These friends led me into the paths of unrighteousness and I eagerly followed. Being a follower, I could not and would not lead anyone, especially to the path of righteousness. After ten years of rebellion to God, I looked back and saw the devastation of my life. I was a drug addict, deeply in debt, homeless, and out of work. I had lost several good jobs. My résumé was so bad that I could not find a job without outright lying to the potential employer about my previous employers. It was a pitiful place to be, far from what I had hoped my life to become and desperately in need of God to intervene. I just wanted "a life" and wasn't looking for God to make great. I just assumed that was an impossibility.

As I explained before, through a serious car accident, God got my attention. I started going back to church and was given time to grow and mature a little before being offered an opportunity to serve in a ministry. When I did finally begin to help, something began to change in my life. I started to really enjoy giving of my time and energies to others. It made me feel as good as living for myself had made me feel bad. I hate to say it, but I became addicted to serving others.

Almost immediately, God gave me a job at a machine shop making $6/ hour. He was beginning to bless me as I gave of myself willingly. I continued to serve others with a passion, and God gave me a fiancée and a $10/ hour job. My passion then became souls. Not just serving people, but reaching people for Christ. I married and my pay rose to $13/ hour, though I had no training in machine shop work, just a good attitude and a servant's spirit.

Shortly thereafter, God put it upon my heart to start a Bible study for addicts called Reformers Unanimous. I began to minister to them on Friday nights. My phone rang one night shortly thereafter. "Are you saved?" was the first phrase I heard. "Yes," I replied.

> The best way to get ahead is to put others ahead of you. To get God to make you great, you must give willingly after this sort. You must make others great, esteeming them more highly than yourself.

"Praise the Lord," was the response of the caller. It was a former employer that I had worked for in my years of addiction. He owned convenience stores and had been saved for just over a year when he read my testimony in an RU tract that had been passed on to him. He decided to call and offer me employment.

For the next five years, I went on a ride that, to this day, I find nearly impossible to believe. Year one our addictions class averaged thirty students, and I earned $30,000 that year. God removed my debt in one year, and my wife and I spent nearly all our time serving others. Year two I moved up to General Manager and $56,000 annually, as RU doubled to sixty students per week. Year three RU doubled again to over 120 students every week, as I daily spent from

4:30-6:30 AM writing what would later be our program curriculum. At the same time, I was promoted to Vice President of Operations and later of Administration, making a six figure income. I am here to tell you that it was within God's power to make great, not mine. Everything I had done with my life on my own ended up in destruction. After five years business and ministry, my pastor suggested that I enter the ministry of Reformers full time. A month later, though at first unwilling, my employer agreed. I jumped from being a junior executive to being a full time servant, making just over $12,000 my first year in ministry. I never could have planned or done all that. Never! God showed me that it is within His power to "make great."

The best way to get ahead is to put others ahead of you. To get God to make you great, you must give willingly after this sort. You must make others great, esteeming them more highly than yourself.

Well, we have seen that God is the One who can give riches, honor, power, might, and to make great. He does it for those who first *offer so willingly after this sort*. Remember these verses when placing your gift in the getter's hands:

> *But this I say, He which soweth sparingly shall reap also sparingly; and he which soweth bountifully shall reap also bountifully. Every man according as he purposeth in his heart, so let him give; not grudgingly, or of necessity: for God loveth a cheerful giver. And God is able to make all grace abound toward you; that ye, always having all sufficiency in all things, may abound to every good work:*
> 2 Corinthians 9:6-8

If you give cheerfully (on purpose, without feeling forced) and in abundance to others, you will have all things in sufficiency and you will *abound* in every good work. Your steps will be ordered by the Lord and He will lead you to give. After you give, then you will receive. And you will learn the age old truth, "It is better to give than to receive."

God Made—It Gives
(Author Unknown)
God made the sun—it gives.
God made the moon—it gives.
God made the stars—they give.
God made the air—it gives.

God made the clouds—they give.
God made the earth—it gives.
God made the sea—it gives.
God made the trees—they give.

God made the flowers—they give.
God made the fowls—they give.
God made the beasts—they give.
God made the plants—they give.

God made man—he took...

Stop taking and start giving. The steps of a *good* man are ordered by the Lord. When God tells you to give, do you give?

- Step One- Be a man of the Book. Read your Bible. Study your Bible. Memorize and meditate on it.
- Step Two- Be a man of prayer. Don't bring God your grocery list; build a two-way communication with Him while you pray

- Step Three- Grow your faith.
- Step Four- Live a separated walk.
- Step Five- Have a compassionate heart.
- Step Six- Be a witness for God.
- Step Seven- Learn to give.

Follow these seven steps and you will find that all areas of your life will be *ordered by the LORD*. You will find delight in His way, too! Don't be discouraged if you fall, because you *shall not be utterly cast down*. Why? *...for the LORD upholdeth* [you] *with his hand. I have been young, and now am old; yet have I not seen the righteous forsaken, nor his seed begging bread* (Psalm 37:23-25). God takes good care of His good men and women.

Chapter 8

EIGHT
"UN" CHARACTERISTICS
OF UNCLEAN SPIRITS

And they came over unto the other side of the sea, into the country of the Gadarenes. And when he was come out of the ship, immediately there met him out of the tombs a man with an unclean spirit, Who had his dwelling among the tombs; and no man could bind him, no, not with chains: Because that he had been often bound with fetters and chains, and the chains had been plucked asunder by him, and the fetters broken in pieces: neither could any man tame him. And always, night and day, he was in the mountains, and in the tombs, crying, and cutting himself with stones. But when he saw Jesus afar off, he ran and worshipped him, And cried with a loud voice, and said, What have I to do with thee, Jesus, thou Son of the most high God? I adjure thee by God, that thou torment me not. For he said unto him, Come out of the man, thou unclean spirit. And he asked him, What is thy name? And he answered, saying, My name is Legion: for we are many. And he besought him much that he would not send them away out of the country. Now there was there nigh unto the mountains a great herd of swine feeding. And all the devils besought him, saying, Send us into the swine, that we may enter into them. And forthwith Jesus gave them leave. And the unclean spirits went out, and entered into the swine: and the herd ran violently down a steep place into the sea, (they were about two thousand;) and were choked in the sea. And they that fed the swine fled, and told it in the city, and in the country. And they went out to see what it was that was done. And they come to Jesus, and see him that was possessed with the devil, and had the legion, sitting, and clothed, and in his right mind: and they were afraid. And they that saw it told them how it befell to him that was possessed with the devil, and also concerning the swine. And they began to pray him to depart out of their coasts. And when he was come into the ship, he that had been possessed with the devil prayed him that he might be with him. Howbeit Jesus suffered him not, but saith unto him, Go home to thy friends, and tell them how great things the Lord hath done for thee, and hath had compassion on thee. And he departed, and began to publish in Decapolis how great things Jesus had done for him: and all men did marvel.

—Mark 5:1-20

We have discussed in great detail how we ought to act when under the influence of the inner man. When God is leading us and our outer man is yielding to this leading we will act right, think right, and feel right. However, when we reject the influence of the inner man, we will act much differently. Sometimes when acting the way we want we will find ourselves behaving like unbelievers, sometimes even like wicked unbelievers. How can this be? In this chapter we will analyze how influences can effect our actions and reactions and cause us to respond to the oppression of evil spirits.

This is quite a unique story we see in Mark 5. Jesus arrived by boat outside a town called Gadara. Immediately upon

His arrival, a man possessed of many unclean spirits ran to meet Him there. This definitely was no ordinary man. He lived in the tombs, his behavior was uncontrollable, and he was naked. I once heard a message preached on this passage entitled, "That Nude Dude in a Rude Mood."

This story seems rather bizarre, but really, it is very sad. This man was so overcome by these spirits that he could not even function in society. But when he met Jesus, He cast the evil spirits out, and there was an immediate change in that man. When the people from the city came to see this phenomenon, they found him *sitting, and clothed, and in his right mind*!

The "right mind" that this man obtained as a newborn Christian is exemplified in Philippians 2:5-7. *Let this mind be in you, which was also in Christ Jesus: Who…took upon him the form of a servant…* As evidenced by his desire to follow Christ and even to willingly depart from Christ (and to testify of His goodness to not only his friends and family, but also to those who were angry and asking Jesus to depart from their coasts), this man's right mind was under the influence of the Spirit of God. It was the mind of man (what man thinks) submitting to the mind of Christ who lives within man. He was being Spirit-led.

Under the blood, we cannot be demonically *possessed*, being under the influence of the Spirit. We can however, be demonically *oppressed*.

That's right. Only unbelievers can be demonically possessed. It would probably be surprising to find out how many Christians were formally possessed by one or more evil spirits before they were saved. However, for a Christian, demonic *possession* is an impossibility. We are the temple of God. He dwells within us. No power can overtake our current resident, the Holy Spirit of God. In Colossians 1:13 we read, [God] *hath delivered us from the power of darkness.* At salvation, we are delivered from the power of Satan. He cannot overpower us anymore. He may still be able to influence us, but not overpower and indwell us. We read in Matthew 12:29, *Or else how can one enter into a strong man's house, and spoil his goods, except he first bind the strong man? and then he will spoil his house.* We are the house of God and *no one* is able to overpower Him. His dwelling place is secure from demonic possession.

Now, on the other hand, demonic *oppression* is possible when we fail to be under the influence of the Spirit of God's leading. In Ephesians 6, we see a study in what is called the "armor of God." This armor is a defense mechanism against the wiles of the devil. Verse twelve tells us that the devil is a combative force in our lives. This verse also explains the ways in which he manages his mayhem. Let's dissect and define this verse. It will show us the influence of the enemy over an unprotected believer.

Ephesians 6:12 *For we wrestle not against flesh and blood, but against principalities, against powers, against the rulers of the darkness of this world, against spiritual wickedness in high places.*

- "Wrestle" means to combat an opposing force.
- "Not against flesh and blood" means not against humans.
- A "principality" is a prince's territory. (Such as Prince Charles is the Prince of Wales. It is his territory that has been given to him to rule. It is his principality.)
- "Powers" means authority figures.
- "Rulers" is an Old English word for the Modern

English word, leader.

- "Darkness of this world" is a phrase describing a movement to restrict light. Light is determined to be spiritual direction. Thus, this phrase means "a movement to restrict spiritual direction."
- "Spiritual wickedness" represents gross demonic plots.
- "High places" means heavenly places.

Lots of words to define, but Paul is telling us lots about our enemy. We must do our homework to understand the devil's ways. Paul says that we combat an opposing force that is not human. Our enemy is a prince who has been given a territory—earth. He is the prince of this world (John 12:31). Paul then explains the devil's chain of command. Directly under him are powers (or, authorities). These powers are given authority over leaders. By definition, then, there must be followers or subordinates of these leaders. This command structure oversees the gross demonic plots that are intended to do one thing: restrict spiritual direction.

The primary focus of the prince of this world is to hide the Light of the world. From the unbeliever, he tries to hide the light of justification; from the believer, he tries to hide the light of sanctification. This command structure is well designed and executed by the devil to keep unsaved people lost and keep saved people defeated! It is around us all the time and at all levels. His influence is trying to permeate my house, your house, the schoolhouse, the church house, and the White House! This is his territory, and he is determined to reign and to rule. Now, after learning all this, do you think it's wise to begin your day without quality time with the Lord? Quality time with the only Power we possess to overcome this evil force? Surely, without a developing relationship with the Spirit of God, we will be heavily influenced by this prince and his territorial leadership. That influence is what is referred to as demonic oppression.

Sad but true, such demonic oppression, whereby a believer submits to the influence of the enemy rather than the influence of the inner man (Christ in us), can lead us to behave in such a manner that will appear to be the same as this crazed lunatic who was possessed. Since Satan can't possess us, he tries to oppress us. If he succeeds, the obvious results will be our destructive behavior. We will still go to heaven when we die, but we will have lived defeated lives, having yielded to the wrong influence. Let's delve into this amazing story and see how we can keep a behavior pattern like that of the Gadarene demoniac from forming in our Christian lives.

In this chapter, we will uncover eight "un"characteristics that were evident in this poor maniac's life, which can also be manifested in our lives should we allow ourselves to be under the influence of the wrong spirit. They are characteristics that the spirit world wants you to adopt in your lifestyle so that whether possessed as an unbeliever, or oppressed as a fleshly-led believer, the devil will have control over you.

> Surely, without a developing relationship with the Spirit of God, we will be heavily influenced by this prince and his territorial leadership. That influence is what is referred to as demonic oppression.

Unclean

...immediately there met him out of the tombs a man with an
<u>*unclean*</u> *spirit...*

The first characteristic of these spirits is that they are
unclean. Whenever the devil gets a hold of something, he
always makes it unclean. It doesn't matter if it is music,
worship, entertainment, young men and ladies,
marriage—the list could go on and on. Anything that is
pure and beautiful, the devil's desire is to defile it.

Another word for unclean is "guilty." When God calls
someone unclean He is calling him or her guilty. God's
Spirit is without sin. He has no guilt and produces no guilt
or condemnation. But in the dark spirit world of the devil,
all are guilty under sin.

The New Testament contains the word "unclean" thirty
times. In twenty of those instances, it is used in reference
to demonic spirits. The other ten times refer to things
which were unholy according to Old Testament Law. So,
we can see that being unclean is something God considers
evil or under the influence of evil.

As believers, we cannot be unclean. We are not guilty of
anything any longer. We are forgiven for everything and
we will receive no condemnation for what we have done. In
Acts 10:9-16, Peter has a vision and hears God's voice. *And
the voice spake unto him again the second time, What God
hath cleansed, that call not thou common.* The word *common*
means "defiled." The animals mentioned in this passage are
symbolic, not of unclean spirits, but of people formerly
under demonic possession or unclean (guilty). Since God
has cleansed us, we cannot be defiled by an indwelling
demonic spirit. We have been cleansed. First John 1:7 tells
us, *the blood of Jesus Christ his Son <u>cleanseth us</u> from all sin.*

Titus 1:15 says, *Unto the pure all things are pure: but unto them that are defiled and unbelieving is nothing pure; but even their mind and conscience is defiled.* The "defiled" are those who are unbelievers. The believers are those who are now pure. First John 3:2-3 reminds us that we are children of God. Though at times we don't appear to be like Him, when He returns, we will be just like Him. He says in verse 3 that those who have this hope in Him keep themselves pure. *Beloved, now are we the sons of God, and it doth not yet appear what we shall be: but we know that, when he shall appear, we shall be like him; for we shall see him as he is. And every man that hath this hope in him purifieth himself, even as he is pure.*

Now, realizing that we are pure and that God sees us as cleansed by the blood of our Lord Jesus, let's look at how the devil can influence us to live as if we were back in bondage and unclean. He cannot make us unclean, but if he can get us to act unclean, we will feel unclean. We can behave as if we were possessed, but the truth is that we are being oppressed and yielding to the oppression.

In chapter seven we discussed friendships that could be considered bad influences. The key verse was 2 Corinthians 6:14. Paul tells us in this verse not to be unequally yoked. He compared this partnership to light and darkness—God's influence partnering with evil influences. Verse 15 continues on to explain that Christ and Satan have no harmony (concord) together, no partnership whatsoever; no positive interaction. They agree on nothing (vs 16). We are His temple and He lives in us. Verse 17 then tells us to come out and separate ourselves from these types of influences that are not in agreement with our inner influence. And then in 2 Corinthians 7:1, we are given the following responsibility: *Having therefore these promises, dearly beloved, let us cleanse ourselves from all filthiness of the flesh and spirit, perfecting holiness in the fear of God.*

This appears to be a request for us to *do* something that will cleanse us. We know that all efforts in our own power to establish a form of righteousness is of no good. So what work is Paul referring to? If we are already clean, then why do we need to cleanse ourselves? Well, in God's eyes, we *are* clean. But that does not mean we act, think, or feel clean. The truth is, we are clean in spite of how we feel. This verse is not talking about our cleanness in our position with God, but rather in our position with man. God can see us as clean, but the world, based on our behavior, can see us as unclean. Paul called it "the filthiness of the flesh and the spirit." Now, that is an odd criticism—calling the spirit unclean. But that is not what this verse means. He is calling "the flesh and the spirit" unclean. Let me explain with a short review from previous chapters on the flesh and the spirit.

> The **Soul** is the outer man; your mind, will and emotions.
> The **Spirit** is the inner man; God's mind, will, and emotions in us.
> The **Flesh** is the members (or body parts) that are under the influence of the soul.

When we walk "after the flesh," we are taking repeated steps under the influence of the outer man. This is our way of thinking, wanting, and feeling. When we walk "in the Spirit," we are taking repeated steps under the influence of the inner man. This is God's way of thinking, wanting, and feeling, manifested as Christ living not only *in* us, but also through us.

If a person is engaging in drugs or alcohol, then we

understand that to be flesh. He is doing what he wants and definitely not what God wants. That is easy to define as flesh. It is unrighteous flesh. However, there is another flesh that hardly anyone knows about. It is not unrighteous flesh, and there is no such thing as righteous flesh, so what other type of flesh could there be? Self-righteous flesh. That's right, acting righteous in our own power. Despite the fact that we have been cleansed by God's power, we try to *act* clean in our *own* power rather than the power of God.

Now, how might that flesh—the flesh of self-righteousness—appear? Here are some examples:

1. A person gives $45 every week in the offering plate on Sunday morning as his tithe. The person never fails to give this offering.
2. A person mows his pastor's lawn every week, without fail, for free.
3. A person sings in the church choir and also sings solos.
4. A person teaches Sunday School.

The list can go on and on. How could we do these things that seem so good, yet do them "after the flesh" rather than in the Spirit? It's simple. Often, we actually begin by doing them "in the Spirit," but then end up doing them "after the flesh" in our own power. Paul warned the church of Galatia about this in Galatians 3:3. *Are ye so foolish? having begun in the Spirit, are ye now made perfect by the flesh?* This is what the outside oppression of the devil can do to believers. The devil has no power within. The only powers within a believer are the power of God and the power of man living together, preferably with the power of man submitting to the power of God. However, the commanding forces of the devil will place outside influences that are oppressive on us to get the power of man to run the Christian life. When we do this we will appear clean to man, but under the conviction of the Holy Spirit we will not feel clean. It makes us feel discouraged and fleshly. Because we are! Let's look more closely at our examples to see how this can happen.

1. A person gives $45 every week as his tithe. But through the years, his income has grown from $450 per week to $600 per week. This person is not a giver, he is a robber. He is doing good (by putting money in the offering), but he is doing it in the power of the flesh.

2. A person mows his pastor's lawn every week. He doesn't expect his pastor to give him money, but if his pastor doesn't thank him regularly and even sometimes from the pulpit, he gets offended and quits. That's not love, the fruit of the Spirit; it is the lust of the flesh, self-love.

3. A person sings in the church choir and also sings solos. She used to beg God for His power to use her gift, but now she hardly practices because she has learned to "perform" in her own power. She doesn't need God's power because she has gotten good enough to sing in her own power.

4. A person teaches a Sunday School class. He used to beg God for His direction in what to teach and for the power to teach it. But now, after a number of years, he doesn't look for God's direction or power. As a matter of fact, he waits until Saturday evening around 9:00 p.m., struts over to the computer to string a few thoughts together and get a few clean jokes off the internet, and off he goes. By starting class late and adding a few "illustrations," he might even turn it into a two-week lesson. What is he

doing? A good work, but in the power of his flesh.

Now, be sure of this, no one else may ever know it, but people such as these will feel unclean. They will not experience the fruit, or outcome, of the Spirit. Their work is not an outcome of the Spirit, it is an outcome of the flesh. (In chapter nine, I will explain the differences between them more thoroughly.) These Christians will not experience joy but, rather, frustration in their work and walk.

That is what the filthiness of the flesh and spirit is in 2 Corinthians 7:1. It is when someone who is indwelled by the Spirit allows himself to be led by the flesh to do "good things." It is when the flesh tries to imitate the Spirit. We often do not realize it, but it is why we get so frustrated in the work of the Lord.

As you may recall, we covered this topic earlier in chapter two. The verse that describes this filthiness is Hebrews 4:12 which tells us that the Bible will divide asunder (or, separate) the soul and the spirit. When the soul tries to act like the spirit, we will feel unclean. We are *not* unclean and we may not even *act* unclean, but we will *feel* unclean. The truth is that when we engage in self-righteous flesh long enough, our frustration will cause us to lower our guard, and that same evil influence will oppress us into unrighteous flesh. The result is doing something in our flesh that is wicked and was once unthinkable. That is the purpose of the oppression—to get us to act in our own power, rather than yielding to God's power within us. Eventually, we will live under the power of the oppressor. Possessed? No, not possible. But oppressed. We will begin to act unclean. Under this influence, we will first *think* unclean, then *act* unclean, then *feel* unclean—yet you *are* clean in God's eyes! To fix this, we need to *cleanse ourselves from all filthiness of the flesh and spirit, perfecting holiness in the fear of God.*

> The purpose of the oppression is to get us to act in our own power, rather than yielding to God's power within us. Eventually, we will live under the power of the oppressor.

How do we do this (and continue to do this) so the evil forces that surround us will not oppress us into submitting to the outer man and eventually to Satan himself? The answer is found in 1 John 1:7 where the Bible says, *But if we walk* (or, take repeated steps) *in the light* (or, spiritual direction)*, as he is in the light, we have fellowship one with another, and the blood of Jesus Christ his Son cleanseth us from all sin.* Now, don't get ahead of the verse and assume that we must re-cleanse ourselves whenever we step away from our spiritual direction. No, the blood of Christ has already done that. Being saved, the blood has cleansed us. But taking repeated steps in the light (spiritual direction from the Holy Spirit) will keep us in fellowship with God. If we are in fellowship with God, we cannot be in fellowship with devils. We cannot be oppressed by them when we walk in the light. First Corinthians 10:20-21 says, *I would not that ye should have fellowship with devils. Ye <u>cannot</u> drink the cup of the Lord, and the cup of devils: ye <u>cannot</u> be partakers of the Lord's table, and of the table of devils.*

Staying in the light of the Holy Spirit's leading will keep us from feeling unclean. Returning to that light will restore the broken fellowship between us and God in us. This will hinder the influence of outside oppression.

Whenever the oppressor wins, we are left thinking, acting, or feeling unclean. God can change all that. Our thinking can be *transformed* and our acting can be *conformed* into His image as we yield to the light of the inner man. We only need to take one step to feel better about ourselves—confession. You see, it is the devil's goal to keep us engaged in or dwelling on unconfessed sin to make us feel guilty, even though we are not guilty. If he can get us to do that, we will remain defeated. God can remove the guilty unclean feelings as well as the thoughts and actions. His remedy is found in 1 John 1:9. *If we confess our sins, he is faithful and just to forgive us our sins, and to cleanse us from all unrighteousness.* *Confess* means "to agree." If we agree with God that the soul is leading the body and that we are not under His influence (even though we are at times doing good) and ask Him to forgive us, we will be cleansed. He removes the guilt and shame that comes from not living under His control. What a blessed way to live!

Don't let the devil oppress you into thinking, acting, or feeling unclean. I have shared with you a biblical method for cleaning up your messes. Now you can be, as John 15:3 says, *clean through the word which I have spoken unto you.*

Uncivilized
Who had his dwelling among the tombs...

The second characteristic of unclean spirits is that they are uncivilized. To be civil or civilized means to be structured, or to have structure. It is to live a structured life. In the case of the Gadarene demoniac, his life was absent of the structure of a house and a home. He was homeless; he had no structure in which to dwell. We know he had family because, after he was in his right mind Jesus told him to go home to them. Presumably, his family had a home and a house to live in, but he rejected this structure to live a life that was uncivilized. Scripture records many examples of possessed unbelievers that were uncivilized. I think devils probably hate structure and accountability.

This characteristic, though, is not reserved for the unbeliever, much less the possessed unbeliever. You see, when the devil gets ahold of the mind, will, or emotions of a believer, that believer can become uncivilized. Of course, this is not a characteristic that is becoming of a Spirit-led believer. It is un-becoming.

This demon-possessed man was first attacked within himself, then within his home, then outside his home, and then he had no home. He became uncivilized. He rejected everything in his life that resulted in structure. Under the oppression of the devil, we will eventually reject structure and accountability.

A home is a structure that is built within and without. We can have multiple homes. There is the home of our Lord, the wonderful body temple. We can build it without through exercise and proper diet. We can build it within by using the five forms of communication with God and yielding to however He leads during those times of communication. There is the home of our emotions, which can be built without through praise and properly motivated good works. It can be built within through proper thinking and humility toward others. There is the home of your family. Not only the structure within and without of a house, including drywall within and siding of some sort without, but the structure of atmosphere that makes it a home. This can be built within through kind, loving relationships, and without through family-oriented activities and public worship.

There are many things in life that are designed to be built both within and without. When they are built from both within and without, they give us structure. They bring civility to our lives. The devil doesn't like civility, and our structure is a hindrance to his goal to restrict spiritual direction. God can work through a structured life that accepts accountability. Without that structure and accountability, man will reject the work of the Lord.

DEMONIC POSSESSION LEADS TO AGGRESSION

It is the devil's intention to get a man to work on only part of his structure or overlook working on another part of his structure. If you are an unbeliever, his primary focus is to gain access to the inside of your structure. As an unbeliever, your spirit is dead and cannot be indwelled or controlled by a devil or demon; God reserves that power and place for the Spirit of Truth (John 16:13) upon conversion. The devil will, however, gladly reside within the soul of an unbeliever, thus placing that unbeliever's mind, will, and emotions under full control by the demonic presence.

This is, of course, where we find the Gadarene demoniac. His soul was actually possessed by many demons. The demons' name was Legion. Legion was a military term used to define a quantity of soldiers. It represented six thousand soldiers. This man may have had thousands of demons inside of him.

Anytime the devil gains possession of a man's soul, that man will begin to behave in an uncivilized fashion, eventually doing so on a regular basis. It is what I call the "Aggression of Possession." Possessed people become very aggressive, especially when believers try to help them. As a society, we do a number of things to try to hinder such people from being a menace to society and to themselves. Society will try to lock them up. We often reject them and send them out to be homeless, like the possessed man in our study. We often medicate them, or they self-medicate using drugs or alcohol. Now, of course, that doesn't mean that every locked-up or homeless or addicted person is possessed of the devil. Yet, I have worked with many, many of them over the years, and I would say a majority of them are at least heavily influenced by the devil. Satan wants to get inside the unbeliever and control the inside (or, soul) of his structure. Once he controls the soul of a man, he will destroy that man's structure, leading to a way of life that will be uncivilized.

DEMONIC OPPRESSION LEADS TO SUPPRESSION

If the devil cannot gain access to possess the inside of a person, then his secondary plan is to gain control of that man's soul through oppression. You see, the devil cannot possess a believer, but he doesn't care to. We are already blood bought and heaven bound. We have God living within us. The devil doesn't want to get anywhere near our inner man. Satan and his demons love the darkness and they hate the light (John 3:19). Since he cannot destroy us and keep us from the kingdom of God, he will try to oppress us to hinder us from advancing God's kingdom. This is what I call the "Suppression of Oppression." He knows the power of the life of Christ living through a Spirit-led believer. He knows the potential impact a Christian's life has to cast light into a dark world. He must hinder us to suppress God's power in our lives. He can't destroy the inside of our structure anymore, so he tries to influence it from the outside. That is demonic oppression and it is the devil's primary weapon against the redeemed of the Lord to influence the soul toward self-control rather than spirit-control. Not satanic control, but self control. Under the control of self, we may not live wickedly like we would if we were controlled by the devil, but we will not be under the control of the Spirit.

Psalm 127:1 reads, *Except the LORD build the house, they labour in vain that build it.* Self will try to build its own structure. It might look good and even be on the right foundation. But it is not the house that God would have built, and it remains vulnerable. Self is only a hearer of the Word and not a doer. It is a vain attempt to obtain righteousness by learning *about* God rather than experience leading *from* God. When in control of self, we might do many good things, but we will not cast light on a dark and dying world. Game, set, match—the devil has won direction of our lives from the Lord, not by evil spirit control, but by evil spirit oppression that led to self control.

DEMONIC IMPRESSION LEADS TO DEPRESSION

If the devil cannot gain access to a believer's outer man, or soul, because that man is under the influence of the inner man, then he will try his third and final option. He will attack the outside of the structure. He will attempt to get the believer to overlook certain areas of the Christian life in order to do damage to the body. His goal is to destroy every believer's testimony. This is an incredibly depressing place for a Christian to be. I often refer to this as the "Depression of Impression." Satan wants to impress upon us a discouragement that will hinder our effectiveness. That is why we must avoid appearances that may harm our testimony. A damaged or destroyed testimony, whether perceived to be that way or that way in reality, depresses a Spirit-indwelled Christian. It causes us to lose our joy when we give others a negative opinion of our Homeowner. That is why I find Holy Spirit-led conviction in areas of worldly separation to be so liberating. Many Christians do not like these views on separation. And, of course, no one should live by man's view of separation, only a God-given view. When a person rejects the Spirit's leading or the Bible's teaching on separation from the world and its influences, then that person has allowed his light to be dimmed by the devil at best, or placed under a bushel at worst. The devil may not possess you or oppress you, but he will look for a way to impress you—to influence you toward his opinion.

The reason most Christians reject the boundaries of separation is because they see it as a form of legalism, and legalism will lead to spiritual bondage. If a Christian follows those boundaries as a way to gain righteousness, that *is* legalism. Legalism is trying to do God's work in the power of the soul, trying harder to do better. However, if someone has developed a dynamic love relationship with Jesus Christ, then the Spirit will direct concerning certain areas of separation from the world, and that Spirit-led believer will accept those standards, even cling to them. To this person, these Spirit-led views are not bondage; they are boundaries that prevent bondage. Be careful! We are not rejecting boundaries because we prefer the bondage of self-propelled righteousness. Our righteousness is as a filthy rag (Isaiah 64:6).

The devil will not only ruin the testimony of a Christian by leading others into attacking him for appearing to be doing something Christians shouldn't be doing, but he will try to influence the believer into losing his testimony by self-inflicted damage to the beautiful body temple. It is sad, but health to many Christians is the least of their concerns. We fail to realize that when we do not take care of the dwelling place of our Lord, it harms our testimony and lowers the effectiveness of our work. This may seem unimportant compared to the alternatives of the devil possessing or oppressing us. But the truth is that any influence the devil can gain over any area of our lives is intended to destroy or deflect our light from shining as brightly as it possibly could.

Civilized people must focus on building proper structures. A proper structure will help protect you from ungodly influences. Begin by opening up your structure as a dwelling place for the Lord—by becoming a Christian. Continue by allowing your inner man to lead your outer man—by being a Spirit-led believer. Your structure is then completed as you develop the outside of the structure to bring honor and glory to its Owner—by taking care of its appearance.

In chapter five, we looked at Jesus' parable of two builders. One built upon the sand (the unsaved), and one built upon the rock (the Christian). The one that built upon the sand never listened to what God said. He was under the influence of another. His structure was destroyed by adversity. The other builder not only built upon the right foundation (by becoming a Christian), but Jesus also called him a wise man. Why? Lets look at the parable again:

> *Therefore whosoever heareth these sayings of mine, and doeth them, I will liken him unto a wise man, which built his house upon a rock: And the rain descended, and the floods came, and the winds blew, and beat upon that house; and it fell not: for it was founded upon a rock* (Matthew 7:24-25).

What made him wise? Well, number one he listened to the right influence—Jesus. (That's the influence of the inner man over the outer man.) Number two, he did what Jesus asked him to do. (That's allowing the body to yield to the inner man.) This man was not possessed and aggressed by someone evil. He was not oppressed and suppressed by someone evil. He was not impressed and depressed by an evil spirit, but rather possessed by God and impressed by His leading. His structure was built from within and without. He was a hearer and a doer, and as a result, the adversity had no negative effect on the structure of his life.

Unmanageable

…no man could chain him, no not even with chains.

The third characteristic of unclean spirits is that they are unmanageable. Look again at the Gadarene demoniac. People were trying to help him. People wanted to help him. People cared about him, and they wanted to keep him from hurting himself. They tried to manage this man, but he kept hurting himself. He refused their assistance. They would come out and try to help him, but he would break free and try to hurt himself yet again.

Several years ago, I was employed in convenience store management. I had several employees under me, some of which I would consider very unmanageable. I would give them specific instructions on things to do. Later, when I would inspect their work, I would find that they had not followed through with my instructions—they didn't get the job done. They were unmanageable. They refused instruction. As a result, they did not rise in the organization. (And they never seemed to understand why!) In some cases it led to termination from the organization. Proverbs 1:7 says, *fools despise wisdom and instruction.* I've heard it said that you can always tell a fool, but you can't tell him much!

I remember when I was the same way. When I was a senior in high school, I began to rebel against authority. One day,

> You can always tell a fool, but you can't tell him much!

while frustrated with my God ordained leadership, I did something really stupid and very much against the rules. To make matters worse, I got caught. I was suspended from school, and my principal turned me over to the senior pastor of our church, Pastor Kingsbury, for further disciplinary action. That afternoon he took me for a ride in his car over to the public high school. We sat there in his car during the lunch hour and watched the teens intermingle. I saw many that appeared to have rebellious attitudes. They were listening to rock music and seemed to be somewhat uncontrolled in their lunch time activities. They were cussing and doing crude things to one another in a joking fashion. As I watched the ugliness of sin influencing their lives, my pastor gently said to me, "Steve, if you don't begin to listen to instruction now, this is how you are going to end up."

The punishment for my wrongdoing was a one-week suspension from school. To ensure that I did not have idle time during my suspension, my pastor sent me to the local mission to do volunteer work. The truth is that I had been caught drinking beer. My pastor could tell I was heading the wrong way, and fast. He really tried to help me, to instruct me, to manage me at a time when I did not want to be managed any longer. As he dropped me off at the mission that following morning, he once again encouraged me, "Steve, this is where a lifestyle of drinking will bring you. If you do not start making the right choices, this is exactly where you are going to end up."

My pastor was giving me wise instruction. He was trying to manage me. But at that time in my life, I was absolutely unmanageable. I refused to listen to godly instruction. As a result, I suffered the consequences. I ended up just like those kids at that high school who were acting so rebelliously. As a matter of fact, those same kind of people ended up being my friends. After I got out of the Christian school, I rejected all the things that I had learned while growing up.

You see, rebellion will cause you to be unmanageable. At first, you will rebel against your parents. Then the next "parent" in your life will be your teachers. You will eventually rebel against your teachers. The next "parent" in your life will be your employer, and you will rebel against your employer. The next "parent" in your life will be the government—the laws of the land. You will break the law and rebel against each and every form of authority that God has placed in your life. Only you yourself will manage you, which will make you unmanageable by another.

That's exactly what I did. I rebelled against authority; I refused to be managed in all aspects of my life. I rejected my parents' authority and my pastor's authority. The instruction of my teachers was forgotten and seldom applied to my life. I was not a good employee, and as a result, I went from job to job. I engaged in drugs and alcohol, breaking the law on a regular basis. To be honest with you, everything my preacher warned me against took place in my life. I became a homeless, unemployed man with over $20,000 in debt. No one wanted to work with me because I was unmanageable. I only wish that I had listened to that instruction.

Whenever the devil gets ahold on or over people, his goal is to get them to reject all forms of management in their lives. All instruction is rejected as intrusive and overbearing. These people may not be possessed by the devil, but they are severely oppressed by him.

The first part of Proverbs 13:18 reads, *Poverty and shame shall be to him that refuseth instruction.* Once the pleasure of sin was over and sin had ruined my life, I became ashamed of the way I was living. I lived in poverty—no money, nowhere to live. My whole life had been destroyed. When I learned to yield to God-ordained authority and allow God to manage my life through these authority figures, the second part of Proverbs 13:18 came true in my life. It is the key to repairing the damage of refused instruction: *...but he that regardeth reproof* (or, listens and obeys when corrected) *shall be honoured* (or, promoted).

Have you become unmanageable? Have you, as a Christian, become unwilling to allow authority to govern the affairs of your life? If you will listen to and obey your God-given instruction, you will be promoted. Your willingness to regard reproof will make you wiser. Proverbs 9:9 says, *Give instruction to a wise man, and he will be yet wiser: teach a just man, and he will increase in learning.* Why? Because you are accepting input from others. You will grow and develop if you are managed by God's management system. You will be marginalized and undeveloped if you try to self-manage your life.

Ephesians 6:1-3 says, *Children, obey your parents in the Lord: for this is right. Honour thy father and mother; which is the first commandment with promise; That it may be well with thee, and thou mayest live long on the earth.* I believe this can not only be applied to our relationship with our earthly parents, but it can also be applied to our spiritual parents. Our "parents in the Lord" are those whom God has given the authority to raise us up in the Christian life. They have a responsibility, given by God, to develop us. If we will obey those in spiritual authority over us, God will bless us. I have been convinced that if we forsake instruction, we will suffer the consequences. However, if we accept instruction under the umbrella of protection—our parents, pastors, teachers, employers and the government—we'll be wiser and we'll enjoy a more productive and longer life.

God will not do anything with an unmanageable, possessed, unsaved person. It's sad to say, however, that the only thing He can do with an unmanageable, oppressed, saved person is to punish him. And He will!

Uncooperative
...often bound with fetters and chains...

The fourth characteristic of unclean spirits is that they are uncooperative. *Cooperate* means "to act jointly with others to produce an expected end." The Gadarene demoniac refused to cooperate. This man would not help people help him. Not only could he not be managed, not even with chains, but when they were able to get the chains on him to try to bring him under control, he still would not cooperate with them. He would reject the people's protective barriers and break free, ironically, into bondage. He rejected the boundaries of the chains of protection in exchange for the bondage of self-destruction. This is not what his friends were trying to produce. They wanted him out of harm's way, but he refused to cooperate toward their expected end. He was uncooperative.

Often, we allow our authorities to manage us and to lead us, but we do not necessarily cooperate. What they have done, we allow to come undone—sometimes on purpose, even realizing the struggle we endured to allow it to become done in the first place!

Whenever we begin to be uncooperative with the outside pressure of God-ordained authority or with the inside pressure of the inner man, we are struggling with "soul-control." If your soul is being uncooperative with God and His management system, you can be sure that you are under the influence of outside pressure or oppression. God's impression on us will always lead us to cooperate with Him. Philippians 1:6 tells us, *he which hath begun a good work in you will perform it until the day of Jesus Christ.* God's work in our lives will continue until Christ returns, but we will need to cooperate with Him and His system of management.

Remember the devil's system of management (a prince, with powers, leaders and followers that restrict light, each one strongly loyal to its leader; well managed, and cooperative)? If the devil's system of management is so well coordinated, how much the more ought Christians be loyal, well managed, and cooperative with God and His system of management?

Proverbs 29:1 says, *He, that being often reproved hardeneth his neck, shall suddenly be destroyed.* When a Christian receives God's warnings, but hardens his neck, he has become uncooperative. His end will be sudden destruction. Look closely at what God is saying. He tells us we will be given a period of time to cooperate. We will be reproved for an uncooperative attitude. Reproof takes time. First comes the outside pressure of authority, then the inside pressure of the Holy Spirit. Finally, there is the time that God allows for us to determine whether we will heed His reproof. Eventually, we will either cooperate or we will "harden our necks" (or, become stubborn and uncooperative). It all takes time. He goes on to say that before He will allow us to be destroyed, He will reprove us "often." This will further increase the amount of time that God will give a stubborn believer to cooperate with His leading. We don't know how long God will suffer through this, but we can assume it will be a long time because we have a longsuffering God. His longsuffering will lead us to cooperate because the goodness of God leads to repentance (Romans 2:4). On the other hand, His longsuffering can be something we tend to take for granted. That is what will bring sudden destruction. He tells us He will give us time and He will remind us often, but eventually He is going to bring the hammer down. When He does, it's going to break that outer man that is so stubborn!

If we do not heed God's warnings, eventually they will seem to go away. The Bible refers to the Spirit's prompting as a still, small voice. It is not active and boisterous like the voice of the possessor/oppressor, the "roaring lion." If we do not hearken to this still, small voice, it will become faint, making it that much harder to discern. If you think it is hard to yield to the inner man now, just remember how hard it is or was when He did not have a place of preeminence in your life. You were trying to live for God without a leading from God. It is easier to cooperate with a still, small voice than to try to discern a leading from a grieved Spirit who has been overruled by your uncooperative soul.

There is a better way. You can develop your sensitivity to that still, small voice to something far more influential in your life. You will not do it by talking more or louder. Rather, you must train yourself to listen better.

Mark 4:23-25 is an exciting passage of Scripture! *If any man have ears to hear, let him hear. And he said unto them,*

Take heed what ye hear: with what measure ye mete, it shall be measured to you: and unto you that hear shall more be given. For he that hath, to him shall be given: and he that hath not (or, he that is not willing to have ears to hear), from him shall be taken even that which he hath.

These verses speak of cooperation. If we will learn to increase our listening, we will learn how to increase our cooperation. Let's do a little dissecting and defining.

- *Take heed* means "to take notice." He tells us to take notice of what we hear.
- *Measure* means "to ascertain a quantity," and
- *Mete* means "the same thing."

It's like saying, "with what measure you measure, it shall be measured to you." For example, if you were to walk up to a drinking fountain with a coffee cup, you will be measured a quantity of water that is equal to the measure that you brought to quantify it. You brought a cup; you'll get a cup. Likewise, if you brought a bucket, you will be measured a lot more because you measured using an instrument that had a greater ability to quantify. You can get more if you have a bigger measuring device!

These verses tell us that the more we are prepared to listen, the more we will receive. If we will listen, and listen in abundance, we will be given more things to hear. As we listen, we will learn. If we do not listen, we will forget even what we have previously learned.

This is a great example of the proper way in which to cooperate with God. The devil's goal in the life of the unbeliever is to get the soul to lead the body—to walk "after the flesh." To do this, he needs to get us away from the Spirit's leading. He wants us to be uncooperative with God and His system of management. To do this, he will oppress to suppress. He will oppress until we are uncooperative with the inner man, and he will suppress us from hearing God's voice of reproof. This will lead to our eventual destruction. But God says to listen to His voice. In fact, increase the quantity in which we are listening. Take advantage of every opportunity to hear. Do not reject opportunities of listening: Bible reading, studying, memorization and meditation, Sunday School, morning service, evening service, mid-week service, preaching tapes, and Christian literature. All of these and many more ways of listening will develop our sensitivity to the inner man and increase our ability to hear and cooperate.

There are a lot of churches today that reject this premise. They will not put an influence on Bible time. Often they say its importance is overblown. They suggest an increase in the music program and a decrease in the preaching, and now they are even cutting church services down to once or twice per week. What are they doing? They are reducing the measure with which they may mete their hearing. They are decreasing the size of the cup. They are hearing less, thus less is being given to them by God. They will struggle, with less feeding, to experience God's leading. Eventually, I believe they will not cooperate with God. Some already aren't. That is why they have made such changes in their churches. In doing so, they have limited the people's opportunities to hear.

The prosperity of your life is dependent on your willingness to hear and to heed God's warnings, to cooperate with God as He tries to protect you from harming yourself. God will never harm you; the oppressor will never help you. With whom are you going to cooperate—the oppressor without or the impresser within?

Unhappy

And always, night and day, he was in the mountains, and in the tombs, crying...

The fifth characteristic of the unclean spirits that we will examine is their emotional state. The Bible tells us that the Gadarene demoniac was unhappy. He was crying all the time. I don't know about you, but there have been times in my life when I was unhappy enough to cry. I have experienced times when I cried into the night. I have even had experiences that caused me to cry throughout the day. But I have never been so sad or dejected that I was always crying both day and night—all the time! This man was miserable!

The truth is that unhappiness is found at the very root of sin. Wherever there is sin, there is sorrow. That doesn't mean that wherever there is sorrow, there is sin. God doesn't withhold sorrow from every saint, but He does release sorrow to those who live in sin, or live after the flesh. Once again, this does not mean that everyone that is unhappy is involved in sin, but it does mean that everyone that is involved in sin is unhappy. They may not seem like it to others. They may not act like it all the time. They may not even know why they feel as miserable as they do. But God has designed a system in which joy comes from yielding to Him and unhappiness comes from yielding to the possessor/oppressor.

Let's take a look at the first example of sin and how it introduced unhappiness into the world at the hands of the oppressor.

> *Unto the woman he said, I will greatly multiply thy sorrow and thy conception; in sorrow thou shalt bring forth children; and*

> *thy desire shall be to thy husband, and he shall rule over thee. And unto Adam he said, Because thou hast hearkened unto the voice of thy wife, and hast eaten of the tree, of which I commanded thee, saying, Thou shalt not eat of it: cursed is the ground for thy sake; in sorrow shalt thou eat of it all the days of thy life;* (Genesis 3:16-17)

Notice some things in this story. After falling for the deception of the oppressor, Adam and Eve disobeyed God and yielded to the pressure of the devil. They ate of the forbidden fruit. As a result of yielding to the wrong influence, they plunged humanity into sin! God then determined their punishment. He told the woman that He would greatly multiply her sorrow. This is an indication of why women are far more emotional than men are. God did not say he would multiply the sorrow of man, but of woman. He then said that He would also multiply her conception. Adding both punishments together, he told her that in her conception of children, she would experience sorrow. He then placed her under the authority of her husband (that's probably where the real sorrow began for the woman!).

Turning to Adam, he pointed out his sin in particular. He did not do this to Eve. As a matter of fact, in verse 14 God blamed Eve's mistake on the serpent, who was possessed. God said to the serpent, "Because thou hast done this..." and then He cursed him. What was the sin that Adam had committed? Was it eating the fruit? No, not entirely. Was it not protecting his wife, since the Bible tells us in verse 6 that Adam was "with her" while the devil sought to beguile her? No. God said Adam's sin was that he hearkened to (or, listened to and obeyed) the voice of his wife, which led him to eat the fruit. He allowed his decision-making process to be influenced by someone that would lead him away from what God had said. This was sin. The first sin. It preceded the eating of the fruit. The devil possessed the serpent, oppressed the woman, and impressed the man into yielding to the wrong influence. This pattern began in the beginning. It continued during Christ's lifetime, as evidenced in the story of the Gadarene demoniac, and that old serpent is still at it today! Man's punishment was that he would experience sorrow as he worked the land to provide for himself and his family.

What does this tell us? In particular, God allows sorrow into our day-to-day responsibilities. For the woman, she will have great sorrow in the bearing and building of her children. For the man, he will work for his food and it will be laborious and will also bring sorrow. These were their new God-given responsibilities to one another, and they were to experience sorrow as they performed them. What a huge price to pay for yielding to a wrong influence!

The unique thing about God's system, however, is that when we live under the influence of the inner man, we will not experience overwhelming sorrow. Oh, it is still there and it comes and goes as a result of the mistakes made back then and the one's we make today, but it can be greatly reduced as God abundantly gives us His love, joy, peace, gentleness, and on and on it goes. As we yield to God's power, we will meet our God-given responsibilities with a different approach and will find great joy in it all. I never enjoyed work—until I got right with God. I have been told by several young ladies that they seldom enjoyed mothering, much less child bearing—until they got right with God. Man's sin introduced the sorrow, but God's grace can overrule it. It is all dependent upon whom you allow to influence you.

King Saul also experienced unhappiness as a result of an evil spirit's influence. Several times in 1 Samuel, the Bible tells us that an evil spirit came upon King Saul. He became very moody and extremely unhappy. First Samuel 16 says the first time that this evil spirit troubled him, King Saul responded correctly. He allowed David, a godly, young, shepherd boy, to sooth his frustration with some beautiful music. First Samuel 16:23 tells us, *Saul was refreshed, and was well, and the evil spirit departed from him.*

> Joy comes from yielding to God and unhappiness comes from yielding to the possessor/ oppressor.

But in 1 Samuel 18, we see King Saul influenced again by an evil spirit, as he had allowed a root of jealousy to invade himself. David came to play for him again. Only this time, he did not accept the influence of the right source to be rid of this evil spirit. You see, his jealousy was toward David. So, while David played the harp for him, King Saul attempted to kill David! Thus began a miserable life for King Saul of revenge toward his perceived enemy, David, the future king of Israel. Why did he perceive David to be his enemy? He was led to believe this from an evil influence, causing himself misery the rest of his life. His unhappiness all started with an evil spirit of influence.

King Saul began as *a choice young man, and a goodly: and there was not among the children of Israel a goodlier person than he* (1 Samuel 9:2). Yet, when he allowed sin in his life, it brought him unhappiness and eventually destroyed his life. Sin is pleasurable for a season (Hebrews 11:25), but once that season is over, the consequences of sin will bring unhappiness and sorrow.

By contrast, we see the formula for happiness in Psalm 1:1-3. It is 100% dependent upon whom we allow to influence us. Let's take a look at this familiar passage and then dissect and define it so that we can understand it better.

> *Blessed is the man that walketh not in the counsel of the ungodly, nor standeth in the way of sinners, nor sitteth in the seat of the scornful. But his delight is in the law of the LORD; and in his law doth he meditate day and night. And he shall be like a tree planted by the rivers of water, that bringeth forth his fruit in his season; his leaf also shall not wither; and whatsoever he doeth shall prosper.*

Blessed is an old English word for the Modern English word "happy." Thus, this is the formula for being happy. It involves three don'ts and three do's. Let's look at the three don'ts:

- Don't #1: Don't walk in the counsel of the ungodly. Don't get advice from those who do not love God. In other words, don't allow ungodly people to influence you!

- Don't #2: Don't stand in the way of sinner. Don't fellowship with people whose course in life will introduce you to sin. People who engage in sinful habits should be avoided. In other words, you don't allow sinful people to influence you!

- Don't #3: Don't sit in the seat of the scornful. Don't take the position of those who are critical of others. In other words, you don't allow critical people to influence you!

Then the three do's:

- Do #1: Delight in God's law. This requires developing an appetite. The three don'ts will suppress your appetite for God's word. The more you eat the greater your appetite.

- Do #2: Meditate on the law all day. This requires a form of memorization that will allow you to be influenced by the inner man throughout the day with the verses you have memorized.

- Do #3: Meditate on the law all night. This requires us to not only use His Word to help us out in our workplace, but also in our homes (or vice versa if you work nights). Such a person does not cease to be influenced by his inner man just because he is in the comfort of his own home.

To put it all together, the formula for happiness in the Christian life (despite our curse of sorrow) is avoiding the negative influence of ungodly, sinful, and critical people, plus devouring God's Word to the point of memorization so the inner man may be a positive influence all day and all night. Happiness is found in influence. Not who you are influencing, but rather who is influencing you.

Influence is a very important responsibility. We all wield a level of influence. At work and at home, we have the potential to influence many people. When we use our influence and people yield to that influence, it is called respect. When someone respects us, they allow themselves to be influenced by us. We must be careful to whom we give our respect, because those same people are who we will allow to influence us.

The Bible talks a lot about respect—respecting God, that is. It is called "the fear of the Lord." It is an imperative ingredient for gaining influence from the inner man. If we do not respect God for who He is and what He can do, then we will not allow ourselves to be influenced by Him.

Remember our story in Genesis? The serpent that was possessed by the devil beguiled the woman, having promised her many great things—things that even God had not offered her. She allowed herself to be influenced by the devil because she respected what he said he could do for her. The devil's opportunities are always smoke and mirrors. He cannot produce the real thing, so he tries to get us to respect him or fear him. If he can do this, than he can influence us.

Proverbs 28:14 tells us, *Happy is the man that feareth* [the Lord] *always.* Psalms 112:1 also tells us, *Blessed is the man that feareth the LORD.* These verses promise us that we will be happy if we fear (or, respect) God. A healthy respect of God brings great joy. Why? Because when we respect God, we will allow Him to influence us. And when God influences us through the inner man, we will experience the fruit of the Spirit, which brings great joy.

With the proper influence, we can actually enjoy our God-given responsibilities. Let's see if God could ever allow us to be happy in child bearing or rearing and in our day to day labor:

- Psalm 127:4-5 *As arrows are in the hand of a mighty man; so are children of the youth.* <u>*Happy is the man*</u> *that hath his quiver full of them: they shall not be ashamed, but they shall speak with the enemies in the gate.*
- Psalms 128:2-4 *For thou shalt eat the* <u>*labour of thine hands: happy shalt thou be,*</u> *and it shall be well with thee.* <u>*Thy wife shall be*</u> *as a fruitful vine by the sides of thine house:* <u>*thy children like olive plants*</u> *round about thy table. Behold, that thus shall the*

man be blessed that feareth [respects and is influenced by] *the LORD.*

Yes, that's right! Whenever the devil gets ahold of someone, he always makes them unhappy. But when God gets ahold of someone, then they always become happy. Like Psalm 144:15 says, *Happy is that people, that is in such a case: yea, happy is that people, whose God is the LORD.*

In conclusion to this characteristic of the devil, unhappiness, a lot of people want to talk about their problems and do nothing about them. I have given you a recipe for happiness, using key verses out of the Bible. I will now repeat what our Lord said in John 13:17, *If ye know these things, happy are ye if ye do them.*

Uncontrolled
...and cutting himself with stones.

The Gadarene demoniac was a possessed unbeliever out of control. His self-destructive behavior was another reason why his friends and family had been trying to tame him, even trying to chain him. Being uncontrolled is the sixth characteristic of unclean spirits. Whenever the devil possesses someone's body that person will lose control. This man was unable to control himself.

I know believers, myself included, who have struggled with this same characteristic. They are not in control of their lives. You see, as a believer, you have a choice. You can yield to the Spirit of God or you can submit to your own desires found within the core of your outer man. Either way, the ability to do choose belongs to you—you're in control. Whether you are walking in the Spirit or walking after the flesh, you are in control. You may be yielding that control to God in you, but that is within your control to do, and you can cease to do so at any time, as we all know. The ability to yield is a form of control, just as much as the ability for self-rule.

However, there is another kind of rule and that is the rule of the devil over us. As children of God, we can yield control, not to an inside persuasion, but to an outside pressure. This is how we become uncontrolled, much like this demoniac. The truth is, the devil desires to control us. If he cannot control us with outside pressure, he will work to get us to lose control by influencing us to reject the inner man's leading and live through soul control—that is, under the control of the outer man.

Romans 6:12 warns, *Let not sin therefore reign* (or, rule*) in your mortal body, that ye should obey* (or, submit to*) it in the lusts* (or, desires*) thereof.* The word *should* is a legal term that means "under obligation." This verse is telling us that if we allow sin to rule within the outer man, then we will be under obligation to submit to its desires. This is a situation of your having a choice, but losing the ability to choose. We are now under obligation to something. We are not in control. We have allowed something to influence us on the inside. An outside pressure took up an inside position and placed you under an obligation of obedience. It began to rule. We have lost control.

> You can yield to the Spirit of God or you can submit to your own desires. Whether you are walking in the Spirit or walking after the flesh, you are in control. The ability to yield is a form of control.

Verse 16 of the same chapter reiterates this truth with a rhetorical question. *Know ye not* (or, don't you know*), that to whom ye yield yourselves* (or, give possession to*) servants to obey, his servants ye are to whom ye obey* (or, submit to*);*

whether of sin unto death, or of obedience unto righteousness? Paul is asking us if we realize that when we yield to something, we are allowing it to possess us.

The word *possess* in the dictionary has many meanings. Yet when it defines the possessing of a life, the word *possess* means "to seize, or to be given power over." Sin, under the outside pressure of the devil, will seize control of us. God will not control us unless that power is given over to Him. The devil will wield control and God will yield control. It is within our power to give possession to the outside pressure or the inside persuasion. When we allow the devil to control us through whatever outside pressure he can muster, we will be under his control and will wish to have that control back. However, when we yield control to the inner man, we still remain under our own control. Christ is living through us, not for us. We can cease to submit. He will not control us without our willing submission to His leading. Of course, being under God's control as a servant of righteousness is such a blessed place to be! But when we cease to yield to His control, we find ourselves out of control. We will not be happy when we take control of the outer man or when we give control to outside pressure.

We have two choices: we can choose to serve sin (which takes control and won't willingly give it back); or, we can choose to serve obedience (which will lead to the paths of righteousness). There is no middle ground. Are you in control of who is leading you? If so, then God is leading you. He is the only presence that will permit you to yield to His pressure. All other forms of pressure will take control of you and leave you uncontrolled.

Unrepentant

And cried with a loud voice, and said, What have I to do with thee, Jesus, thou Son of the most high God? I adjure thee by God, that thou torment me not.

This demoniac came out to meet Jesus, but not necessarily to repent of his evil possessions or positions. When he came to Jesus, he, in his own power, tried to worship Jesus. However, the very act of his worship was tormenting the demons within him. They were unrepentant, which is the seventh characteristic of unclean spirits. In fact, they cried out to Jesus to stop it! He was causing them much anguish (the definition of torment). If you are possessed, you will have to find your necessary repentance toward God and faith in our Lord Jesus Christ (Acts 20:21) to escape the influence of your possessors. They will not stand idly by as you seek to change. You will need God to free you from this possession before you can gain the power within yourself to repent of who you are and what you have become. After this, and coupled with the saving step of belief in Christ's substitutionary death, God will no longer need or expect you to exercise your power. He will come to live within you. You will never be overcome with evil again. Only He can give you the power to overcome evil with good (Romans 12:21).

This man may have wanted to be helped, he just could not control himself enough to get help or accept the help that was being given to him. However, when he saw Jesus and realized that Jesus would not bind him with chains but would rather break the inner bondage of his possessors, he "changed his mind" about wanting help. So he ran to Jesus! His demonic possessors mockingly cried out on his behalf, "What have I to do with thee?" There was no repentance found within the voice of the possessors, neither was their repentance in the voice of the man. He was more worried about the plight of the demons, hoping they would not be forced to leave the country, but rather to keep them nearby in the mountains (within the pigs).

Jesus, however, knew the man's condition. He knew the man was out of control, wanting help, and in need of the only type of help that sets free—Jesus the Truth. He is the same way with many of us. He knows our hearts. Proverbs tells us that He ponders them. That means He is considering our hearts. Repentance is a change of mind, but not a change of mind that leads to only different thinking. Rather, it is a change of thinking that leads to a different belief. This change is not found in the mind, it is actually found in the heart.

I know a lot of people that have changed their minds about their behavior, but they don't turn and run to Jesus, much less worship Him! The repentance or change of heart that leads to belief is simply a correction of the mistake in the Garden of Eden.

Adam and Eve chose the acquisition of information (tree of knowledge) over the development of a personal relationship. Since then, man has needed to repent of thinking that knowledge is power, when in fact, knowing God is power! You see, since we know the difference between good and evil, we need to reject or repent of our own methods of trying to control them. We try to control good and evil by gaining more knowledge. Instead, we need to develop a personal relationship with God and, as a result of this personal relationship, He will control the good and the evil in our lives. We will be free from the bondage of knowledge. This does not mean that ignorance is bliss, it means a focus on knowledge will cause us to miss! We fall short of His glory. We are unable to make Him look good.

As Christians, we can allow an unrepentant attitude toward sin to permeate and weaken our spiritual walk. Our repentance toward God and faith in our Lord Jesus Christ will get us to heaven eventually. It is a benefit of justification that we can look forward to, but we will not experience it until we arrive there. However, another benefit of our repentance and faith is sanctification. This is a benefit that is available right now! However, when an unrepentant believer allows sin to reign in his body and his soul to follow "after the flesh," he will not experience the full benefits of his conversion here on earth. He will get his sanctified body in heaven, but he will not have experienced the beauty of a sanctified life that was yielded to Christ—the hope of glory (and our only hope of making God look good).

The outside oppression of the devil in the life of a believer is intended to interfere with this glory being beheld. We discussed earlier the opposing force and it's subordinate leaders and followers. Their goal is to restrict light. When we are living the sanctified life and repenting of sin that would weaken our walk we are casting light. His light is what reveals His glory! If you will allow your outer man to be broken by the circumstances of life, it will blow a hole in your soul. From that hole, the inner man can flow through and shine as a light unto the world. But it takes a hole—that is, an opening in the outer man that allows the inner man to flow through. While under the influence of an outside pressure, you may at times yield to your outer man. You may engage in sin. But the hole in your soul will lead to God's glory if formed by your repentance!

If we will not repent of being under soul control, then we are not allowing our weakness in our walk to be a channel for the inner man to flow through (*when I am weak, then am I strong*. 2 Corinthians 12:10). This is what Paul is referring to in Galatians 2 when he says we can frustrate the grace of God. God wants even our temporary rebellion to bring about good. But if we are rejecting His conviction, we will not allow Him to do His work of grace on our behalf. This type of rebellion to the inner man will lead to chastening by God. This failure to repent will not send us to hell, but it may make us feel like we've been there!

Yes, repentance is not just for the unbeliever. It's for the believer as well. Repentance is for anyone who sins. Matthew 9:12-13 says, *But when Jesus heard that, he said unto them, They that be whole need not a physician, but they that are sick… for I am not come to call the righteous, but sinners to repentance*. Sure He calls the unsaved sinners to repentance, yet He also calls those who are no longer sinners, but saints who sin; we are whole but in need of a hole—the hole of repentance that will keep us whole.

Unclothed

And they come to Jesus, and see him that was possessed with the devil, and had the legion, sitting, and clothed, and in his right mind: and they were afraid.

The eighth characteristic of unclean spirits is their trademark fashion statement—unclothed. Mark makes a point of telling us that when the people around Gadara came to see Jesus, they saw this now formerly possessed man sitting and clothed. This indicates that he was *unclothed* under the possession of the evil spirit. Once again, this is a perfect example of our society today. We see how the possession/oppression of an evil spirit can lead one to do irrational things.

Why do you think that it is noted that this man is now clothed? Simply because when the inner man is given control over the outer man, we will automatically see a person "change." Not only will there be a change in our behavior, but also a change in our *standards* of behavior.

I have found whenever the devil gets a hold on people, he will always lead them into poor standards of morality until he can eventually get them into immorality. We see this to be true in the Bible: Noah, Lot, Abraham, Jacob, Samson, David, Solomon—the list goes on and on. The truth is, in all the Biblical examples of immoral opportunities, only one person is named as having been able to abstain—Joseph.

How was Joseph able to abstain? I believe it was because he had high standards of morality. He would not sin against God. He just would not do it.

> Whenever the devil gets a hold on people, he will always lead them into poor standards of morality until he can eventually get them into immorality.

The devil understands the domination that immorality can have over people. He seeks to place that power over people, even over God's people if they will let him. The devil begins his work on people early. He knows that if he can get young people to give up their morality, he can eventually get them to give up anything until they have given up everything, including themselves (possession).

The Bible tells us in 2 Timothy 2:22, *Flee also youthful lusts.* These youthful lusts are desires that we obtained as young people. I think Paul knew that young Timothy had struggles with some desires like all young people have. He told him to flee them. Everyone else that Paul wrote concerning temptation, he instructed to fight against it or to resist it. But when it comes to sins or desires of the youth, he says that we ought to flee. *Flee* means "to run with rapidity;" to run as rapidly as we can and as repeatedly as we need to. Don't mess with youthful lusts! In 1 Peter 2:11, we are told that lusts will war against the soul. That's the outer man. Therein lies the battle! The outside pressure, unable to take up an inside possession, will accept an inside persuasion that is meant for the inner man to give. Satan will apply his outside pressure to produce an inside persuasion within us. He will do it by waging war with the outer man, placing pressure on us to get us to live under the control of the soul. He will use lusts or desires, especially youthful lusts and desires.

Paul continued his exhortation to by telling him to, *follow righteousness, faith, charity, peace, with them that call on the Lord out of a pure heart.* Wow, what a contrast! One influence needs to be run from, the other needs to be followed. Youthful lusts begin as entertainment but eventually control us, leaving us lonely and impure in heart. The alternatives allow us to follow (within our control) others (he says, "with them"; we won't be alone) as we seek God's help with a heart that is kept pure.

It is probably too late for most of us to avoid the creation of the desires or lusts of our youth. We probably have sown those seeds and are reaping the desires that those lusts created. What was it in your life? Did you make compromises as a young person? Were you saved and persuaded by this influence of the devil, or unsaved and possessed by his influence? What lusts did you develop? You were not the first and you will not be the last. In fact, most young people will face exactly the same temptations.

The steps to destruction for a youth are often (not always, but often) the same.

Step One: Bad attitude or bad music that leads to…

Step Two: Rebellion toward authority that leads to…

Step Three: A loss of protection from evil influence that leads to...

Step Four: Possession or oppression from that evil that leads to…

Step Five: Self-centeredness that always leads to…

Step Six: Lowering the moral code that almost always leads to…

Step Seven: Immorality!

As adults, we not only must protect our children from these seven steps to destruction, but we need to avoid them ourselves. We allow the devil's outside pressure to lead us to rebel against God's outside pressure (ordained authorities). This will lead us to allow the devil to tempt us with the inside persuasions of the outer man—the soul. When we yield to the soul, we rebel against the inner man—the Spirit. We are not possessed but are experiencing oppression. It controls us from the outside in.

Why do you think the possessed demoniac of Gadara was led of his possessor to remove his clothing? Do you see how we (and the young people in our churches) are driven by the outside pressure of society to wear less and reveal more? It is often fought in churched societies. Adults and young people often get frustrated by leadership's demands of high standards of dress. Why is it such a big deal? They're often asking the wrong people. Go ask the devil; he is the one that's trying to get people to take their clothes off. But when God gets ahold of a man, he will clothe himself with the right mind—a pure one.

CONCLUSION:

Possessed Unbelievers are:
1. Unclean
2. Uncivilized
3. Unmanageable
4. Uncooperative
5. Unhappy
6. Uncontrolled
7. Unrepentant
8. Unclothed

These eight characteristics of the Gadarene demoniac are certainly un-Christ-like. It goes without saying that something is missing in our lives when we behave in any way similar to this man. Yet, we have seen in our study of this passage that these characteristics can be found in our own behavior at times. Why? Why would people with the presence of God living in them and the power of God coming upon them ever settle for anything less than the abundant, Spirit-led life?

I cannot answer for sure in every person's case, but I think that the primary reason is an overall lack of appreciation. A failure to appreciate what God has saved us from and what He has subsequently prepared for us. Let us notice the level of appreciation that the former demoniac had in Mark 5:18-20.

> And when he was come into the ship, he that had been possessed with the devil prayed him that he might be with him. Howbeit Jesus suffered him not, but saith unto him, Go home to thy friends, and tell them how great things the Lord hath done for thee, and hath had compassion on thee. And he departed, and began to publish in Decapolis how great things Jesus had done for him: and all men did marvel.

Here is a man that just experienced a major miracle whereby he was healed of his possession and saved by his faith in the Lord Jesus Christ. His natural response was to be with Jesus. He wanted to follow Him, go with Him, be with Him, and learn from Him. But the Bible tells us that Jesus would not allow him to accompany Him as He left their coasts. He had something more important for this man to do than to tag along with Jesus. What was that something? *Go home to thy friends, and tell them how great things the Lord hath done for thee, and hath had compassion on thee.*

Jesus asked this man to turn back to the very crowd that was running Him off, to play a role in their understanding of God's goodness to him. This must have been an incredibly difficult thing to do. Yet, he did it. The Bible says, *he departed, and began to publish in Decapolis* (the ten-city region around Gadara) *how great things Jesus had done for him.* His response of obedience was one of gratitude for Christ's work in his life. This man not only got saved, but he appreciated his salvation.

Jesus gave the same assignment to His disciples (and subsequently, to us) when He ascended into heaven. He did not permit them to leave with Him, though I am sure they would have liked to have gone. Rather, He instructed them to "go," the same word He used with the Gadarene man. Their response to Jesus' instruction was equally miraculous, especially once the power of the Holy Spirit came upon them.

This is what He wants us to do, as well—go! He wants us to go home to our friends and our families, to the cities in which we live, even to the cities that surround us and beyond.

Is that too much to ask? It is sad to say, but for many of us, the answer is yes. But if we really understood what Jesus is asking and really appreciated what Jesus has done for us, then nothing that He would ask of us could be considered too much.

The reason most people reject their God-given responsibilities to witness (as covered briefly in chapter seven) is because they are afraid to share with others the message of heaven and hell. They are afraid to share their faith. But this fear is simply an outside pressure that we have identified throughout this chapter as "oppression." Surely, what Christ is asking of us is not too difficult in reality. He is not asking us to go to our family and friends and community and force the Gospel on them. He is not asking us to share with them the dangers of rejecting the Gospel—eternity in hell. Sure, that is an important message, one that needs to be shared as a motive for *believers* to share the Gospel, but not a motive for unbelievers to be saved. The Bible tells us the goodness of God leads to repentance (Romans 2:4). Eternity in hell is not the Good News. Hell is the "bad news"! We are not here to spread the bad news; we are here to share the *Good News*!

> Eternity in hell is not the Good News. Hell is the "bad news!"

Jesus told this man from Gadara to tell his friends and those at his home the great things the Lord had done for him and how Christ had compassion on him. That's exactly what he did. The Bible tells us in verse 20 that the result of this witness of God's greatness and compassion was that *all men did marvel*. *All* men did marvel! Now that's much fruit!

If we would reject the outside pressure to withhold our

witness when inside pressure to share it is present, then we would see the same result by simply sharing God's goodness and compassion toward us with those who need it. The truth is, there are many people that *really* need God to be good to them and to show them compassion, but they don't even know it is available. So many of us who have seen it don't appreciate it enough to share it with them. That is the great goal of the devil—the former possessor of many Christians and the current oppressor of all Christians. He wants to pressure us into believing that what has been done for us is not that great or that compassionate. What a lie! As we have seen in this study, we had most of these characteristics in our lives before Christ changed us. Even now, when we cease to submit to what we have previously experienced, we tend to yield to some of those same characteristics. Yet God never leaves us nor forsakes us. Hallelujah! What a Savior!

There are those who are saved and there are those who appreciate their salvation. Which one are you? Let me ask you, have you gone home to your friends? If you will, they will marvel and so will others. When the good news is shared, people, as a result of your influence on their lives, will become clean, civilized, manageable, cooperative, happy, controlled by the Spirit, clothed, and repentant. Aren't you? If not, then why not? You're allowing your outside pressure to overrule your inside presence. Let the circumstances of your life blow a hole through your soul that the Spirit of God might flow through you. I promise you—*everyone* will marvel!

Chapter 9

9 Fruits of the Spirit

This I say then, Walk in the Spirit, and ye shall not fulfil the lust of the flesh. For the flesh lusteth against the Spirit, and the Spirit against the flesh: and these are contrary the one to the other: so that ye cannot do the things that ye would. But if ye be led of the Spirit, ye are not under the law. Now the works of the flesh are manifest, which are these; Adultery, fornication, uncleanness, lasciviousness, Idolatry, witchcraft, hatred, variance, emulations, wrath, strife, seditions, heresies, Envyings, murders, drunkenness, revellings, and such like: of the which I tell you before, as I have also told you in time past, that they which do such things shall not inherit the kingdom of God. But the fruit of the Spirit is love, joy, peace, longsuffering, gentleness, goodness, faith, Meekness, temperance: against such there is no law.
—Galatians 5:16-23

This chapter will be our longest. However, all the lessons learned from previous chapters form the basis of truth supporting this key chapter. Teachers, I strongly suggest that you spend one whole class on each fruit and it's opposing work of the flesh. This will take you at least nine weeks to teach. To the casual reader, this chapter may be harder to digest on the run. Please allow yourself time to study and understand each of these truths. At first, they may seem hard to follow. But, if you will read slowly and study carefully, I believe you will come to understand them completely. First, ask God to help you understand this chapter in its entirety. Ask Him to give you the grace to apply these truths to your day-to-day life. By doing so, you will be living freely in a bound world.

Throughout our chapters we have discussed the role of the inner man. The inner man is God in us, looking to live through us to produce power for us, that we might do great exploits for Him. If God is going to be living His life in us, and as a result of our submission, through us, as well, then we ought to be able to determine, by observation, when He is actually leading us and when we are instead leading ourselves.

In retrospect, we have learned that when the outer man is in submission to the body, then we are in the flesh. Even if we are doing good, we are in the flesh because we are doing good in our own power rather than the power of God.

In Galatians 2:21, Paul told the church of Galatia that this type of behavior will frustrate the grace of God. Grace is where God is doing His work. *Frustrate* means "to interrupt." Thus, Paul is charging the church members of Galatia with interrupting God's work on their behalf. How were they doing this? In the third verse of chapter three, Paul writes, *Are ye so foolish? having begun in the Spirit, are ye now made perfect by the flesh?* The church of Galatia, which had been greatly used by God, had ceased to submit to the Spirit's work in their lives and were trying to develop themselves spiritually in their own power. This is an incredibly frustrating place to be. It frustrates us when we live this way because despite our efforts to do good, we are living absent of joy and it frustrates our God that is living in us. Why does this frustrate God? Because He is trying to do a good work, but we will not allow Him to perform it. We are not under the Spirit's control; we are exercising soul control!

> The inner man is God in us, looking to live through us to produce power for us, that we might do great exploits.

In Galatians 5:17-23, we see an explanation of this battle between our flesh and the Spirit of God. Verse 17 begins, *For the flesh lusteth against the Spirit, and the Spirit against the flesh...* This tells us that our soul desires to yield to the body rather than yield to the Spirit's leading. It also tells us that the Spirit wants to lead the soul of man, rather than for the body to lead the soul.

Paul goes on to say, *and these are contrary the one to the other.* He is telling us something that is very obvious. These two desires of the body and the Spirit are contrary, or opposite, of each other. There is no middle ground. The Spirit will lead as the soul submits to Him. If not, we will be ruled by the body, as the soul rebels against the Spirit's leading. This is otherwise known as self-control. Many people think self-control is good, but it's not. It is better than no control, but the only good option is Spirit control. Remember,...*in me (that is, in my flesh,) dwelleth no good thing...*(Romans 7:18).

The last phrase of Galatians 5:17 gives us the biggest struggle of the Christian life, yet explains it at the very same time. It reads, *ye cannot do the things that ye would.* The biggest struggle of the Christian life is *trying* to do the things that we would like to be able to do. We want to do the right things and we try to do the right things, but that is our biggest problem. We are *trying* hard to do good. We also see the reason why this effort is so futile. Paul tells us that we *cannot* do the things that we would. Have you ever seen this before? You cannot do it. You cannot live the Christian life in your own power. Only Christ can live the Christian life. We have to stop trying and let God do the work. That's grace! Grace is when God does the work; the law is where man does the work. If you are trying to do what you would (or should), you will ultimately fail and lose your joy, as well! However, if you would let God do what you would like to be able to do, then victory is certain.

Further explanation of this truth is given in the next verse, where Paul tells us, *But if ye be led of the Spirit, ye are not under the law.* If God is leading us and we are following Him in step, then we are walking in the Spirit. We will not be under the law (where we must try to do the work, yet where we cannot do the work), but we will be under the influence of the Spirit (where God will do the work for us).

So we see that when God is in control of our lives, the soul is in complete submission to the Spirit, and we can accomplish things that we cannot accomplish when the flesh is in control. As a result of this truth, Paul tells us of the actions or reactions that we might find in one who is under the leading of the soul. Now, understand that when someone walks after the flesh, their fruit, or outcome, may appear good or bad. There is good flesh and there is bad flesh. We will discuss the good flesh during our later discussion of the fruit of the Spirit. For now, let's look at the bad flesh that is discussed in verses 19-21.

Now the works of the flesh are manifest, which are these; Adultery, fornication, uncleanness, lasciviousness, Idolatry, witchcraft, hatred, variance, emulations, wrath, strife, seditions, heresies, Envyings, murders, drunkenness, revellings, and such like.

The phrase *works of the flesh* means "the efforts of the soul under the influence of the body." *Manifest* means "to make evident." Therefore, when the body is in control of our soul, it is often evident by our behavior. Let us define some of this behavior.

Adultery: sex outside of marriage
Fornication: sex before marriage
Uncleanness: sexual deviance
Lasciviousness: sexual excess

These behaviors describe fleshly acts that are sexual immorality. Now consider this fact, lest we believe we are too moral to behave in such wicked ways, Paul then lists some other lusts of the flesh that may at times seem attractive to the soul.

Idolatry: valuing something more than you value your relationship   with God.
Witchcraft: Sorcery; being under the influence of demonic forces
Hatred: Having a great dislike for another
Variance: Argumentative
Emulation: An unhealthy desire for superiority
Wrath: Revengeful feelings of getting even
Strife: Spreading angry contentions
Sedition: Raising commotion
Heresies: Errors in the fundamentals of religion
Envying: A general uneasiness with the happiness of others
Murders: Premeditated killing of another human

Drunkenness: To be habitually overpowered with intoxication   from alcohol
Reveling: Uncontrolled feasting and carousing in a party-like atmosphere

Now, I see that some of these things have been and are at times problems for me.   And when they are, it is made evident, that I am exercising the lusts of my flesh. I am obviously following after the flesh, because I am doing bad things of the flesh.   If this is a consistent problem in your life and there is no conviction or chastening from God, then you should question your salvation.   That's what I believe Paul means when he says, *of the which I tell you before, as I have also told you in time past, that they which do such things shall not inherit the kingdom of God.*

This is the second time this church has been explained this truth.   We don't know exactly the circumstances in which it was previously used.   Maybe it was in an unmentioned sermon that Paul preached to this church (he had been there once prior to this letter), or possibly that the churches would share their letters that Paul wrote to them.   If that were the case, then he could be discussing the nearly identical passage that he wrote to the church in Corinth in which he said: *Know ye not that the unrighteous shall not inherit the kingdom of God? Be not deceived: neither fornicators, nor idolaters, nor adulterers, nor effeminate, nor abusers of themselves with mankind, Nor thieves, nor covetous, nor drunkards, nor revilers, nor extortioners, shall inherit the kingdom of God* (1 Corinthians 6:9-10).

These fleshly behaviors are qualities of one who is *not* submitting to the inner man, God is *not* in control of their lives, and the soul is *not* in complete submission to the Spirit.   There is, however, an alternative.   I call it "a little heaven on earth."   That alternative is the victorious

Christian life! This means that God lives through us, giving us an opportunity to live a heaven-like lifestyle here while guaranteeing us a future in heaven.

Unfortunately, all of us have been guilty of one or more of these sins at one time or another. But verse 11 gives us hope! *And such were some of you: but ye are washed, but ye are sanctified, but ye are justified in the name of the Lord Jesus, and by the Spirit of our God.*

Wow! What a marvelous opportunity! God has offered to clean house. Mine and yours. He can wash us from the filthiness of our sins through justification and sanctification. We are justified by belief in the Lord Jesus and sanctified through the influence of the Spirit of God.

Let's dig into these behaviors just a little bit more, so that we can better understand God's alternative to these behaviors. In chapter six, we discussed the difference of "being in the flesh" and "walking after the flesh." They seem similar, but as a point of reminder, a believer cannot walk *in* the flesh, but can intentionally follow *after* the flesh. This is taught to us in Romans chapter 8. (A good study of Romans 8 is found in the Reformers Unanimous Challenger Workbook. I would suggest you understand Romans 6 and 8 clearly to understand the loss of power and influence that sin experiences over a new believer.) To explain the problems that some believers may have with some of these aforementioned sins, let us look at a few verses in Romans 8 to better understand the difference between being "in the flesh" and walking "after the flesh." This is not a complete study, but rather a short explanation of these two terms. Do not skim the verses. That will hinder your study. Read each verse slowly, meditate on the meaning, and notice especially the emphasis added where underlined.

- Romans 8:1 *There is therefore now no condemnation to them which are* <u>in</u> *Christ Jesus, who* <u>walk not after the flesh</u>, *but* <u>after the Spirit</u>.

- Romans 8:2 *For the law of the Spirit of life* <u>in</u> *Christ Jesus hath* <u>made me free</u> *from the law of sin and death.*

- Romans 8:3 *For what the law could not do, in that it was weak through the flesh, God sending his own Son in the likeness of sinful flesh, and for sin, condemned sin* <u>in the flesh</u>: (Re-read verse one, then continue to verse four.)

- Romans 8:4 *That the righteousness of the law might be fulfilled in us, who walk not* <u>after the flesh</u>, *but* <u>after the Spirit.</u>

- Romans 8:5 *For they that are* <u>after the flesh</u> *do mind the things of the flesh; but they that are* <u>after the Spirit</u> *the things of the Spirit.*

- Romans 8:8 *So then they that* <u>are in the flesh</u> (those that are unsaved) *cannot please God.*

- Romans 8:9 *But ye are not* <u>in the flesh</u>, *but* <u>in the Spirit</u>, *if so be that the Spirit of God dwell* <u>in you</u>...

- Romans 8:10 *And if Christ be* <u>in you</u>, *the body is dead because of sin; but the Spirit is life because of righteousness.*

Verse one tells us that if we are in Christ, we will not be condemned. It goes on to indicate that if we walk after the flesh and not after the Spirit, we *could* experience condemnation. And we do! Not from God, but from the devil. That is how we can explain such horrible *feelings* of condemnation when we behave badly. That does not come from God, it comes from the devil. But if we are walking after the Spirit, those feelings of condemnation will be an impossibility. There is a big difference between the Spirit's conviction and Satan's condemnation.

This new law (verse two) of the Spirit brings us emancipation from the power of sin and freedom from God's condemnation. The word *law* means "rule of conduct." He is telling us that if we will yield to the rule of conduct that now lives within us, we will experience the benefits of being free from the power of sin. If we don't yield to the Spirit's rule for conducting ourselves, we will instead walk "after the flesh." We are free from sin's power, but as a result of our "walk," we will not exercise or experience the benefits of this freedom. We are willfully walking after it, following it as it is leading us astray.

This is often a result of the presence of fear or a weakness in our faith. Either we fear failing in our new-found freedom so we choose to remain in unbound bondage, or we lack faith that God is really going to do what He said He will do.

I have heard it said that after the *Emancipation Proclamation* was signed, a large number of former slaves became afraid of the ramifications of their new freedom, and they determined to remain "slaves." Free as they were, they chose to remain in bondage and under tribute to their "masters." This did not change the fact that they were free, but they remained as they had been.

That is exactly what we are capable of doing after conversion. Though God has freed us from the power of sin, we can still choose to follow it. It has no power over us except what we give it. To stop following after this illegitimate master, all we have to do is exercise our faith in the law that liberated us. For the law of the Spirit of life in Christ Jesus has made us free from the law of sin and death!

Verse 3 reminds us that those that are "in the flesh" are condemned. Verse 4 proves that we can live the Christian life by yielding to the inner man and not going after what is already dead (verse 10). Verse 8 tells us that those in the flesh cannot please God; to please God we must walk in the Spirit by faith. Verse 9 reminds us of our position in Christ and His position in us.

Now, let's get back to Galatians 5 and our study on the lust of the flesh. It is usually obvious when someone is engaged in these sins. Many, if not all of them, are noticeable by outward demonstrations of behavior. That is why Paul said that these works of the flesh are manifest, or made evident. It's bad flesh. The fruit of the Spirit contrasts it. However, I want to tell you about another type of flesh. It is a flesh that hardly anyone knows anything about. Paul alluded to it in Galatians 3:1 as a type of flesh that bewitches, or fascinates, Christians. It is not a flesh that is evident by our behavior. As a matter of fact, it is very hard to discern. It is less evident. It is the biggest problem, in my opinion, in Christianity today. I call it "doing good in the flesh." Galatians 5:19-21 lists bad flesh (or, unrighteousness) and verses 22-23 list righteous behavior. This "good" flesh is neither *unrighteous* behavior, nor *righteous* behavior. So what was Paul referring to? It's *self-righteous* behavior.

You see, the devil knows that believers are not going to be comfortable with the Holy Spirit convicting them of engaging in the works of the flesh mentioned in verses 19-21. God's people may vary from the Spirit's leading and walk after the flesh, but being in Christ, this type of behavior brings great conviction as well as chastening from the Lord.

So, the devil has created a more subtle type of flesh that hardly anybody realizes. The Bible says that Satan is transformed into an angel of light (2 Corinthians 11:14). He can appear as a provider of spiritual direction. He uses this imposter-like spiritual direction to lead us into doing good in our own power rather than in the power of God. That is good flesh. Doing good under the influence of the soul instead of under the power of the Spirit is a fascinating place to be.

> If we don't yield to the Spirit's rule for conducting ourselves, we will instead walk "after the flesh." We are free from sin's power, but as a result of our "walk," we will not exercise or experience the benefits of this freedom.

Now let us look at each of these alternatives that are created and offered up by the angel of light as alternatives to righteousness but are actually self-righteousness. The devil realizes that his good flesh alternatives must look like God's fruit of the Spirit or at least, when not similar in appearance at least acceptable to the believer and to those whom he or she interacts with.

Let us now look at the fruits of the Spirit as listed in Galatians 5:22-23. (This study is best learned by participating in the Reformers Unanimous Strongholds Study Course. This is an intense discipleship course created for the purpose of understanding the differences between righteous fruit and self-righteous flesh.) *But the fruit of the Spirit is love, joy, peace, longsuffering, gentleness, goodness, faith, Meekness, temperance...*

Fruit means "outcome, or result." Thus, the *fruit of the Spirit* means "the outcome, or result, of the Spirit's leading in our lives." By design, God has limited Himself in the way in which He will respond to all forms of adversity. This was

His decision. The Spirit will lead you to respond in one of these nine ways, or He will not lead you to respond to a circumstance whatsoever. It is His choice how to respond, and it is our choice to yield to that response.

Realizing that God has nine actions or reactions to all the circumstances in life and the devil is an angel of light that mimics false spiritual direction thereby offering an alternative to each of these fruits, then how many potential actions or reactions do we have to choose from? Of course that would be 18. It is actually 20 when you consider that God may ask you to not respond and the devil leads you to respond anyway, or He may ask you to respond and you decide not to. So there are basically twenty options for every circumstance in life. I know that makes life problems sound simplistic, but that is an aberration. The majority of the flaw in Christian evangelism of the lost can be traced to Christians inability to develop a dynamic enough walk with God to determine the difference between righteous responses under the influence of the Spirit and self-righteous responses under the influence of the flesh.

Let's look at these eighteen potential actions or reactions of a Spirit led or self led Christian to all the circumstances in life. We will look at them in breakdowns of three and as listed in order in the Bible. They will be categorized using the following descriptions.

1. Transforming—Love, Joy and Peace. That is inner being transformation.
2. Conforming—Longsuffering, Gentleness, and Goodness. That is outer being conformation.
3. Reforming—Faith, Meekness and Temperance. That is new being reformation.

The first breakdown and first three fruits of the Spirit, I call inner being transformation. Remember chapter three's discussion on transforming proceeding conforming (Romans 12:2)? A person will never change the way they act until they change the way they think. God must change the inside of the man, first and foremost.

If you will notice, the first three fruits of the Spirit, as listed in the Bible are all fruits that deal with the inside behaviors of a man. If a man does not love, or have joy or peace, it can go undetected. It is an inside problem. Before you can get a man to act right on the outside, you should get him to act right on the inside. God wants our inner being to act right. He offers these three fruits to be our inner man's response to adversity. If our soul will yield to our inner man than we will respond properly. Let's take a look at God's three internal responses found within our inner man.

1a. GOD OFFERS THE FRUIT OF THE SPIRIT~LOVE.

There are different types of love mentioned in the Bible. Unlike in the English language, there are several Greek words for love. *Eros*, from which we get the word *erotic*, means "physical love." In Greek mythology, Eros was the god of love, which we would associate with the Roman god, Cupid. The word *eros* is not used anywhere in the New Testament. *Philadelphia* means "brotherly love." It is derived from the root word *philos*, which means "affectionate regard; fondness." It is the type of love shared beween close friends. *Philostorgos* means "family affection" and is translated as "kindly affectioned" in the New Testament. It is the type of love we have for our parents or our children.

There is another Greek word for love in its highest form and that is *agape*. It is the word Paul used when he listed the fruit of the Spirit~Love. The best definition of *agape* is "the willing, sacrificial giving of oneself for the benefit of others without thought of return." That is God's kind of love, and it is available for us to demonstrate to others by the power of the Holy Spirit.

This type of love is evident in many places in Scripture, but never was more love shown to us than by our Creator, the God of heaven. In John 3:16 we read, *For God so loved the world, that he gave his only begotten Son, that whosoever believeth in him should not perish, but have everlasting life.* What did God do to demonstrate His love toward us? He willingly, sacrificially gave of Himself for the benefit of others without thought of return. That is the greatest gift of all! He did not even require us to change before He would offer this gift to us. In Romans 5:8 we read, *But God commendeth his love toward us, in that, while we were yet sinners, Christ died for us.*

> **Love** is the willing, sacrificial giving of oneself for the benefit of others without thought of return.

Yet God was not alone in this demonstration of love. His only begotten Son was a willing sacrifice for God's plan to redeem sinful man. Though Christ desired for another way instead of His own death, He was willing to lay down His life for us. Christ, under the influence of the Spirit, yielded to the fruit of the Spirit~Love and gave Himself for us. In Ephesians 5:2, Paul encourages us to walk in love like Christ walked in love. He is indicating a "following after." Christ followed the Spirit's leading and expressed God's love toward us. We ought also to follow Christ's example and follow the Spirit's leading to express God's love toward others. As Paul worded it, *And walk in love, as Christ also hath loved us, and hath given himself for us an offering and a sacrifice to God for a sweetsmelling savour.*

As a matter of fact, if we do not yield to God's leading to demonstrate love toward others, they will not be convinced that we are believers in and followers of Christ. This is taught, by Jesus himself in John 13:34-35. *A new commandment I give unto you, That ye love one another; as I have loved you, that ye also love one another. By this shall all men know that ye are my disciples, if ye have love one to another.*

We are commanded throughout the Word of God to love others and one another. God the Father set the perfect example. Christ, in the power of the Holy Spirit, yielded to that example, and we ought to, also. It is a command for us to love. (And, the truth is, all true love comes from God; it is simply yielded to by man.) First John 3:23 says, *And this is his commandment, That we should believe on the name of his Son Jesus Christ, and love one another, as he gave us commandment.* And Matthew 22:37-40 says, *Jesus said unto him, Thou shalt love the Lord thy God with all thy heart, and with all thy soul, and with all thy mind. This is the first and great commandment. And the second is like unto it, Thou shalt love thy neighbour as thyself. On these two commandments hang all the law and the prophets.*

He is asking us to willingly and sacrificially give of ourselves for the benefit of God and others. Love is God's tool for showing unselfish favor to undeserving people. We can do many things for undeserving people. We can make many sacrifices. Yet if those acts of kindness are not done under the influence of the Spirit's love, we will not bring a positive effect into that person's life, no matter what our level of sacrifice.

Let's take a look at 1 Corinthians 13:1-3 to see what God says about sacrifices that do not demonstrate His love.

Though I speak with the tongues of men and of angels, and have not charity, I am become as sounding brass, or a tinkling cymbal. And though I have the gift of prophecy, and understand all mysteries, and all knowledge; and though I have all faith, so that I could remove mountains, and have not charity, I am nothing. And though I bestow all my goods to feed the poor, and though I give my body to be burned, and have not charity, it profiteth me nothing.

Fleshly Sacrifice: Eloquent speaking of various languages
End Result without Yielding to Love: They are of no more value to the hearer than notes of a trumpet or the crash of a cymbal.

Fleshly Sacrifice: Great understanding of God and His ways as well as an ability to communicate those truths and to live them as well
End Result without Yielding to Love: You amount to nothing in their eyes. They will not be impressed with our apparent spiritual gifts.

Fleshly Sacrifice: Give all my possessions to feed the weak and needy and sacrifice my life for the same
End Result without Yielding to love: These great sacrifices will be of no profit to the giver in this life nor in the next life.

However, we then read in verses 4-8 of the great value our works will be if we add to these sacrifices a yielding to the fruit of the Spirit~Love. Let's take a look at this:
Charity suffereth long, and is kind; charity envieth not; charity vaunteth not itself, is not puffed up, Doth not behave itself unseemly, seeketh not her own, is not easily provoked, thinketh no evil; Rejoiceth not in iniquity, but rejoiceth in the truth; Beareth all things, believeth all things, hopeth all things, endureth all things. Charity never faileth:

> **suffereth long, and is kind**: puts up with inconveniences

envieth not: lifts up others; not self
vaunteth not itself: is not stuck up
doth not behave itself unseemly: acts right
seeketh not her own: looks for what is right
is not easily provoked: responds right
thinketh no evil: thinks right
rejoiceth not in iniquity: doesn't get excited about what's not right
rejoiceth in the truth: gets excited about what is right
beareth all things: carries the weight
believeth all things: gives the benefit of the doubt
hopeth all things: hopes for the best
endureth all things: keeps on keeping on
never fails: works every time!

Now, let's think about our forms of service for God and others. Honestly, does our service for God manifest itself in the proper behaviors listed above? Sometimes, yes; but other times, no. It's as if our love is genuine and our hearts are pure, yet we tend to behave in a somewhat selfish manner when we are expressing love. Why is this? It is simple to explain but not so readily recognized in our lives. The opportunity to yield to the fruit of the Spirit~Love has a fleshly alternative. This fleshly alternative to God's love flowing through us is not something that will appear to be the opposite of love. We would not easily fall for the devil's influence to yield to doing the work of the flesh—hate! The devil knows this, so he stimulates a flesh that is so often misunderstood by both the doer and the receiver of the good deeds. Once again, it's the flesh of self-righteousness. The devil's option for us is to show love in our own power. It is not God's love. It is our love. It is otherwise known as self-love.

1b. WE OFTEN PREFER THE WORK OF THE FLESH~SELF-LOVE

Our expressions of the fruit of the Spirit~Love, when understood by the recipient, will rarely be rejected. When love is misunderstood or rejected it is because there are so many false manifestations of it. Those false manifestations (listed in 1 Corinthians 13:1-8) are nothing more than self-love. Remember, love is the willing, *sacrificial* giving of oneself for the benefit of others *without* thought of return. However, the fleshly alternative of self-love is the willing or unwilling giving of oneself to benefit others with selfish thoughts of return.

Do you know someone who serves God with a great deal of time, energy, and self-sacrifice? However, if the pastor doesn't thank this person at least once every ninety days from the pulpit, he gets offended, or quits. He has to be consistently praised for his sacrifice or he becomes complacent in his service or ceases serving at all. Such people are not serving others, they are serving self. They are probably good people, but they are acting like bad Christians. They are doing good works, but they are doing them in the energy of the flesh. The true test of a servant is if he acts like one when he is being treated like one.

I once had a student who had slipped in his recovery and engaged in drug use. He appeared genuinely repentant for what he had done. I asked him to explain the events that led up to his relapse. He said it was because he did not believe that his wife loved him. Well, I found that hard to believe. While he was away on his binge, his wife had demonstrated her love for him in many ways both toward him and even toward me as she sought my advice and help. I asked him, "What makes you think that your wife does not love you?" He replied, "Because, I work hard all week long at my job and provide a good living for my family. All I ask for is a hot meal and some clean clothes. I come home tired at night and have to eat something she just threw together or picked up at a drive through. She never does laundry until after it piles up, and the house is *always* a mess!"

Now, I knew something he had failed to mention. His wife worked full time as a nurse, twelve hour shifts and often up to 60 hours per week. Of course, his forty hour a week office job did not afford him time to mow the lawn or take out the trash, so he paid a neighbor boy (out of his wife's wages) to do his exterior work. And, she also cared for her three children that were all under the age of eight. I wouldn't know, but I am told that men can surely be pigs!

> **Self-love** is the willing or unwilling giving of oneself to benefit others with selfish thoughts of return.

Now, ladies, stop showing this last paragraph to your husband; I am not talking about him! But, suffice it to say, both parties in that marriage seriously misunderstood each other's problems. She believed that his biggest problem was that he had a drug addiction, and he believed that his wife did not love him. Both conclusions were wrong. The primary problem was that the husband did not love his wife—that is, not the way God wants him to love her. You see, he was somewhat willingly (yet begrudgingly) and sacrificially giving for the benefit of his wife, but he had selfish thoughts of return. (His wife probably did, too.) He gave to his wife, but he wanted her to give back. And that seems fair, but self-love, when given, demands a return. By contrast, God's love demands *nothing* in return.

This man is a Christian, but in this instance, he was not being a good one. Why? Most people would say because he was doing drugs. But the truth is, it was because he was not yielding to the Spirit. He was trying to do good in his own power which produces love that profits nothing. By yielding to the fruit of the Spirit~Love, he will give to his wife unselfishly. This will most likely lead to reciprocated biblical love from his wife (and even if it doesn't, another fruit of the Spirit can be applied to keep him from discouragement).

Jesus was not merely making a suggestion when He said, *This is my commandment, That ye love one another, as I have loved you. Greater love hath no man than this, that a man lay down his life for his friends.* John 15:12-13

2a. GOD OFFERS THE FRUIT OF THE SPIRIT~JOY.

The fruit of the Spirit~Joy is, of course, one of the most enjoyable fruits to experience, but also one of the most difficult fruits to yield to. It is strange to realize and difficult to understand that when we lack joy, it is only because we have failed to yield to it. *Joy* is "a cheerful, calm delight in all the circumstances of life."

As we have seen in previous chapters, God will place each of us in situations that will try our faith, produce some patience, and generate a joy found only in the Holy Spirit. We will only grow and develop when the outer man is wounded by circumstances in life and we are given opportunities to yield to the inner man. Those circumstances are intended to break the outer man and develop the inner man. As a result, we will become less carnal and more Spirit-led. The more Spirit-led we are, the more like Christ we are and the more power we experience. Living a Christ-like life under the power of the Holy Spirit is the best way to influence others for Christ, maximizing our God-given gifts for the benefit of family, the church, and the kingdom. It is the life of Christ flowing through us.

We see this truth taught in Romans 8:28-29. This has been covered in previous chapters, but I would like to revisit it. Let's dissect and define these verses.

> *And we know that all things work together for good to them that love God, to them who are the called according to his purpose. For whom he did foreknow, he also did predestinate to be conformed to the image of his Son, that he might be the firstborn among many brethren.*

All things: refers to everything, good and bad
work together: produce a result
for good: in a way that is advantageous
love God: willingly give of oneself without thought of return
called..to his purpose: to be conformed to the image of His Son
foreknow: know in advance
predestinate: pre-plan, or ordain, in advance
conformed: poured into a mold
image of his Son: the likeness of Christ
firstborn: the first in the order of birth
among many brethren: others who become brothers after and as a result of birth

This passage sheds light on the whole subject of Christians experiencing adversity, trials, and persecution. It tells us that everything that happens to us, both good and bad, is intended to produce an advantageous result. But we must give of ourselves for God's benefit and allow ourselves to be molded into the likeness of Christ. God knew in advance that He would effect this type of development in our lives. This method is designed by God to draw others to Christ because of our example.

I have explained all of this to help you understand the danger of rejecting the Spirit's gift of joy. You see, when a difficult circumstance arises, we are actually being blessed with the opportunity to experience the fruit of the Spirit~Joy. We can rejoice and calmly delight in that circumstance. A moment of meditation will serve to remind us that it is for our good and God's glory. It will further serve to remind us that by yielding to the fruit of the Spirit~Joy and rejoicing in that circumstance, we could be leading another person closer to becoming a fellow brother or sister in Christ.

> **Joy** is a cheerful, calm delight in all the circumstances of life.

Responding with joy in a particular circumstance will likely result in the wounding of the outer man and the shining forth of the inner man. More often than not, the light of the inner man shines brightest when beaming through a wound in the soul that was created in the outer man through the cheerful acceptance of and calm delight in a difficult circumstance.

Often, we will see circumstances fade away or become easier to manage when we allow all things to work together for good—properly responding to adversity. However, the devil has an alternative to all of this, a different way to face difficult circumstances. Though it is not a fruit of the Spirit, it unfortunately is still an acceptable response by many Christians. They often embrace it, condone it, and sometimes compliment it. Why is this? It is simple to explain, but not so readily recognized.

The opportunity to yield to the fruit of the Spirit~Joy has a fleshly alternative. It is not something that will appear to be the opposite of joy. We would not easily fall for the devil's influence to yield to the work of the flesh~regret! The devil knows this, so he stimulates the flesh of self-righteousness. Satan's option is to respond to bad circumstances in our own power. It does not produce God's joy; it produces our own level of contentment. It is otherwise known as frustration, and it is the devil's preferred response to every circumstance in life.

2b. WE OFTEN PREFER THE WORK OF THE FLESH~FRUSTRATION.

Our expression of the fruit of the Spirit~Joy, when observed by others, will always impress. To review, joy is a cheerful, calm delight in all the circumstances of life. The fleshly alternative is frustration, which is "a rejection or unhappy refusal in the cicumstances of life."

When we face an unwanted circumstance, we can either respond with joy or frustration. The truth is that most of our brothers and sisters in Christ will accept either response. Others will either appreciate and respect us for our willingness to respond to the fruit of the Spirit~Joy when faced with adversity, or they will pity us as we respond to the circumstance with feelings of frustration. It is sad but true that most Christians do not see frustration as a work of the flesh. However, it is a response generated by the soul. It stems from a negative thought, desire, or emotion. When the heart responds to adversity by looking to the soul for a response, we are guaranteed to act after the flesh. That is why the position of the heart is so important. This trigger must be protected with all diligence, for every important issue in life stems from it!

It has been said by many when counseling, "I understand your frustration." That's like saying, "I understand your crack cocaine addiction." Good flesh is as bad as bad flesh. Flesh is flesh and we cannot please God if we are walking after the flesh, no matter how much good we are doing, no matter how much we believe our frustration is justified.

To this end, we must understand God's purpose for adversity:

- To wound the outer man.
- To allow the inner man to shine through.
- To display our love for God.
- To conform us to be like Christ.
- To lead others to salvation in Christ.

If we respond after the flesh in a difficult circumstance, then we will be forced to continue facing this circumstance over and over again to bring about God's determined results. Furthermore, if we will not yield to joy, we may suffer more *severe* circumstances. God is faithful to break down our flesh and develop His Spirit. If you want to be like Christ, you can be! But you must allow God to place you into circumstances that will wound you. Then, you must respond properly to that circumstance. When you do, you will come forth a vessel for the finer (Proverbs 25:4).

> **Frustration** is a rejection or unhappy refusal in the circumstances of life.

I understand that this is easier said than done. Oh, how many times have I remembered this truth much too late to apply it! I think the same is probably true for most Christians. Even if you did not understand these truths before reading them, you can probably look back and see that this has been the routine of your life. Accept it and it gets better, or reject it and it gets worse. Though you may have never known the reason why it was that way, now you do. Praise the Lord! Yielding to joy brings Christ-likeness and the conversion of unbelievers.

You have a choice: the fruit of the Spirit~Joy, or the work of the flesh~Frustration. It is not a work of the flesh that is obvious. It is often hard to discern. But a refusal to rejoice in the circumstances of life is the lust of the flesh~frustration.

3a. GOD OFFERS THE FRUIT OF THE SPIRIT~PEACE

The fruit of the Spirit~Peace is a most necessary fruit to which we must yield when facing adversity and persecution in the Christian life. *Peace* is "to be safe from harm in spirit, mind, and body."

Why is this such a necessary fruit? Christians who yield to the fruit of love and joy are under the influence of God. They live godly lives because they are "in Christ." And what does the Bible say about Christians who live godly in Christ Jesus? I think you know, but let's look at 2 Timothy 3:10-12:

> *But thou hast fully known my doctrine, manner of life, purpose, faith, longsuffering, charity, patience, Persecutions, afflictions, which came unto me at Antioch, at Iconium, at Lystra; Yea, and all that will live godly in Christ Jesus shall suffer persecution.*

Paul explained to Timothy that if he lived a godly life under the influence of the Spirit, then he could expect to suffer persecution. Persecution in the twenty-first century is one of the most misunderstood of Christian experiences. If we were to ask most godly believers if they suffered persecution, they would say "no." They think of persecution as maybe being stoned to death or maybe martyred in some other way for the cause of the Gospel. And while it can include those types of horrible experiences, the basic definition of *persecution* is "a pursuit, for the purpose of oppression."

In chapter eight, we looked closely at the demonic force called oppression. It is intended to get us to step away from the Spirit's leading and to walk "after the flesh." The devil will pursue all godly, Spirit-led believers in an effort to oppress and render useless. There is no doubt about it, he will persecute. But *how* will he persecute? Does persecution (or oppression) involve non-physical attacks? Take note of verses 12 in the previous passage. Paul's godly living led him to be persecuted in three places: Antioch, Iconium, and Lystra. Let's look at what Paul referred to as "persecution" during his trips to these three cities.

Persecution in Antioch

> *And the next sabbath day came almost the whole city together to hear the word of God. But when the Jews saw the multitudes, they were filled with envy, and spake against those things which were spoken by Paul, contradicting and blaspheming.* (Acts 13:44-45)

Here we see Paul being contradicted and blasphemed by the Jewish religious leaders because they were jealous. Why were they jealous? Because almost the whole city came out to hear Paul preaching the Word of God. He was effective at reaching a crowd because he did it the right way. As a result, He and Barnabas experienced criticism and disagreements by the Jewish people who were lovers of God but non-believers in Jesus. And in 2 Timothy 3, Paul called this type of behavior persecution!

But where were the stones? Where were the physical assaults? They threw nothing but verbal attacks. Paul said that because of living godly in Christ, they were persecuted. He considered this verbal

> **Peace** is to be safe from harm in spirit, mind, and body.

abuse to be persecution. They could have responded by quitting the ministry. They could have at least ceased to submit to the Spirit's leading and brought an end to their verbal persecution, but they did not.

Instead, Paul responded to the fruit of the Spirit~Peace. The next verse says that they "waxed bold." This means they grew in courage in the face of persecution. God was in control, Paul knew that he was safe from harm in his spirit, mind, and body. The word *spirit* here in our definition is speaking of temperament. It is the seat of passions. Paul didn't get overly excited that he might be in harm's way. He didn't begin to fret in his mind or fear for the protection of his body. He responded by continuing to minister, but, as God must have led, to a different strain of people—the Gentiles. *Then Paul and Barnabas waxed bold, and said, It was necessary that the word of God should first have been spoken to you: but seeing ye put it from you, and judge yourselves unworthy of everlasting life, lo, we turn to the Gentiles* (Acts 13:46)

What if Paul had not loved, with joy, those to whom he ministered, experiencing great peace as a result? He could have selfishly focused on his own benefit and responded with frustration, missing God's plan for his life. No, he lived godly in Christ Jesus, and under His influence, he suffered a non-physical pursuit of oppression by jealous religious legalists. Paul and Barnabas continued in the peace of God.

Persecution in Iconium

And it came to pass in Iconium, that they went both together into the synagogue of the Jews, and so spake, that a great multitude both of the Jews and also of the Greeks believed. But the unbelieving Jews stirred up the Gentiles, and made their minds evil affected against the brethren. Long time therefore abode they speaking boldly in the Lord, which gave testimony unto the word of his grace, and granted signs and wonders to be done by their hands. But the multitude of the city was divided: and part held with the Jews, and part with the apostles. And when there was an assault made both of the Gentiles, and also of the Jews with their rulers, to use them despitefully, and to stone them, They were ware of it, and fled unto Lystra and Derbe, cities of Lycaonia, and unto the region that lieth round about: And there they preached the gospel. (Acts 14:1-7)

Here we see what the Bible describes as a "stirring up" of the Gentiles. But notice what led up to this popular uprising. Paul and Barnabas had been extremely effective. Many Jews (on whom Paul was less focused as a result of his trip to Antioch) and Greeks (Gentiles) believed their message.

Lo and behold, here comes the persecution! But not with flying rocks or even verbal assaults? No, this time it was the unbelieving Jews inciting the Gentiles. (Notice they did not try to persuade the multitude of believing Jews—it was too late; they had already believed!) They instigated a tumult among the people by poisoning their minds with criticism against Paul and Barnabas. Yet another pursuit of oppression against these Spirit-led believers!

Their response was the same as before, but in a different direction this time. Verse three says, *Long time therefore abode they speaking boldly in the Lord.* The word *therefore* brings two statements together. Because of their effectiveness, they decided not only to stay in Iconium, but to also continue speaking—*boldly*! They relied on the fruit of the Spirit~Peace to help them face persecution while they continued preaching. Consequently, God's power became even more evident as He granted these godly men the ability to perform signs and wonders.

God's hand was on their ministry despite their persecution. They stood strong and responded to the critical attacks and the uprising with the fruit of the Spirit~Peace. It was manifested by their great boldness. But things only seemed to get worse.

The people became divided: the believers versus the unbelievers. In verses 4 and 5, we see this division reaching the boiling point. *But the multitude of the city was divided: and part held with the Jews, and part with the apostles. And... there was an assault made both of the Gentiles, and also of the Jews with their rulers, to use them despitefully, and to stone them.*

To use them despitefully means "a reproach that attempts physical injury." This conflict had grown from openly verbal contradiction in Antioch to verbal criticism behind their backs and led up to a desire for physical injury. This mob wanted to stone them for what the Jewish leaders considered blasphemy.

Paul responded in the same way that Jesus did when He was faced with popular uprisings: He and Barnabas left Iconium and they did so in a hurry. They yielded to the fruit of the Spirit~Peace by retreating, thus rejecting its alternative. Had they stayed, there would have been a riot of sorts between the believers and the unbelievers.

What was God's higher purpose for this persecution? We find one answer in Acts 16:1. *Then came he to Derbe and Lystra: and, behold, a certain disciple was there, named Timotheus, the son of a certain woman, which was a Jewess, and believed; but his father was a Greek.*

As a result of their stalled work in Iconium and the

resulting physical pursuit of oppression, they went to these cities in Lycaonia and met young Timothy. What a blessing and benefit Timothy became to these persecuted believers! Yet, the persecution followed them, and this time it actually led to physical injury. Let's take a look at Acts 14:19-21.

Persecution in Lystra

And there came thither certain Jews from Antioch and Iconium, who persuaded the people, and, having stoned Paul, drew him out of the city, supposing he had been dead. Howbeit, as the disciples stood round about him, he rose up, and came into the city: and the next day he departed with Barnabas to Derbe. And...they... preached the gospel to that city; and had taught many.

The same troublemakers from Antioch and Iconium caught up with Paul, but did he fear? No, not at all. Stoned and left for dead by these attackers, he revived and returned to the city to preach the gospel. What an unbelievable measure of peace God gave Paul! He was so free from worry of harm to his spirit, mind, and body that he had no fear of man. He and Barnabas then *returned again to Lystra, and to Iconium, and Antioch, Confirming the souls of the disciples, and exhorting them to continue in the faith, and that we must through much tribulation enter into the kingdom of God* (verses 21-22).

Unbelievable! They returned straight into the fire! They went right back to the same places where they had come under great persecution (verbal and physical), encouraging fellow Christians to continue in their bold belief of God's system of management (faith). Seeing these truths helps me understand better what Paul was saying when he wrote to the church of Phillipi, *And the peace of God, which passeth all understanding, shall keep your hearts and minds through*

Christ Jesus (Philippians 4:7).

How does Paul's lesson on Peace in the face of persecution conclude? Let's look at 2 Timothy 3:11-14.

Persecutions, afflictions, which came unto me at Antioch, at Iconium, at Lystra; what persecutions I endured: but out of them all the Lord delivered me. Yea, and all that will live godly in Christ Jesus shall suffer persecution. But evil men and seducers shall wax worse and worse, deceiving, and being deceived. But continue thou in the things which thou hast learned and hast been assured of, knowing of whom thou hast learned them;

Paul opens our eyes about living godly under the influence of Christ. As a Christian, you will suffer pursuits of oppression from people you try to help. It may be verbal to your face and/or behind your back. If you respond properly, God's power will be on your life. You may also be attacked physically, but do not worry and do not retaliate. Plunge into God's perfect peace and boldly continue to do what God leads you to do, and you will be delivered.

Below, I have included part of a song that so eloquently reminds us of the truth of God's ability to protect us in times of persecution and adversity.

God on the Mountain
(Tracy Darrt)
Life is easy when you're up on the mountain
And you've got peace of mind like you've never known.
But then things change and you're down in the valley.
Don't lose faith for you're never alone.

For the God on the mountain is still God in the valley.
When things go wrong, He'll make it right.
And the God of the good times is still God in the bad times.
The God of the day is still God in the night.

3b.   WE   OFTEN   PREFER   THE   WORK   OF   THE
FLESH~WORRY

There is nothing more attractive to a lost person than someone who loves unconditionally, expresses great joy in life's adversities, and exhibits a peace that surpasses understanding in the face of opposition. At the same time, there is nothing more hypocritical to a lost person than self-centered, frustrated people that call themselves Christians. Of course, it is possible for Christians to behave this way by living under the influence of the soul rather than the Spirit. Such people, however, will not only fail to experience the joy of the Lord, but they also will not experience the fruit of the Spirit~Peace. They certainly will not feel free of harm in spirit, mind, and body.

Once again, for every fruit that God offers, there is a fleshly alternative. The alternative to the fruit of the Spirit~Peace is the work of the flesh~Worry. Worry is "to live in fear of harm in your spirit, mind, AND body." This alternative to the fruit of peace is a poor testimony to those who are observing our walk with the Lord.

I have met a lot of Christians who live much of their lives worrying about things. I am guilty, at times, of yielding to my soul's fear of harm, as well. I believe the reason we struggle with fear is because our godly living is sometimes done under an influence other than the influence of Christ.

The most realistic way to differentiate between peace and worry is found in the eye of the beholder. God is the true judge of what is harmful for us. He will not harm us. Everything is going to work together for our good. As a result, the persecutions of life will never bring us harm in God's opinion. However, when we look at our circumstances, we will tend to see them as potentially harmful to us. But this is a lack of faith based on a wrong perspective—the view of the outward man, not the inward man. The promises of Scripture will not be broken, even to get our attention or to bring us back into fellowship with God. It is simply true that God will not harm us. Once again, we may view it as harm, but God does not. He views it as good for us. We are then safe from harm in all areas.

> **Worry** is to live in fear of harm in your spirit, mind, and body.

To this end, whenever we are faced with persecution, we must remember to look at our circumstances "in Christ Jesus." We must view our perceived trouble under the influence of the Holy Spirit. He will always lead us to be at peace, to trust Him, and to have faith in Him and His Word. When we do, we will find ourselves responding to our persecution without a shred of worry.

Do you worry that God may take your spouse or your child? Do you worry that God may take your job or your home? Do you worry about things that if they were to happen, you feel they would bring you great harm? Well then, you are human. I do not mean to suggest that these are not terrible things to endure. I am simply saying if God allows them in your life, they are not going to bring you harm—not in God's eyes. And they won't bring you harm in your eyes, either, if you are living godly in Christ Jesus.

I am not trafficking in unlived examples. I have personally experienced this blessed truth in my life. I have failed to experience it, as well, for the very same reasons listed above. But this one thing is for sure: when we experience such situations, we will find that they produce within us the ability to respond to oppression with the fruit of the Spirit~Longsuffering, the fourth of ten actions or reactions of our Lord.

I refer to the first three fruits of the Spirit as "inner being transformation" because Romans 12:2 indicates that transformation must come before conformation. We cannot change the way we act until we change the way we think. God must first change the inside of man. The devil begins his work on the outside. He uses outside influences of the lust of the flesh to play on the mind, the lust of the eyes to play on the will, and the pride of life to play on the emotions. The devil's work always begins with outside influence and attempts to destroy us on the inside. God works from the inside out. The inner man is the part of man that communicates with God. The Spirit influences the inner man, and when we yield to that influence, it always conforms the outer being to the image of Christ.

So, if a man does not love or have joy or peace, it can go undetected; it is an inside problem. Before God can get a man to act right on the outside, He must get him to act right on the inside. He offers these three fruits to be the inner man's response to adversity.

Let us now look at the conformation process as we yield to the second three Fruits of the Spirit. I refer to these as "outer-being conformation." They are evidenced by our outward behavior. Remembering back to chapter three, after a transformation of the mind has begun, these three fruits will cause us to un-conform from the world and conform to the image of Christ.

4a. GOD OFFERS THE FRUIT OF THE SPIRIT~LONGSUFFERING.

For me, longsuffering is one of the most difficult fruits to yield to. When I do respond to someone with longsuffering, I am certainly aware of the fact that God is doing the work! Longsuffering is "an enduring temperament that expresses itself in patience with the shortcomings of others."

Let's dissect and define this definition. *Temperament* refers to a person's make up—the passions, attitudes, and other elements of temper that combine to produce a level of irritability, whether high or low. *Enduring* means "to continue without perishing" or "to last long, even to permanence." *Patience* means "calm in temper." Thus, longsuffering is made up of a combination of attitudes that expresses itself in long, lasting calmness. To whom is this combination of attitudes to be expressed? Well, by definition, this spirit of calmness should expressed toward people who have shortcomings. *Short* meaning "not of sufficient length," and *comings* meaning "to advance toward a target."

I know this is a long explanation of a definition, but I use it to show how God intends for us to respond to those who fail to reach our expected targets. You see, we all have expectations of what other people should be doing and how they should be acting. Too often, we feel let down by people. Whether they are wrong in falling short, or whether our expectations for them are unrealistic, God's intention for us is to always respond with the fruit of the Spirit~Longsuffering. He wants us to respond with an enduring temperament expressed by patience with the shortcomings (or, faults) of others.

Now, let's briefly review the fruits we have studied to this point and notice how each fruit flows out of the previous one. When we love people without thought of return, we experience an absolute rejoicing in all circumstances. This joy leads to freedom from worry in mind, body,

> **Longsuffering** is an enduring temperament that expresses itself in patience with the shortcomings of others.

and spirit. Therefore, when responding properly to others, we might think that it would naturally yield a great willingness on their part to meet our objectives for them. However, if the devil fails to influence us to react in self-love, frustration, or worry toward people, circumstances, or pursuing pressure, then he will work on others whom he can get to react fleshly toward us. His goal is to get them to influence us away from the influence of the Spirit. He will do this by swaying them to fall short of our expectations. In other words, the more we do for others, the more they may knowingly or unknowingly let us down.

So, what good does it do for us to respond properly to the needs of the needy, to express joy in difficult circumstances, and to rest in absolute peace in the face of pursuing oppression only to react in a fleshly manner toward those we are trying to help? It makes no sense! Can it be true that the more we allow proper responses to flow through us from the Holy Spirit, the higher our expectations are of those people? The more godly we respond, the more godly we expect others to respond? After all, if we can yield to the Spirit's leading, is it asking too much to demand the same of those who are benefiting from our godly responses to their needs? In a word, yes.

Pastors are in a position to experience this probably more than anyone else. I have heard countless pastors tell how they have helped the hurting in their church. They have done everything they can. They have poured out their hearts in their preaching, in one-on-one counseling, in offering encouragement, and even in providing for personal needs, only to have these same people let them down by leaving without so much as a thank you. Too often they exit the church hurling insults and spewing critical statements, all the while trying to take others with them.

Why does this happen? Well, I believe it is a part of the spiritual warfare that we all face. You see, the devil knows that the best witness is one that is willing to lift up Christ. When Jesus is lifted up, He draws all men unto Himself (John 12:32). When we respond in Christ, under the influence of the Holy Spirit, we bring great glory to God; we make Him look good. This allows the inner man to shine through us unto others. Being an effective witness for our Savior is a great detriment to the devil's kingdom of darkness. Remember, his goal is to keep the gospel hidden from the lost. Second Corinthians 4:3-10 explains how the light shines and how the devil seeks to hide it.

But if our gospel be hid, it is hid to them that are lost: In whom the god of this world hath blinded the minds of them which believe not, lest the light of the glorious gospel of Christ, who is the image of God, should shine unto them... For God, who commanded the light to shine out of darkness, hath shined in our hearts, to give the light of the knowledge of the glory of God in the face of Jesus Christ. But we have this treasure in earthen vessels, that the excellency of the power may be of God, and not of us. We are troubled on every side, yet not distressed; we are perplexed, but not in despair; Persecuted, but not forsaken; cast down, but not destroyed; Always bearing about in the body the dying of the Lord Jesus, that the life also of Jesus might be made manifest in our body.

The devil hides the truth from the lost by blinding their hearts so they cannot see the image of God shining unto them. Anytime people are able to recognize the image of God, it is good news for them. That is why God has created us in His image, so others will see His image in us and thus the gospel shines into the darkness. God helps those who see His light in us to realize His power is in us. Certainly, Christians will go through all kinds of attacks, troubles, disappointments, and persecution, but we can respond to all of this adversity by suffering (for a long time, if necessary) without expressing our disappointment. Our godly response of longsuffering will cause (vs. 10) the light of Christ within us to be made evident to others.

The only way to let our light shine in a dark place is for things to happen to us that will bring attention to the image of Christ within us. Such things may cause us to want to react with fleshly selfishness, frustration, or worry. But if we do, the light of Christ will never shine through. He cannot shine through us unless we allow those circumstances to wound the outer man and let the inner man display the image of God. By rejecting the influence of the Spirit to respond properly, we place a bushel over our candle (Luke 11:33).

Many people believe "putting a candle under a bushel" refers to not being willing to tell people about Christ. That is partly true, but we hide our candle under the bushel of the outer man far more often than by not witnessing. We do so by reacting improperly to difficult circumstances. It is usually our inconsistency in yielding to the Spirit that actually leaves us embarrassed or unwilling to share our faith.

The truth is that there is no other fruit that leads more people to Christ than yielding to the fruit of longsuffering when faced with disappointment in others.

As a matter of fact, God's longsuffering toward us was probably a driving force behind our own salvation. His light shone in such a way that we changed our minds from unbelief to belief in Jesus Christ.

> *And thinkest thou this, O man, that judgest them which do such things, and doest the same, that thou shalt escape the judgment of*

God? Or despisest thou the riches of his goodness and forbearance and longsuffering; not knowing that the goodness of God leadeth thee to repentance? (Romans 2:3-4)

These verses remind us how easy it is to condemn those who fall short of our expectations. And not only do we judge the weaknesses of others, but we often are guilty of the same shortcomings. By judging them, we show a disrespect for the wealth of goodness, forbearance, and longsuffering of God. We overlook the fact that God's proper responses to our own shortcomings is what led us to repentance.

In other words, God expresses a calm attitude toward our shortcomings for long periods of time, and we experience great benefits from that longsuffering attitude. However, we often turn around and judge those who come short of our expectations of them. God tells us that this type of behavior is "inexcusable" (Romans 2:1) and that as a result of our judgmental attitude, we shall not escape God's judgment.

God's longsuffering toward us ought to motivate us to be more willing to respond properly to the shortcomings of others. Satan knows if he can get us to react with a fleshly alternative to longsuffering, less people will repent. The less we respond properly, the less His light will shine from our hearts. If the devil cannot get us to let God down in the face of adversity, then he will get others to let us down in disappointing ways. That is when it is most critical that we respond under the influence of the Spirit to the fruit of longsuffering. To battle against this fruit, the devil has what he considers a more self-satisfying alternative. It is a reactionary work of the flesh, fulfilling the soul's desire to be quick-tempered.

4b. WE OFTEN PREFER THE WORK OF THE FLESH~QUICK-TEMPERED.

Temper refers to the seat of our passions and desires. It is similar to the word temperament. *Temper* is "a combination of passions that produces a level of irritability or contentment." Quick-tempered, then, would indicate that it takes very little or a short amount of irritability to excite our passions in a negative way. Often, a quick temper will be the biggest reason for our unwillingness to share the gospel with others.

As I mentioned, longsuffering is a fruit to which I am just now learning to yield. I have resisted this fruit and had no idea how it hindered God's work in my life. I never realized how gun-shy I was becoming to do things God had called me to do. This fear to serve as God was leading was a direct result of the shame of reacting to people with a short temper.

Before I came back to Christ in 1993, I was an incredibly unproductive disappointment to many people who had invested in me. My parents, after ten years of sacrificing for my Christian education, watched with sadness as I went out into the world and rejected a Spirit-led lifestyle. Yet, they always responded in a loving, longsuffering way. My employers, seeing great potential in me, over and over again invested in training and preparing me for positions of influence within their organization. Despite their efforts, I never met my potential. To me, their longsuffering spirit toward my shortcomings was nothing more than a form of flattery that led me to take more advantage of them. Eventually, I had a résumé so poor that it left me basically unemployable. Having rejected my Christian upbringing, I set out for a self-satisfying lifestyle that led to drugs, alcohol, and other crippling addictive sinful habits.

Through it all, I received longsuffering responses from God. My list of grievances against my parents, preachers, teachers, employers, and the government was so long that it would be a ridiculous ritual to try to remember them all. Despite it all and the more I transgressed, it seemed the longer that people would suffer for my benefit. Then came that fateful day when God allowed a near-fatal auto "accident" to open my eyes to the impending judgment of God.

> **Quick-Tempered** is irritability that negatively excites our passions.

As I lay in that hospital bed reading the gospel of John, I came to realize that my shortcomings were costing many people a great deal. I changed my mind, repenting of the way I had perceived the benefits of the many longsuffering responses of those who tried to help me. I began to realize that if I continued to take advantage of the kind gestures of others, God was going to bring my life to an end. He began to work in my heart to establish a healthy fear of the Lord and a genuine spirit of gratitude toward those who were trying to help me.

When I got out of the hospital, my life began to change quickly as a direct result of my repentance and new attitude. I became very productive in my new job, I began to grow in my spiritual life, and in my service to God at church. From that point forward, it just seemed like everything I did went well. It was a very exciting and enjoyable time in my life as I was gaining favor with God and He was giving me favor with man. I went from being one of the most unproductive Christians alive to now being a very productive Christian and full-time servant in the ministry of Reformers Unanimous.

Nevertheless, up until recently I have had one quality about me that nearly everyone who has ever worked under, with, or over me is aware of—the work of the flesh~Quick Tempered. It was incredibly embarrassing when I came to this realization. It took a lot of bad circumstances in my life to finally break this stubborn lust of my soul to react in a quick-tempered, irritated way to others.

Here is how it happened in my life. Maybe my struggle will open your eyes to a similar situation in your life. I had spent nearly all my life being unproductive and disappointing nearly everyone in authority over me. When I gave my life back to God, He began to bless me. Seeing the results of my productivity, I increased my expectations of myself, not realizing that the productivity I was experiencing was not a result of me, but of God *in* me. As I raised my expectations of myself, I also raised my expectations of others.

Shamefully, I was not willing to do for others what God had done for me for so long. I became obsessed with attaining spiritual productivity that no one was able to produce at a level that brought me satisfaction.

I expected a level of perfection from my wife and the mother of our children that I was unable to meet myself as a husband and a father. My staff, though working countless hours, was often reprimanded for being unable to get their jobs done or to do them at a standard that I would accept. I became overbearing. I placed heavy and unscriptural burdens on my family, my staff, and our volunteers. These were all fleshly reactions to what I perceived to be the shortcomings of others. Though I had never experienced this fleshly alternative from others when I was failing in every area of my life, I took up this evil temperament of being quick-tempered with those who, I thought, were letting me down. What a sad commentary on a Christian leader!

I did not realize my error for the first three years of my Christian ministry. It wasn't until God led me to write and teach messages on anger that I began to realize I had a very serious problem. I would write the message and study the message, but I could not preach the message. I knew beyond a shadow of a doubt that I would be a hypocrite. I was working hard and so were my staff, but I was disappointed. It brought great discouragement, but I didn't realize the problem until I found myself unable to teach on subjects that God was obviously leading me to teach.

I came to see that I was not expressing a proper temperament toward others. I was putting expectations on them that God was neither putting on them nor on myself. I came to understand that despite the fact that I was quick-tempered with everyone else, God was still being longsuffering toward me. His goodness in response to my badness was very convicting and it led me to repentance.

Believe it or not, this lesson came to me just a few, short months ago. I have now, to the glory of God, done a 180-degree turnaround in this area. I am not out of the woods when it comes to my fleshly desire to react with my quick temper, but I must say God has given me a great grace to realize my flaw. It wasn't when people quit over the pressure, which people have. It wasn't because people distanced themselves from me, which they did. It wasn't because students felt like under achievers, because I am sure they did, and we probably lost some of them because of it. It was when I realized that as a result of my fleshly reactions to people's shortcomings, I had hindered God's ability to speak through

> The discretion of a man deferreth his anger, and it is his glory to pass over a transgression.
> —Proverbs 19:11

me on certain subjects. My light was shining less and less. In my zeal to be productive, I became less productive with others.

How about you? Do you have a quick temper with the shortcomings of others? If so, it will hinder God's work through you. The devil knows this. If he cannot hinder your productivity by getting you to be selfish, frustrated, or worried, then he will try to lead you to be proud of your God-given productivity. And nothing interferes with the productivity of God like the pride of man.

If you struggle with the work of the flesh~Quick-Tempered, I encourage you to memorize and meditate on Proverbs 19:11. *The discretion* (or, proper judgment*) of a man deferreth* (or, delays) *his anger; and it is his glory to pass over* (or, overlook) *a transgression* (or, violation).

If we will use proper judgment, then we can delay our anger with those who let us down. By delaying our anger, we can eventually overlook their violation altogether. Our willingness to let these violations go will make us look good and will in turn make God look good. By yielding to the Spirit, we will always be willing to suffer for a long time with the shortcomings of others. The inner man will flow through, and God will look good as He lives through us.

5a. GOD OFFERS THE FRUIT OF THE SPIRIT~GENTLENESS.

The Bible indicates that *gentleness* means "softness in manners." *Softness,* when coupled with *manners,* means "mildness." Our manners are the way in which we act in relation to our duties of life, behavior, demeanor, conduct, and management. In other words, gentleness means being mild mannered.

Do you know people who are mild mannered, whose manners are soft and genteel? Of course, we are not talking about having good manners at the dinner table, though that is important. We are talking about a manner of mildness as we face our day-to-day responsibilities. *Mild* means "tender." Thus, a person who is under the influence of the Spirit will act and respond in a tender and mannerly way.

There are people in my life who excel in yielding to a particular fruit. When I think of the fruit of the Spirit~Gentleness, I am reminded of my pastor, Dr. Paul Kingsbury. He is the most gentle man I have ever met. He is mild in every area of his life. Dr. Kingsbury is the father of twelve children. He is the pastor of a church of about a thousand members, the board chairman of RUI, a husband, and a Christian. He seems to be the busiest man I have ever met. Yet, despite that busy-ness, he is always joyful, kind, considerate, patient, and willing to listen to anyone who approaches him with a problem.

Recently, I was out of town when I received a call from his daughter Joy, who works for our ministry. She informed me that Joey, her brother, had just been diagnosed with leukemia. This young man had graduated from high school only one month earlier. Joy told me that Pastor Kingsbury was out of town and would be unable to get back for five days.

When he returned home, he was faced with even more tragedy. One of his deacons, a pillar of our church for thirty years, had been diagnosed with cancer and was given four weeks to live. The following day, a married couple from our church was involved in a motorcycle accident, resulting in the death of the wife—a shocking event that rocked our church family! When I arrived home and attended the following Wednesday night's service, most of the congregation were hearing about all three of these situations for the very first time. Oh, how oppressed I felt that evening! But, as I watched our pastor as he led the service in testimonies and prayer, I was amazed at his gentle manner. I watched him listen intently to so many prayer requests that paled in comparison to the heartaches he was facing. He preached with a soft spirit and with all his heart.

Afterwards, I stood in line in the auditorium to speak with him. As I waited while he talked with the final three people ahead of me, I heard what each of them were talking to him about. I observed as these people brought their seemingly petty problems to him and appeared to have no regard for the burdens he was carrying on this particular day. Yet the whole time, he looked them in the eye. He listened and smiled, committing to help and taking notes of things he needed to do to help these members of his flock who were piling more personal problems onto his current load.

When he approached me, he smiled even more broadly. Before I could offer my condolences for the sorrowful circumstances, he rushed up to me, gave me a hug, and told me he had missed me. He then quickly asked me to give him a quick update on all our ministry's problems! Wow, talk about big shoulders! That is a true man of God. How does he do it? Well, he doesn't; God does. When confronted with adversity, he is able to face his responsibilities and conduct himself in a tenderly mannered

> **Gentleness** is softness in manners.

way. That is God acting and responding to the circumstances of life. That's the fruit of the Spirit~Gentleness.

I have asked my pastor how he is able to be so mild mannered toward people. He told me that his ability to respond to his day-to-day duties under the influence of the fruit gentleness is a result of his decision to forgive people for their insensitivities.

I have, as a result of his example, learned this lesson, as well. You see, I must admit I at times do struggle with these three fruits that deal with conformity of the outer man: longsuffering, gentleness, and goodness. A few years ago, I took steps of action to offset my struggle to yield to the fruit of the Spirit~Gentleness. Not that I have attained, but I have learned a lot about God's ability to handle my problems and my discouragements.

Some time ago, I started to become abrasive when dealing with my responsibilities of counseling fallen students. I place much effort into each of my students and love them dearly. I struggle when I see them fall, and when they do, I want to help them. However, with some it seems that after they fall, they want to talk about their problems and do nothing about them. I am very careful not to allow my time to be abused by those who are not serious about recovery. I had a few students that were beginning to fall somewhat regularly. I had placed a great deal of time into counseling and teaching them. Over and over again, they would call asking, "Wondered if you have a few minutes?" "Of course I do," was always my reply. When they would arrive, they would give me the news. We would cry, talk, cry, and pray. I would encourage them. It seemed to do no good. Over and over again, they would fall and call. This went on for about five months.

I got to the point that I was anything but gentle in my daily duties. I would come to work discouraged. I would look at my schedule only to see the same names over and over again. To top it off, after some students would fall away and stop asking for help, their slots on my schedule would be replaced by newer students that had been doing well but now were not. Oh, the frustration that I felt! It showed in my mannerisms. My secretary would tell me an appointment had arrived and I would just roll my eyes and think, "Here we go again." I was critical and negative to the repeating offenders. I was harsh and unkind to those that would not follow my counsel quickly and correctly. I was not pleasant to work with and I was not pleasant to counsel with. I did not want a ministry that was steeped in daily devotions of defeat. I wanted our students to only experience a victory that was sustainable and enjoyable. I didn't want the problems that my students were bringing me.

Here is when I realized that I had a problem: I was counseling a woman who was bitter at her husband for his continual defeat in his road to recovery. She was mean to him and often unrelenting in her personal criticism of him. I took her to the book of Ephesians to show her how she needed to respond to her husband's failures. While doing so, I realized what was causing me to yield to the fleshly alternative to gentleness. I was struck with conviction and had to excuse myself from our meeting. I asked the Lord to give me the strength to do what these verses say to do. The Bible says to forgive anybody who hurts me, in any way, no matter what they do or how often they do it.

My friend, that is the key ingredient that will release you from the fleshly alternative to gentleness and will allow you to respond in a mild mannered, tender, and gentle way to your day, your duties, and your disappointments.

What was the passage that did this for me? It was Ephesians 4:31-32. *Let all bitterness, and wrath, and anger, and clamour, and evil speaking, be put away from you, with all malice: And be ye kind one to another, tenderhearted, forgiving one another, even as God for Christ's sake hath forgiven you.*

In a previous chapter, I explained the meaning of these verses. However, in review, I would like to look at them again. I think it is important to fully understand how the application of this exhortation can totally change the way we look at our daily duties and our daily disappointments. You see, it is not a sin to be disappointed. It is a sin to allow disappointment to cause you to yield to a lust of the flesh. Let's take a look at the dissected and defined version of these verses on forgiveness.

bitterness: compressed feelings
wrath:feelings of getting even
anger: passions of the mind
clamour: argumentativeness
evil speaking: gossiping
malice: desire for physical injury
kind to one another: outward demonstration of gentleness
tenderhearted to one another: inward demonstration of gentleness
forgiving one another: upward demonstration of gentleness

These verses teach us about actions and reactions that are not mild mannered. In fact, they are just the opposite. These actions and reactions to others or occupations are actually the actions and reactions of the work of the flesh~Harshness!

5b.   WE OFTEN PREFER THE WORK OF THE FLESH~HARSHNESS.

Ephesians 4:31-32 explains how most people react to those who they feel are violating them. It is the antithesis of the fruit of the Spirit~Gentleness. If we fight back, tell others off, argue, get violently passionate, attempt revenge, or even suppress our feelings and do nothing about them, then we are not yielding to the fruit of the Spirit~Gentleness. We are exercising the work of the flesh~Harshness. The dictionary defines *harshness* as "roughness in manner, temper, or words." The desire to do these things can cause us to dislike everybody and everything in our relationships and responsibilities. If we act on these desires, then it will cause others to hate everything about us. Harsh personalities are not enjoyed; they are destroyed. They either self-destruct or are avoided by others and held back from promotion.

David said in Psalm 18:35, *Thou hast also given me the shield of thy salvation: and thy right hand hath holden me up, and thy gentleness hath made me great.* The fruit of the Spirit~Gentleness will lead people to consider you a great person. Harsh people are never considered great guys or great gals.

God wants us to respond in a gentle way when faced with tough decisions. Especially when those decisions are caused by the failure of another. Under His leading, we will always respond gently, never harshly. In James 3:17, we see that when God gives us wisdom in direction, it comes with some uniquely tender responses. *But the wisdom that is from above is first pure, then peaceable, <u>gentle</u>, and easy to be entreated, full of mercy and good fruits, without partiality, and without hypocrisy.*

That's a far cry from my actual reactions to the people who were falling and calling. Was it because I wasn't asking God for help in responding properly? No, my harshness was a direct result of being offended. I was offended that I had worked so hard to help them and yet they were letting me down. I was taking their failures personally and it was destroying my moods and my manners.

That reminds me of another passage I once studied. It is found in 2 Timothy 2:24-26. It reads, *And the servant of the Lord must not strive; but be <u>gentle</u> unto all men, apt to teach, patient, In meekness instructing those that oppose themselves; if God peradventure will give them repentance to the acknowledging of the truth; And that they may recover themselves out of the snare of the devil, who are taken captive by him at his will.*

Strive means "to put forth great effort." The Bible is telling us that we should not have to work hard, but rather we need to be apt or willing to teach in a gentle, patient fashion. Surely, to teach in such a genteel fashion without having to work hard, it must be referring to working with people who are easy to work with—people who don't require hard work because they respond well to our gentle and patient teaching. Nope! The next verse says that we need to be willing to teach ...*those that oppose themselves*, meaning those that do great harm to themselves or those who seem to not care if they follow our teaching or not. Also, those who need to repent to the truth that we are giving them but often refuse. Such people are snared by the devil and in captivity to him.

> **Harshness** is roughness in manner, temper, or words.

Now, I don't know about you, but that seems impossible to me. It would seem these are the people that would need the *most* effort, the *most* striving. Yet they are not. If we are willing to teach them in a patient and gentle fashion, then we won't have to work hard to keep them. We might even lead them to the position of repentance that will bring them out of captivity!

So, how do we do this? How do we stop trying so hard and instead simply yield to the fruit of the Spirit~Gentleness? By forgiving people in the manner that Paul teaches in Ephesians 4:32. To do this, we must follow his directions. It begins in reverse order of the list. If we start with bitterness, we may never forgive; but if we start with forgiveness, we will never be bitter.

To show an outward demonstration of gentleness, to be kind to one another, we must begin by forgiving the alleged perpetrator. We will never be kind to others until we forgive them. God knows our hearts. If we don't ask Him to give us the grace to forgive them, then we will never receive the benefit of a forgiving heart. That benefit is the second step to responding in a gentle fashion. It will lead us to be tender hearted. If we will forgive them, then we will experience the tender heart we need to continue to the third and final step to responding in a gentle fashion: being kind one to another. That's right. If we forgive others, God will give us tender hearts; and a tender and forgiving heart will be kind to others.

Let me remind you of Titus 3:1-2. *Put them in mind* (remind them) *to be subject to principalities and powers, to obey magistrates, to be ready to every good work, To speak evil of no man, to be no brawlers, but* <u>*gentle*</u>*, shewing all meekness unto all men.*

6a.   GOD   OFFERS   THE   FRUIT   OF   THE SPIRIT~GOODNESS.

Some would say the fruit we just studied, gentleness, is identical to our next response of the inner man, the fruit of the Spirit~Goodness. They would be wrong. Though each fruit does have similarities, they are each different responses to different circumstances of life.

Gentleness is a response from God, but goodness, like love, is an action by God! The Bible indicates that *goodness* is "conforming our lives and conversations to behave benevolently toward others." Goodness is when we allow a conformation (or, a pouring into a mold) to take place in our lives. The mold that we are being conformed into is one that produces benevolent behavior, both in word and deed. Let's see how that manifests itself in human behavior.

A synonym for goodness is benevolence. According to Webster's 1868 Dictionary, *benevolent* means "having a disposition to do good; possessing love to mankind, and a desire to promote their prosperity and happiness."

Benevolence is a quality of one who is seeking to promote prosperity and happiness in others. That's really the world's definition of a "good" person. For Christians, it's a person who yields to the fruit of the Spirit~Goodness. Spirit-led Christians are molded to act and talk in such a way that they promote happiness and prosperity toward everyone. The Bible is full of examples of God's goodness. Let's take a look:

- *Oh how great is thy goodness, which thou hast laid up for them that fear thee; which thou hast wrought for them that trust in thee before the sons of men!* (Psalm 31:19)

- *Oh that men would praise the LORD for his goodness, and for his wonderful works to the children of men! For he satisfieth the longing soul, and filleth the hungry soul with goodness.* (Psalm 107:8-9)

- *And Jethro rejoiced for all the goodness which the LORD had done to Israel, whom he had delivered out of the hand of the Egyptians.* (Exodus 18:9)

- *And on the three and twentieth day of the seventh month he sent the people away into their tents, glad and merry in heart for the goodness that the LORD had shewed unto David, and to Solomon, and to Israel his people.* (2 Chronicles 7:10)

There are so many other verses, both in the Old and New Testaments, that speak of God's unending and undeserved goodness. Do you see how closely related goodness is to the inner man transforming fruit of love? Goodness is actually an outer demonstration of the inner yielding to the fruit of love.

I think one of the best passages that speaks of God's goodness to us is found in Psalm 23.

The LORD is my shepherd; I shall not want. He maketh me to lie down in green pastures: he leadeth me beside the still waters. He restoreth my soul: he leadeth me in the paths of righteousness for his name's sake. Yea, though I walk through the valley of the shadow of death, I will fear no evil: for thou art with me; thy rod and thy staff they comfort me. Thou preparest a table before me in the presence of mine enemies: thou anointest my head with oil; my cup runneth over. Surely goodness and mercy shall follow me all the days of my life: and I will dwell in the house of the LORD for ever.

Notice David's closing statement. He indirectly points out that this goodness is undeserved. Remember, mercy is not getting what we deserve. So, David is saying that he doesn't deserve the goodness that he is getting. He is getting it because God is not giving him what he really deserves. I believe mercy is the primary catalyst for yielding to the fruit of the Spirit~Goodness. Goodness is allied when mercy is applied. It is God's mercy that leads Him to promote happiness and prosperity in our lives despite our failures and frustrations. God's mercy leads Him to be benevolent. Our willingness to yield to the inner man's desire to show love will cause the outer man to conform in behavior to be benevolent. A heart of love produces an action of goodness.

> **Goodness** is conforming our lives and conversations to behave benevolently toward others.

This is what will help people to change their minds about the way they act. When they see goodness demonstrated by others toward them, it leads them to repentance. (Romans 2:4 *the goodness of God leadeth thee to repentance.*)

This fruit is incredibly evangelistic. Unfortunately, many of us struggle to yield to this fruit. I believe the reason is because of our unwillingness to offer to others the response of mercy. We often prefer judgment over mercy. God never gives us permission to judge anyone but ourselves! Judgment is reserved for God, not us. We are encouraged throughout Scripture to demonstrate mercy. We are even told to offer grace, giving to people what they don't deserve.

God's command to demonstrate mercy and grace are seemingly tough demands when responding to those who have done us wrong. But consider: If we are unforgiving, God will be unforgiving; if we do not show mercy, God will not show mercy to us; if we are not willing to give grace to others, God will withhold His grace from us.

One reason we prefer to judge others rather than show mercy is to justify indulging in a fleshly alternative. An obvious alternative to the fruit of the Spirit~Goodness is the work of the flesh~Meanness.

6b. WE OFTEN PREFER THE WORK OF THE FLESH~MEANNESS.

The definition of mean is often assumed to be synonymous with angry, hateful, or vengeful. While those could be attributes of someone who is mean-spirited, that is not the type of meanness I mean.

You have probably heard the phrase, "a man of many means," or, just the opposite, "a man of no means." *Meanness* is the antithesis of the fruit of the Spirit~Goodness. It is defined as "refusing to be liberal with charity, thus avoiding any personal expense." These two contrasting types of behavior—being benevolent and being stingy—are often assumed to either refer to the giving or hoarding of money. Of course, in a society that is so obsessed with acquiring money, it is understandable if we only think of benevolence and charity as the giving of financial resources. Yet, there is so much more to benevolence than simply giving away money.

For God's work to be done through men, He needs us to demonstrate goodness with our money, time, energies, gifts, and talents, even in our actions and responses to the mistakes of others. God's work is hindered when we act or react to the failures of others refusing to share God's many resources that we have at our disposal. How can we advance the kingdom of God when we focus on the acquisition of and the refusal to expend any valued resource for the sake of the "kingdom of me"?

In Jesus' Sermon on the Mount, He laid out what God thinks about choosing covetousness over benevolence.

(Take the time to read the whole passage so that our dissecting and defining will be fully understood.)

> *Lay not up for yourselves treasures upon earth, where moth and rust doth corrupt, and where thieves break through and steal: But lay up for yourselves treasures in heaven, where neither moth nor rust doth corrupt, and where thieves do not break through nor steal: For where your treasure is, there will your heart be also. No man can serve two masters: for either he will hate the one, and love the other; or else he will hold to the one, and despise the other. Ye cannot serve God and mammon. Therefore I say unto you, Take no thought for your life, what ye shall eat, or what ye shall drink; nor yet for your body, what ye shall put on. Is not the life more than meat, and the body than raiment? Behold the fowls of the air: for they sow not, neither do they reap, nor gather into barns; yet your heavenly Father feedeth them. Are ye not much better than they? Which of you by taking thought can add one cubit unto his stature? And why take ye thought for raiment? Consider the lilies of the field, how they grow; they toil not, neither do they spin: And yet I say unto you, That even Solomon in all his glory was not arrayed like one of these. Wherefore, if God so clothe the grass of the field, which to day is, and to morrow is cast into the oven, shall he not much more clothe you, O ye of little faith? Therefore take no thought, saying, What shall we eat? or, What shall we drink? or, Wherewithal shall we be clothed? (For after all these things do the Gentiles seek:) for your heavenly Father knoweth that ye have need of all these things. But seek ye first the kingdom of God, and his righteousness; and all these things shall be added unto you.*
>
> —Matthew 6:19-21, 24-33

Jesus tells us that we should not focus on the acquisition of temporary things that will be of no value to us when we die. Instead, we should lay up treasures in heaven. The word *treasure* is "a great quantity of anything that is collected for future use." This is the proper focus of life. But Jesus goes even further in telling that we should not worry about accumulating resources for day-to-day living! In our advanced society, that may seem like no big deal, but in those days, that was the central focus of life!

As I write this, I have spent the last seven days in a third world country. In that time, I have observed the townspeople as they struggle to survive. My wife and I gained a friendship with a lady who braids the hair of travelers who come to her village. As she spoke to us in broken English, she told of how she begins her days at 8:00 AM and finishes at 11:30 PM, seven days a week. Over a hundred hours a week! As she was braiding the hair of a young middle-eastern girl and nearing her 11:30 quitting time, her husband walked up to her stand and began placing beads on the little girl's hair to help his wife. He had been at work in the port since 6:00 that morning!

Meanness is refusing to be liberal with charity, thus avoiding any personal expense.

I could not believe that they worked so hard and so long for so little! She told me that they do this to put food on the table for their three pre-teen girls. I was astonished that it took that much effort to provide the basic necessities of food, clothing, and shelter in this impoverished country. Not to acquire more stuff, but to provide week-to-week. Because she can work year-round, she did not need to store up provisions for her family during the winter months. Thus, she and her husband work with a focus only on meeting the basic needs of their family day by day, week by week.

In Jesus' day, there was not a Wal-Mart® on every street corner. There was no government aid, no unemployment insurance, no welfare, no return-to-work programs. So, when He told these people to not focus on necessary resources, He seemed to be telling them to abandon their existence! Actually, He was not teaching them to *forsake* the provision of their daily needs, but rather to get their focus off of that and onto the kingdom of God. As we do, God will provide our every need in abundance.

However, it is not enough to merely focus on the kingdom of God. There is another step to having our needs met while here on earth. Jesus says that we must also seek His righteousness. Now what does this mean? Remember, when we do good under the influence of the Spirit, then we are involved in righteousness. Therefore, doing good under the influence of His Spirit is seeking His righteousness. In other words, to gain God's provision, we must experience justification and sanctification. No change in His philosophy here. God's desire is for people to accept Christ's sacrifice and then allow Him to lead them to reach others. Over and over again, Scripture confirms this as God's plan for us. To this end, He offers us the fruit of the Spirit~Goodness.

Naturally, the devil tries to suppress this fruit of goodness by frustrating us into focusing on meeting our own needs, thus bumping God out of the equation. If we can meet our own needs, then we will not learn to depend on God.

Just as God's tool of mercy is what creates a desire for Spirit-led believers to respond with a Spirit of goodness to the needy, the devil's tool of meanness is to get flesh-led believers to react to them with judgment. When God would have us give the merciful response of goodness, the devil would have us give the judgmental reaction of meanness.

The primary ministry of Reformers Unanimous

International is to impact the lives of the addicted with the Gospel. Of course, as with any ministry, this type of outreach requires benevolence on the part of God's people. To see the lives of the addicted rebuilt, I must do as Nehemiah did when he wanted to rebuild the walls of Jerusalem. I must ask God to meet our every need financially, and then I must petition those whom God has given kingdom wealth to loosen their purse strings. I must request benevolence on the part of God's people.

I enjoy doing this because I get to minister to both the givers and receivers of the benevolence. It is a great privilege because there are often great needs on both sides of a gift. However, sometimes I come across people who are obviously in a position to give, yet their reactions to my requests show the undisguised Work of the Flesh~Meanness. Let me explain why I believe this happens so often.

I have always been told that working with addicted adults is an incredibly hard ministry to raise benevolence for. I am also told that if I would run a ministry for battered women or underprivileged children, then I would have no problem raising money; no one could justify meanness to such victims. But since I minister mainly to grown adults with self-inflicted problems, many potential givers can justify their meanness (that is, avoiding personal expense by supplanting charity with judgment). They judge the needy to be unworthy of their merciful benevolence. That is not a right response. It is a sinful reaction. Spirit-led believers should respond in one of two ways: By not giving because God leads not to give (and since He may not give a reason, neither should that person be required to give a reason); or, by giving as much as God leads to give, thus yielding to the fruit of the Spirit~Goodness. By obeying, givers show mercy while laying up treasures in heaven.

I don't know about you, but I don't want my treasures consumed by moths and rust and thieves. But distributing benevolence with a heart of mercy to the undeserved, I know I will receive that same mercy back from God, both here and in His kingdom to come. As a child of God you have the fruit of the Spirit~Goodness available to you. I would strongly encourage you to use it to benefit others. Let it be said of us even as Paul said of the church in Rome, *And I myself also am persuaded of you, my brethren, that ye also are full of goodness, filled with all knowledge, able also to admonish one another* (Romans 15:14).

7a. GOD OFFERS THE FRUIT OF THE SPIRIT~FAITH.

Our final three fruits of the Spirit deal with what I call "new-being reformation." It should be evident by these final three fruits being observed and yielded to in our lives that we are indeed "new creatures" in Christ (2 Corinthians 5:17).

Faith has been dissected, defined, and diagramed so many times in our textbook that I find it very difficult to write anything about faith that you may not already fully understand. So, we will only cover a few other aspects of faith that may shed more light on this ever-important fruit. You see, justification from the penalty of sin and sanctification from the power of sin are both experienced by faith. Without it we cannot please God. We have studied faith more than any other topic because it is what allows believers to live freely in a bound world. Every victory in the Christian life is experienced because of the fruit of the Spirit~Faith. By contrast, every defeat in the Christian life is experienced because of the work of the flesh~Doubt.

We have defined *faith* as "a personal measurement of the level of confidence in what Christ has done and will do in, through, and for us." All Christians have a personal

> **Faith** is a personal measurement of the level of confidence in what Christ has done and will do in, through, and for us.

measure of faith, and it should be evident in the life of a Spirit-led believer.

I want you to see that justification is dependent upon faith in information, but sanctification is dependent upon faith in a personal relationship. When Eve responded improperly to the outside influence of the possessed serpent, she did so because she doubted God's goodness to her. She thought God was holding something back and she wanted to know more information about God and being like God. Thus, she ate of the Tree of Knowledge and plunged mankind into utter darkness. Since then, man has set off on a journey to know more about doing good in his own power so he may be like God. Man has rejected a personal relationship for the acquisition of information. To this day, man assumes that knowledge is power, but it is not. Knowing God is power. In the garden, man knew God, but after the fall, man could no longer know God; he could only know *about* God.

To satisfy man's penchant for knowing how to be like God, he was given information in the form of laws, commands, statutes, and judgments. This was to take God's people out of the bondage of barbaric behavior and to civilize them. The purpose of each covenant God made with man was to picture the day when the acquisition of information would become secondary to the development of a personal relationship with Him.

That day came after Christ died and rose again. Since then,

man can by faith accept Christ's atonement as payment for his sin, experiencing justification—freedom from the penalty of sin. Believers are new creatures who, though dead, can live in Christ, by faith. Our key verse for this entire book shows us that truth. *I am crucified with Christ: nevertheless I live; yet not I, but Christ liveth in me: and the life which I now live in the flesh I live by the faith of the Son of God, who loved me, and gave himself for me* (Galatians 2:20).

To live this life dead to self and alive in Christ, we must live it by faith. Yielding daily to faith will allow God to work in our lives. This makes us uncomfortable and God's power comes upon us to make us comfortable when we respond in faith—hence the term, Comforter.

However, we often run from the leading of faith and cling to the fleshly alternative of doubt. This causes us to make decisions based on information rather than on our personal relationship with God.

7b. WE OFTEN PREFER THE WORK OF THE FLESH~DOUBT.

Too often, Christians actively doubt the many truths that we have examined throughout this book. Truths that have been proven with Scripture and examples of personal experience. Humanly speaking, doubt is easier to rationalize than faith is to internalize. The Bible indicates that *doubt* is "an attitude of unbelief, characterized by rebellion and disobedience toward God." In other words, by choosing the work of the flesh~Doubt in a given situation, we declare God to be a liar and presume to take control ourselves. You see, the soul can be very convincing, and it always desires to be in control. The soul would rather reject the boundaries of authority and choose instead to indulge in what the flesh thinks, wants or feels. To this end, when we choose to doubt and reject taking the next step of faith led by God, it's because we are yielding to one of the three aspects of the soul.

Some fail to live by faith because they are mind driven. They doubt things because of intellectual reasons. They are thinkers. There are churches that are focused too much on knowing *about* God because they are led by fleshly pastors who are driven by their minds. There are even whole denominations that are intellectually driven.

Another reason some fail to live by faith is because they are emotionally driven. They doubt what they know to be truth because of emotion created by doubt, and the rejection of faith is more pleasing and acceptable to their flesh. There are churches that are focused way too much on emotionalism because they are led by fleshly pastors who are driven by their emotions. There are even whole denominations that are emotionally driven.

The third reason some fail to walk by faith is because they are driven by the desires of their wills. They doubt certain truths because faith may

> **Doubt** is an attitude of unbelief, characterized by rebellion and disobedience toward God.

disqualify them from doing what they want or from doing something the way they want to do it. Their wills are their masters. There are churches that are led by fleshly pastors who are driven by their wills, placing a huge burden on God's laborers and refusing to allow change in any way. There are even whole denominations that are driven by strong-willed leadership.

This is the devil's design not only for God's people in general, but specifically for pastors and church leaders, as well. When God's pastors and our church leaders yield to the lust of the flesh~Doubt individually, their followers will do likewise. When a church is fleshly led, the members will struggle to yield to the fruit of the Spirit~Faith.

Here is the basic contrast between faith and doubt: When we yield to doubt, we are depending on desire, knowledge, and reasoning to make our decisions; when we yield to faith, we are depending on God through our personal relationship with Him to make our decisions.

This brings me to some final thoughts on the subject of faith. We often ask God to give us more faith. As believers, this is actually an unrealistic request. We have all the faith we need to live the victorious Christian life. The only way to experience the measure of faith that changes our behavior is not to ask God for more faith, but rather to ask God to help us *yield* to the measure of faith that we already have living within us.

In looking at the actions and responses of the Holy Spirit, do you consider any of them to be impossible for you to manifest in your life? Do you consider them to be such unlikely choices when faced with the realities of adversity that you reject even the truths themselves? Have you been focused on knowing *about* God rather than *knowing* God?

If you answered "yes" to any of these questions, you are being driven by your soul and trying to be like God in your own power. You are using the acquisition of information to justify the failure of your personal relationship. Reject your thoughts, desires, and feelings of doubt, and have faith in the God that took up residence in you. If you do, your faith will bring great power from God—not because you know more *about* Him, but because you *know* Him (Daniel 11:32 *the people that <u>do know their God</u> shall be strong, and* *do exploits.*).

Develop your personal relationship with God by yielding to the fruit of the Spirit~Faith. You will then be conforming to His image by allowing the Holy Spirit to do the transforming. However, if you focus your righteousness on the acquisition of information that yields to the work of the flesh~Doubt, then you will be conforming by performing. Performance is never God's design; conformance is. Man performs, God conforms. If you're performing for God, your willingness to yield to faith is weak. Ask God to conform you as you trust and obey, for, as the song goes, there's no other way to be happy in Jesus, but to trust and obey.

8a. GOD OFFERS THE FRUIT OF THE SPIRIT~MEEKNESS

Meekness is a fruit that is seldom noticed but usually appreciated when applied. Most people probably do not even recognize this fruit unless they were to realize the thought process of the person that is yielding to it. You see, meekness is a fruit that is applied when someone is trying to assist a person who is actually engaged in a work of the flesh. For most of us, meekness is a difficult fruit to yield to.

I have been told that when the translators were interpreting the Greek New Testament into the English language, they could not readily agree on a word that adequately defined the word *praotes*. At first, the closest they could come was the word *weakness*, but that was far from accurately capturing the essence of this Greek word. The true meaning relates to the practice of adding saliva to help someone get a grip on something. For example, if you were to grasp a baseball bat, you might spit into your hands to get a better grip on it. The word literally means "to add a lubricant in order to reduce friction."

So, how is this manifested in Christian character? The word *meekness* means "the ability for God's people to negotiate among others without causing friction." Where is *that* in our churches? When God's people respond to each other and to a lost world in the spirit of meekness, it is sure to produce a level of respect and curiosity.

As I mentioned earlier, when I struggle with yielding to a particular fruit, I try to find people who seem to be stronger in yielding to that fruit, someone who exhibits that fruit with apparent ease. I try to learn from them how they attained the grace and faith necessary to become so successful in yielding to that particular fruit.

> **Meekness** is the ability for God's people to negotiate among others without causing friction.

At a certain point in my secular career, I was promoted to the position of General Manager. It was the first time that I actually had the privilege of managing other people since my re-dedication. In this management position, I soon found out that meekness would be an excellent fruit to master! Unfortunately, yielding to this fruit was just one of life's mysteries to me. However, my employer Dan Arnold, who even now is one of my teachers and counselors, excels in exhibiting this fruit. He is simply the meekest man I have ever met.

Mr. Arnold knows the value of people. He knows they have many weaknesses and understands that each of them has particular strengths that offset their weaknesses. He realizes that if his people's strengths are to ever be a benefit to his organization, he will have to overlook some of those weaknesses. He will have to especially overlook weakness in the area of personality flaws. Most importantly, he realizes how important it is to get a person's co-workers to also overlook those weaknesses of character.

He once told me that there are three things working against the relationships of our people: their weaknesses, our weaknesses, and Satan, who seeks to get us to react to each other's weaknesses improperly. In other words, we have very little chance that people will just naturally get along. These relationships require a spiritual man to add a lubricant to reduce the friction. Dan realizes the value of helping people get along with one another for the sake of keeping the "working family" together. His organization is very much like a family, and he is truly loyal to his people. He does not want to see them leave the organization, especially over personality weaknesses that could be improved with time.

He once told me that the key to running a successful organization is to develop people daily. He has that slogan on a tab in his day planner, and he moves that tab forward every day. His goal is to always utilize people's strengths, but not stop there. He also works diligently to help them overcome their weaknesses.

However, his ways were not my ways. I did it quite differently. When I would see a weakness in someone, I would "share" it with them. I would give them flack for it and often "encourage" them to shape up in that area. I actually created more controversy than their weakness ever created. I caused a *lot* of friction with my leadership style. But I knew of no other.

So, I watched Mr. Arnold and I saw a different type of "people development" going on. I would observe him as he would discuss something with someone who was frustrated with another staff member. He would never criticize the weaker employee to the person who was complaining.

Actually, he would try to explain why that person may have acted the way he did and would encourage the complaining employee to be patient and to overlook the mistake.

Then, in a day or so, he would work with the person with the weakness, not deriding him or telling him how much trouble he was causing with the other staff member. Rather, he complimented him on his areas of strength. Dan would then give that person work assignments that were well thought out. They were tasks that would expose that employee's weakness to himself. Dan would be right there to encourage and advise as necessary. Not only that, he would also point out to the weaker employee the strengths of the person who had complained, as an encouragement to both employees.

This type of leadership produces a wonderful spirit of "people development" in the workplace. It took me years to even understand what was happening. Only recently was I able to even define it, much less apply it to my own "people development" skills.

Some would call Dan Arnold a "flat liner." Nothing gets him excited. He is neither emotionally up or down, no matter what type of people-failure he's facing.

Why is meekness so valuable in our professional lives (as well as in our relationships with God's people)? As Mr. Arnold pointed out, we have three things working against us: their weaknesses, our weaknesses, and Satan himself. Without our willingness to yield to the fruit of the Spirit~Meekness, we will never apply the lubricant necessary to get along with our co-workers or our co-laborers in Christ. Plus, the burden lies on us to get along with *all* people. How else will we be called upon during their times of great need? How else can we show them the love of God in the face of affliction? Let's take a look at the biblical role we have when faced with a weakness on the part of a fellow believer.

> *Brethren, if a man be overtaken in a fault, ye which are spiritual, restore such an one in the spirit of meekness; considering thyself, lest thou also be tempted. Bear ye one another's burdens, and so fulfil the law of Christ. For if a man think himself to be something, when he is nothing, he deceiveth himself.* —Galatians 6:1-3

This passage gives us the biblical precept for restoration of an erring Christian—to restore him to his former standing in fellowship with Christ using the spirit of meekness. When someone's personal weakness is made evident to us, we should begin a healing and repairing process. This does not mandate a public proclamation of that person's sin.

What Paul is telling us here is that when someone steps forward with a fault, we should restore that person in a way that doesn't cause friction! If we don't, then we ourselves may face similar situations that could cause us to be overtaken. Our fall will surely be met with the same discord that we applied to those who needed our spirit of meekness.

God's people should always be willing to encourage others in a way that reduces friction. That means we cannot just say what we feel like saying to those who have glaringly obvious personality flaws. Doing so would not be exhibiting the fruit of the Spirit~Meekness.

And if meekness means getting along with people without causing friction, then the opposite would be *not* getting along with people by *causing* friction. This is the work of the flesh~Discord.

8b. WE OFTEN PREFER THE WORK OF THE FLESH~DISCORD

As the leader of a ministry that produces adult converts, I have seen the damage done by the work of the flesh~Discord. It can bring great harm to a baby believer, and that is the devil's design. I have heard it said many times that the Christian army is the only one that shoots its own wounded. I don't want to believe that saying, but, as is often the case with such clichés, there is some truth to it.

Discord is one of the most damaging works of the flesh that we have studied. Webster's 1828 Dictionary defines *discord* as "any disagreement which produces angry passions, contest, disputes, litigation, or war." Discord may exist in any relationship. Problems have been in families since Cain and Abel. It is no wonder that they permeate our church families, as well.

Let's look at the words of James, one of the Bible's best educators on human behavior, to see what he says about the value of meekness and the dangers of discord. After giving several illustrations of what great damage can be done by the tongue, James offers this cure:

> *Who is a wise man and endued with knowledge among you? let him shew out of a good conversation his works with meekness of wisdom. But if ye have bitter envying and strife in your hearts, glory not, and lie not against the truth. This wisdom descendeth not from above, but is earthly, sensual, devilish. For where envying and strife is, there is confusion and every evil work. But the wisdom that is from above is first pure, then peaceable, gentle, and easy to be intreated, full of mercy and good fruits, without partiality, and without hypocrisy. And the fruit of righteousness is sown in peace of them that make peace.* (James 3:13-18)

It is the job of wise and knowledgeable teachers to teach others with meekness how to live right by example. The teacher, because he has the works to back up the words, can explain to believers that busybody conduct is not from God, but devilish and sensual (that is to say, it stimulates certain senses of our emotions). Without this type of leader in the church working with our tongue troubles, then we will experience confusion and evil work within the body of Christ. God doesn't create confusion, the devil does! Verse 17 explains the sweet spirit that God will send to permeate the church if the people will invest in opportunities to make peace whenever possible.

This type of leadership would yield wonderful results. Anything short of having a "tongue police" within our church would be of great value! However, I think a good way to apply this truth would be to have someone within the church train others. This teacher should be someone who has proven himself to be exceptional at yielding to the fruit of the Spirit~Meekness. The lessons would include how to develop faith, grace, and obedience in learning to yield to the fruit of meekness. It could save a lot of problems in our churches.

In my opinion, my home church, North Love Baptist Church in Rockford, IL, is one of the meekest churches in America. Yet, it was not always that way. God used our pastor to foster such an atmosphere because God knew He needed an environment at our church that was conducive for baby Christians to grow; for surely, God intended to send many of them our way.

> **Discord** is any disagreement which produces angry passions, contest, disputes, litigation, or war.

When Reformers Unanimous first began in 1996, I had a

student who, for the sake of her privacy, I will call "Joan." Joan attended class nearly every Friday for six months. She seldom missed. However, no matter how many times my wife and I invited her to church, she would kindly respond, "No, thanks." I knew she was not attending church anywhere else, so one day I asked why she would not even try to attend our church. She explained that she did not have a dress and she was waiting to save up enough money to buy one. Then she would attend. I explained to her that she did not have to wear a dress to attend our church; she could wear her nicest outfit and no one would say anything to her. She agreed that she could, but insisted that she wanted to have something special to wear the first time she went to church. Being impressed with her desire to give God her best, my wife and I offered to buy her a dress, but she refused. "God wants me to buy it myself!" Well, out of ammunition, I surrendered.

About six weeks later, Joan exclaimed to me with gladness that she had saved enough money to buy a dress. She would be at church the following Sunday. My wife and I were overjoyed. That Sunday, when Sunday school dismissed, Lori and I anxiously headed upstairs to meet Joan. When we got to the top of the stairs, we saw Joan hanging her coat up. As I turned the corner toward her, my heart sank. She had purchased a very short mini skirt. I sympathetically thought to myself, "She doesn't know any better." So, we told her we were so glad to see her and welcomed her to our church. We took her to our usual seats near the front of the church. Everyone was kind to Joan, and she received no stares or glares for her "way-too-short" skirt. As the choir walked onto the platform, Joan began to realize that her choice of dress was not like what the other Christian ladies were wearing. She tugged on the hem of her skirt, trying to bring it toward her knees. She was uncomfortable but that was okay. She was still observing and learning. I knew her heart was in the right place.

After the service, however, things went downhill fast. As I was talking with someone else, Joan was approached by one of our church's "finest." This wonderful woman took it upon herself to inform Joan of the inappropriateness of her clothing. She exclaimed how her husband "could not keep his eyes off your nakedness" during the service and chided her on her rebellion of indecency in the house of God. Joan fled in tears. She has never been back to class or our church since then.

Indeed, several situations like this happened in the early days of the RU ministry. In hindsight, it was a necessary period in our church's history. It was especially challenging for me. But, these types of situations, coupled with what I was learning at work from Mr. Arnold, taught me the value of being a leader who yields to the fruit of the Spirit~Meekness. To be effective at work and in ministry, I had to learn to submit to the Holy Spirit's direction to reduce friction between people.

When I told my pastor about Joan's experience, he was absolutely heartbroken. Immediately, his preaching shifted toward what we see in James 3. He drew on his own experiences of taming his tongue and began to teach others how to as well. Within a short time, the very spirit and atmosphere of North Love Baptist Church changed. Since that time, it has become fertile soil for baby fruit to grow, developing to incredible levels of maturity beyond what many might find possible to experience in most churches today.

Why? Because a wise man, our pastor, with knowledge

showed others how it ought to be done. If we are going to destroy discord, we must teach ourselves to restrain our tongues. We must yield to the Spirit's leading to reduce friction between others. And finally, we must take what we have learned and teach it to others. As Mr. Arnold taught me, we must develop people daily!

9a. GOD OFFERS THE FRUIT OF THE SPIRIT~TEMPERANCE.

As we near the end of our study of the fruit of the Spirit, we find a fruit that some think should be mentioned first. But under the influence of the Spirit, Paul listed it last—not because it is the least of all the fruits, but because it is the completion of all the fruits. It takes temperance to put us into a position of being Spirit-led believers.

Temperance is essential to keep the passions of the mind, will, and emotions suppressed, allowing the Holy Spirit to rule our lives.

When questioned on the definition of temperance, many people would describe it as "self-control." Even children's songs teach the value of temperance and define it as "self-control." Nothing could be further from the truth! We have seen in so many lessons throughout this book that we ought never to be in control of ourselves. Actually, "self-control" is an oxymoron. There is nothing about me that I can control that will gain God's acceptance of me. I must stop trying to control myself. The more I control myself, the less God is in control of me. Thus, the true definition of the fruit of the Spirit~Temperance is Spirit-control, or more specifically, "Spirit-controlled in all of life's pleasures."

Life as given by God offers many pleasures. However, the devil seeks to take those pleasures and turn them into objects of lusts. His goal is to get us to enjoy all of God's pleasures in a lustful way, creating appetites that are ungodly and out of control. The absence of Spirit-control is the single most fleshly action that produces habitual sins.

To fully enjoy the benefits God offers, we must yield to the fruit of the Spirit~Temperance. Many Christians fail to cultivate this fruit, opting rather to reject most of life's pleasures in an attempt to control the temptation to fuel fleshly lusts. I believe this leads God's people into spiritual bondage, otherwise called legalism. True, legalism is the belief that people can get to heaven by doing good works. Though Christians do not believe this, we tend to strive toward obtaining a level of righteousness in our own power that ultimately makes us self-righteous. I call this "legalistic sanctification." As I have mentioned before, we readily accept that justification that comes by God doing all the work, but when it comes to sanctification, we act as if we need to row our own canoe. We believe we need to help God out.

This is a mistake in Christian development. Although we avoid the obviously unrighteous sins listed in Galatians 5:19-21, we still find ourselves over indulging in the natural affections of the flesh. This leads to discouragement and frustration in the Christian life, so we try hard to do better. We serve until we're half-dead, but we receive little joy in return. So the mind, will, and emotions begin to tell us that our lack of joy is due to not acting righteously enough, and *that* failure is because we are allowing ourselves to enjoy too many of life's pleasures. To compensate, we reject all forms of enjoyment to try to please God, much like a monk trys to gain God's favor through abstinence. This is a perversion of God's designed intention of pleasure.

Admittedly, then we should avoid situations that could lead

us to compromise our Christian walk. Nevertheless, we must be willing to allow God to put us into circumstances that will permit us to yield to the fruit of temperance. When we do so, God is in control of the pleasures of life and His Spirit can monitor our enjoyment of them.

I know people who refuse to own a television. They will not eat any food that might be nutritionally weak. They will not go to a fireworks show in the City Square on Independence Day. They will hide in their basements with all the lights out on Halloween (which might not be that bad of an idea). They will not permit their kids to play organized sports. They will not go to the mall. They will rip out pages from magazines before their husbands can see them; and many, many more things that are done to prevent themselves or those they care about from being tempted.

Now, before you start thinking that I feel it is acceptable to carelessly place yourself or those you love in harm's way, please notice the context of my statements. This entire book was written in such a way as to prove that I am a strong proponent of avoiding the snares of the devil. However, God wants us to endure temptation. It is His design. Remember when Jesus fasted for forty days in the wilderness? The Bible says He was led there by the Spirit to be tempted by the devil himself (Matthew 14). Jesus taught us that when we pray, we ought to ask God to not lead us into temptation. How could we request such a thing if God is not in control of whether or not we must endure temptations?

To be sure, God wants to develop our souls to yield to the inner man's leading of temperance. God wants us to be under His control in the unpleasurable circumstances of life as well as in all the pleasurable circumstances of life.

The only way to avoid temptation completely is to sever your relationship with the outside world, and many religions require just that. However, we cannot do that and function in society, much less be effective in evangelism. So the devil will try to get us to give up all interaction with the pleasures of life and to do good *in our own power.* Then, as we are performing instead of transforming, he will place an incredibly appealing temptation in our way, and overcoming it in our own power will not be enough to sustain victory. We will eventually indulge in our fleshly desire because it is impossible to endure the temptations of the devil indefinitely in our own power. We are no match for Satan without the power of God.

We will remain crippled in our evangelistic outreach if we avoid any interaction with this world. Being laden with

> **Temperance** is Spirit-controlled in all of life's pleasures.

hidden desires and secret sins that make us feel dirty and defeated is spiritual bondage. It is the soul of man controlling the spirit of man.

God has a better way. His plan is for us to face temptation with the confidence of knowing that He has provided a way of escape. That way of escape is revealed by the inner man. God, communicating by His Spirit, will enable us to walk away from a pleasure temporarily or to abstain from it all together. When we allow this type of spiritual interaction between the soul and spirit to take place, we are exercising our faith. It will grow and strengthen just like a muscle. It is called spiritual development. It means giving every bad thing and every good thing to God, staying under His control in all things.

Let's revisit some verses in Romans that help explain God's demands for abstinence from sinful behavior.

1. As a result of God's work on our behalf, sin should be decreasing in our lives, not increasing.

    What shall we say then? Shall we continue in sin, that grace may abound? God forbid. How shall we, that are dead to sin, live any longer therein? Romans 6:1-2

2. God destroyed the power that sin had over us so that we could serve someone other than self. This someone that we would serve (through submission to His leading) will bring us freedom.

    Knowing this, that our old man is crucified with him, that the body of sin might be destroyed, that henceforth we should not serve sin. For he that is dead is freed from sin. Romans 6:6-7

3. God does not want us to yield to those old desires anymore. The power is gone, but the desire is still there. To destroy the desire, we must yield to God's power in our life.

    Let not sin therefore reign in your mortal body, that ye should obey it in the lusts thereof. Neither yield ye your members as instruments of unrighteousness unto sin: but yield yourselves unto God, as those that are alive from the dead, and your members as instruments of righteousness unto God. For sin shall not have dominion over you: for ye are not under the law, but under grace. Romans 6: 12-14

4. If we indulge fleshly appetites, they will grow stronger. If we feed our Spirit-led appetites, they will grow stronger, as well. Be careful! God will never feed a fleshly appetite, but we will – after we tire of performing in our own power.

    Know ye not, that to whom ye yield yourselves servants to obey, his servants ye are to whom ye obey; whether of sin unto death, or of obedience unto righteousness?

Being then made free from sin, ye became the servants of righteousness. Romans 6:16,18

So, we could never justify willfully placing ourselves in harm's way, making it harder for us to avoid sin. Certainly, God is against feeding our sinful appetites. But, we equally need to guard against placing ourselves in positions conducive to developing the outer man's self-righteous lifestyle. Allowing this form of self-development hinders God's work on our behalf. Friend, our Heavenly Father will rip the cover off of your self-righteous behavior, and I would hate to see what He will permit you to endure in your own power, eventually bringing about a much-needed lesson in your life. For whom the Lord loves, He most certainly chastens.

Rather than utterly rejecting my view on Spirit-control of life's pleasures versus self-control consider the following conclusion: If we control life's pleasures, then life's pleasures will control us; but, if God controls our pleasures, then we will be safe from harm in the face of temptation, because His plan includes our way of escape.

9b. WE OFTEN PREFER THE WORK OF THE FLESH~SELF-INDULGENCE.

The reason that soul-control, or what people refer to as self-control, is often taught in our churches is because when we are weak spiritually, we will reject the fruit of the Spirit-Temperance and instead engage in the work of the flesh~Self Indulgence. So, to offset spiritual weakness as church members, many people assume it is best for us to learn how to control ourselves. Then, if we reject God's control, we can fall back on our own control and not engage in sinful self-indulgence. But remember when we try to control ourselves, it is just the flesh trying to control the flesh. It's not the flesh of self-indulgence, but good flesh is just as bad as bad flesh. Therefore, self-indulgence is when self control ceases to control itself. We will lose the battle of spiritual warfare when we indulge appetites on a regular basis, hindering our spiritual walk.

To help illustrate the difference between temperance and self-indulgence, I'd like to present an explanation of appetites. Appetites are the determining factor in every good or bad decision that we make. There are basically three types of appetites in life. Let's take a look.

Some appetites need to be satisfied. These are good appetites. Most people do not naturally have appetites for things that are good. To gain good appetites, we must determine what creates those appetites and then feed them. Feeding them, then they will be temporarily satisfied. It is good for them to be satisfied. The reason that they do not remain that way is good, as well. You see, if they remained satisfied, we would never need to feed them again. As a result, we would lose our appetite for that which is good. Thus, when we feed a good appetite, it will become temporarily satisfied, causing our good appetite to grow. As it grows, so does the necessity for feeding it. Consequently, good appetites should never be over-fed or starved, but rather should be fed on a regularly scheduled basis.

Some examples of good appetites that need to be created and fed are a daily "God and I" time, church attendance, serving, soul winning, family time, work ethics, nutritional food, physical exercise, etc. Notice Matthew 5:6. *Blessed are they which do hunger and thirst after righteousness: for they shall be filled.* This verse tells us that God will

> **Self-indulgence** is when self control ceases to control itself.

completely provide for our yearning to yield to the inner man (i.e., righteousness). Obviously, these are appetites that must be regularly filled or else the cares of this world will eventually draw us dry. However, Jesus assures us that whenever we seek to be filled with the Spirit's leading, we will always be fed by God. Such an appetite will lead us to even greater blessings.

Some appetites need to be starved. These are the appetites that are sinful and should not be fed at any time. These appetites will grow to be insatiable with just the slightest feeding. They are small appetites that require little food to grow; a look here, a thought there; a point there and a click here. If we indulge these appetites, they will quickly control us. They are never fully satisfied and always require more feeding to keep them alive. When they want to be fed, they will bring us nagging misery as they attack our minds.

Examples of these appetites include the sins listed in our key passage in Galatians 5, as well as the sins of our fleshly works (i.e., the alternatives to the fruit of the Spirit.) Other examples may involve drugs, alcohol, gambling, pornography, anger, pride, or possession-centeredness. Still, other examples may look right but are equally wrong such as self-love, frustration, worry, doubt, etc. These behaviors must be strictly avoided. If you have a problem in any of these areas, follow RU Principle number four to protect yourself, and then develop your inner man to reject these sinful, insatiable appetites of the soul. They will destroy your life sooner rather than later.

Let's look at what the Bible says about the dangers and disappointments of feeding appetites that God intends for us to starve.

- *All the labour of man is for his mouth, and yet the appetite is not filled. Better is the sight of the eyes than the wandering of the desire: this is also vanity and vexation of spirit.* Ecclesiastes 6:7,9

- *He that loveth silver shall not be satisfied with silver; nor he that loveth abundance with increase: this is also vanity. When goods increase, they are increased that eat them: and what good is there to the owners thereof, saving the beholding of them with their eyes?* Ecclesiastes 5:10-11

- *And have no fellowship with the unfruitful works of darkness, but rather reprove them. For it is a shame even to speak of those things which are done of them in secret.* Ephesians 5:11-12

These verses remind us that all of our efforts to satisfy our wrong desires will be to no avail. Whether we get what our appetite desires or whether it is withheld from us, we will not be satisfied with the consequences of these appetites either way.

Some appetites need to be suppressed. Each of the three appetites listed requires us to yield to the fruit of the Spirit~Temperance to feed, starve, or suppress as needed. This third type of appetite is for those things which God gave us a natural need, drive, or use for and intended for our good pleasure, but these appetites, when indulged in with abandon will lead to lusts that will eventually control us. These are good, yet potentially dangerous appetites of the soul which the inner man will monitor as we yield to temperance. Abuse of these appetites will probably not destroy your life sooner but if fed without temperance, they will destroy your life later.

Once again, these appetites are not designed by God to

generate sinful behavior. They are God-given appetites. Actually, many of them are a necessity to live, yet they can still lead to great bondage if we are not careful. Examples of these appetites that must be suppressed from controlling us are for things like food, sleep, relaxation, possessions, money, sexual relations with your spouse, work, play, sports, news/talk radio, television, reading, etc.

In 1 Corinthians 6:12, Paul speaks of these appetites. *All things are lawful unto me, but all things are not expedient: all things are lawful for me, but I will not be brought under the power of any.* He realized the importance of controlling good appetites and was careful to do so. He did not feed appetites that were not beneficial. He starved appetites that would be considered fleshly. Why? Because he refused to be the servant of anything other than the Spirit of God.

Remember, control over these appetites will require an effort on our part. Not effort to do the work ourselves, but rather an effort to allow God to do the work for us. Temperance is just that—being under the control of the Spirit. Appetite control will require a putting off of the old man and a putting on of our Lord Jesus Christ. *But put ye on the Lord Jesus Christ, and make not provision for the flesh, to fulfil the lusts thereof.* (Romans 13:14)

In Conclusion:

In Galatians 5, the words that Paul wrote just before and just after listing the works of the flesh and the fruit of the Spirit will bring our entire study of the abundant Christian life together quite nicely. Verse 16 says, *This I say then, Walk in the Spirit, and ye shall not fulfil the lust of the flesh.* And, concerning the fruit of the Spirit, verse 23 says, *against such there is no law.*

To be Spirit-led believers, we must take repeated steps "in the Spirit." Though we will occasionally reject or overlook the Spirit's leading and may actually fulfill a lust of the flesh, we will never, ever need a law of God or man to get us back in line. The God who saved us and the God who changes us is also the God who keeps us. He is able to keep us from falling - if we will let Him. To paraphrase what Paul said, "If you will simply abide in Christ, God will do all the work for you."

I would like to add one final thought concerning the Nine fruits of the Spirit. In chapter two we say how Christ summed up the Old Testament and the Law with two basic commandments. They were to love God and love others. *All* the Law and commandments hung on these two commands, which were to LOVE.

I suggest to you that it is quite probable that with the elimination of the Law (where man did all the work) and with the implementation of Christ's Grace (where Christ does all the work) that all the fruits that permit us to live without "the Law" are equally predicated and hang on this one fruit, which is to LOVE!

Many Christians, for the sake of judging others or to at least avoid the self-sacrifice of offering mercy to them, have rejected the verse that tells us that God is love. They prefer to remind us all that God is judgment and God is righteous and God is jealous and God is Holy; and He is. He is every one of them. Many people seem to get upset when reminded of the fact that God is love. But He is! A brief study of Scripture will show that the attribute that God and His Son Jesus used when describing their self-portraits was LOVE.

If you were to ask me, "How can I develop my inner man to

the position where I am abiding in Christ effectively enough to act and respond under the influence of the nine fruits of the Spirit?" I would suggest the following commitments on your part, and let God do all the rest:

- Pray every day that God will allow circumstances in your life that will break your outer man.
- Pray that those circumstances will cause you to yield to the inner man, allowing God's light to shine through that hole in your soul.
- Cultivate a heart for knowing God by developing your relationship with Him early every day. (Don't eat until you have prayed; don't sleep until you have read. Feed no fleshly appetite before your spiritual appetite if full.)
- When you become aware of someone with a need, ask the Spirit how you should respond. If you are led to give, always respond with the fruit of the Spirit-Love. Give of yourself willingly, without *any* thought of return.
- If you will yield to love, then more often than not, the other fruits will fall in line and become easier to yield to, as well. Why? Because the greatest of these is LOVE.

Nine Fruits of the Spirit and Works of the Flesh

LOVE: *the willing, sacrificial giving of oneself for the benefit of others without thought of return.*
SELF-LOVE: *the willing or unwilling giving of oneself to benefit others with selfish thoughts of return.*

JOY: *a cheerful, calm delight in all the circumstances of life.*
FRUSTRATION: *a rejection or unhappy refusal in the circumstances of life.*

PEACE: *to be safe from harm in spirit, mind, and body.*
WORRY: *to live in fear of harm in your spirit, mind, and body.*

LONGSUFFERING: *an enduring temperament that expresses itself in patience with the shortcomings of others.*
QUICK-TEMPERED: *irritability that negatively excites our passions.*

GENTLENESS: *softness in manners.*
HARSHNESS: *roughness in manner, temper, or words.*

GOODNESS: *conforming our lives and conversations to behave benevolently toward others.*
MEANNESS: *refusing to be liberal with charity, thus avoiding any personal expense.*

FAITH: *a personal measurement of the level of confidence in what Christ has done and will do in, through, and for us.*
DOUBT: *an attitude of unbelief, characterized by rebellion and disobedience toward God.*

MEEKNESS: *the ability for God's people to negotiate among others without causing friction.*
DISCORD: *any disagreement which produces angry passions,*

contest, disputes, litigation, or war.

TEMPERANCE: *Spirit-controlled in all of life's pleasures.*
SELF-INDULGENCE: *When self control ceases to control itself.*

But the fruit of the Spirit is love, joy, peace, longsuffering, gentleness, goodness, faith, Meekness, temperance: against such there is no law.   —Galatians 5:22-23

Chapter 10

10 Principles
To Conquer Stubborn Habits

This final chapter is to explain to you some principles for God's valuable commodity of freedom. This freedom was granted to Adam and Eve at the time of the perfect world. Yet mankind was not able to maintain that freedom because of our failure to observe the measuring device for that freedom.

You see, freedom is measured by its boundaries. Freedom is not to do whatever you want; freedom is the ability to do what God wants. The boundaries for the freedom of Adam and Eve was to not eat of the Tree of the Knowledge of Good and Evil. They had the freedom to eat of every other tree, but they chose to exercise their freedom of the will and violate those boundaries.

Oftentimes, we reject boundaries because we think they are too restrictive. My friend, remember this truth: When we reject the boundaries of freedom, we will *always* exchange those boundaries for the bondage of slavery. We only have two choices in life—boundaries, or bondage. God has designed for man to live within boundaries.

We have thus learned that, through Christ, we are given another opportunity to experience freedom that releases us from the bondage of sin. However, this freedom comes with boundaries. For sake of illustration, let's remember back to our childhood days and our boundaries that gave us freedom.

For a newborn babe, the first freedom he is given is the freedom of the crib. He can cry, scream, play, sleep, and all those other things babies do, as long as he stays within the boundary of that crib.

When he grows a little more, he is given the freedom of the playpen. This is much better because here he can play with toys, make a lot of noise, crawl around, and see all that is going on around him. The next big step is the freedom of the living room. This gets even better because now he can explore his surroundings. But he must stay within the boundaries of the living room. When he violates that freedom by attempting to crawl up the stairs, what happens? Mom puts him back in the playpen. He lost his freedom because he violated his boundaries.

As the years pass, the freedoms grow—the freedom of the back yard, then the neighborhood. But what happens when he violates his boundary of staying in the neighborhood? He is restricted once again to his own yard.

Sweet Sixteen is here. Do you remember your glorious day? With tears in Mom and Dad's eyes, what freedom was given to you? The freedom of the car. This is so much better than the playpen, or the back yard, or even riding bikes through the neighborhood! But the moment those flashing lights pull up behind the speeding teenager, that freedom is taken away. He is now back to the bicycle. Why? Because he violated his freedom of the car.

Such is God's system for distributing the commodity of freedom. As we grow within our boundaries, those boundaries will grow with us. However, when we violate or reject these boundaries, those freedoms are taken away.

Our final chapter covers the boundaries of ten biblical principles that guarantee prosperity and freedom. They are ten boundaries that I have followed since God showed them to me nearly ten years ago. I learned these under my pastor's preaching and from various authors. Two such books that God used to mold these principles was *Bread for Believers* by Dr. Curtis Hudson and *The Way Back* by Elizabeth Rice Handford. They have helped me understand the value of a system of obedience that is measured by remaining within boundaries.

The ten principles will keep you within the boundaries of your new-found freedom in Christ.

Principle #1-
If God's Against it, So Am I.

Now the works of the flesh are manifest, which are these; Adultery , fornication, uncleanness, lasciviousness, Idolatry, witchcraft, hatred, variance, emulations, wrath, strife, seditions, heresies, Envyings, murders, drunkenness, revellings and such like: of the which I tell you before, as I have also told you in time past, that they which do such things shall not inherit the kingdom of God. Galatians 5:19-21

Throughout the Bible we see passages indicating behavior that God is against. He has asked that we avoid behaving in this way. He warns that participating in certain behavior will bring sorrow, punishment and can even lead to a shorter life. We have seen this to be true in not only our own lives, but in the lives of many others, as well. It is called the law of sowing and reaping. This simple law says if we sow (or, spread) destructive behavior, we will reap (or, receive) destruction in our life. But if we spread good behavior patterns, we will receive blessings from God.

As we have learned in previous chapters, the Bible was written to tell us what is right, what is not right, how to get right and how to stay right. If God's intention was to inform us of what is, what is not, how to get and how to stay right, then it is our responsibility to conform each area of our lives that is revealed to be wrong. He will help us do this. He gives new believers His Spirit and a hunger to be right.

This new presence and new desire for good is what God uses to mold our new Christian character. If we draw a line and do not overstep this line of behavior that is considered by God to be wrong, then He will reveal more and more things that He would like to change in our lives. As we continue to adopt these revelations of God's will for us, we will find ourselves farther and farther from the original line (which is to not indulge in our addiction). Eventually, we will find ourselves so far from our original line in the sand, so to speak, that even when we have a bad day, the thought of using or engaging in our addiction is not even a remote possibility. This is a joyous place to be.

To this end, we see that all who want to be unanimously reformed in their lives must accept Christ's offer for salvation first and foremost. Then we must draw a line and say, "If God is against it, so am I!"

Principle #2-
Every Sin has its Origin in our Hearts.

Before I came to Christ, I tried to overcome my addictions over and over again through regular attendance to group meetings in society. I would spend hours upon hours sulking in my coffee, smoking cigarettes, and discussing my endless desire to drink. Sound familiar? Why didn't this type of activity help me?

Ephesians 5:11-12 reminds us to *have no fellowship with the unfruitful works of darkness, but rather reprove them. For it is a shame even to speak of those things which are done of them in secret.* Our sins of the past must be forgotten. To meditate and discuss them openly only gives place to the devil. I decided a long time ago I would rather tell people what God has done for me than to tell people what I had done to God.

Constant meditation (or, thinking) on our desire to fulfill a fleshly lust will ultimately lead to acting out our desire. If we're fortunate to avoid it physically, we will seldom avoid it mentally. Proverbs 23:7 reads, *For as he thinketh in his heart, so is he...* For me to avoid the seemingly unending desire to fulfill my desire to feed my addiction, I needed to discipline myself to avoid talking about it (in a desirous way) and avoid thinking about it. By thinking about it, I was actually making it easy for myself to do wrong. Romans 13:14 states, *But put ye on the Lord Jesus Christ, and make not provision for the flesh, to fulfil the lusts thereof.*

I saw an old friend at a local grocery store. He had heard that I had stopped using drugs and had "found religion." I explained how Jesus had changed my life and given me power over my addictions to both drugs and alcohol. He exclaimed his gladness and went on to tell me that he had been sober for three weeks. He had finally quit his job that led to after-hours drinking and had moved out of his buddy's house (who liked to have drinking parties regularly). Realizing these were both good first steps, I encouraged him to visit church and offered to pick him up. He gave me his address. Unfortunately, the young man had chosen to take up residence in an apartment that was directly adjacent to a popular bar in town. He never made it to church. Why did this man fail in his recovery? He made it easy for himself to do wrong. Even if he never left his house, the constant sounds of the music in the bar beneath him would never let the thought of drinking leave his mind!

You see, the heart can accustom itself to sin. An act that once would seem terrible and undeniably wrong can, by contemplating it too often, become attractive. Proverbs 4:23 reads, *Keep thy heart with all diligence; for out of it are the issues of life.* Everything I ever searched for in life—the important issues of life: love, joy, peace, happiness, friendship, financial freedom—were always withheld from me during my times of addiction. Why was that? Because the important issues of life are given by God and He never entrusts them to those who do not work hard (diligent) to keep (guard) their hearts from being hardened from the deceitfulness of sin.

Remember, before you ever did it, you thunk it!

Principle #3-
It is Easier to Keep the Heart Clean than it is to Clean it after it has been Defiled.

Oh, what a truth this is! When my wife and I were first married, I had quite a few lessons to learn. I was a 28-year-old bachelor and was not accustomed to cleaning up after myself. My favorite meal was Chili-n-Fries Surprise (the recipe is available for a small charge). My wife refused to cook it because of the extreme mess that the grease and chili sauce would make on her white stove. I was forced to suffer. However, a friend of my wife's asked her to work a few hours every Monday afternoon at her beauty supply store. She consented and I was left to fend for myself to obtain dinner on Monday nights. Praise the Lord, Chili-n-Fries Surprise! In my desire to consume this long awaited meal, I overlooked the cleaning of the stove. When the next Monday rolled around, I found the chili sauce and grease stains from the previous week's delicatessen still splattered on my wife's stove. It was gross, and there was no way I could prepare a meal on this filth.

When my wife arrived home later that evening, I asked her when she was planning on cleaning the stove. BIG MISTAKE. Our first fight. I learned a valuable lesson that night. After an hour of scrubbing, I learned it is easier to keep a kitchen stove clean than to clean it after it has been stained.

This is the same truth we are taught in the Bible. Over and over again we are faced with examples of people who chose to associate with sin in hope that it would not lead them to a sinful condition. Lot was a righteous man (2 Peter 2:8) yet he chose to associate with ungodly men (Psalm 1:1a), he had day to day contact with sin (Psalm1:1b), and he allowed the people around him to decay into moral wickedness with no good use for God (Psalm 1:1c). Yes, Lot's life was ultimately spared by God. However, he in no way prospered (Psalm 1:3). The last we hear of him, he is getting drunk and committing terrible sins (Genesis 19). How can this mistake be avoided in your life? Follow these three simple verses:

Proverbs 22:3 *A prudent man foreseeth the evil, and hideth himself: but the simple pass on, and are punished.*

Proverbs 6:27-28 *Can a man take fire in his bosom, and his clothes not be burned? Can one go upon hot coals, and his feet not be burned?*

Proverbs 4:23 *Keep thy heart with all diligence; for out of it are the issues (important things) of life.*

Remember: If you do what you've always done, then you will be what you've always been.

Principle #4-
We Cannot Fight a Fleshly Appetite by Indulging in it.

Disregarding this principle has caused such great pain and failure for many years. It is also this very same principle that God will bring to our remembrance every time we feel like indulging in any fleshly desire. This principle has done more to discourage the desire to wander than any of the others. If the truth be known, the failure to recognize and apply this principle to our lives is usually at the core of every besetting sin.

An appetite is a dangerous thing. If disciplined, it can be controlled. If not, it can control an individual. God has given within each of His children a power to control our appetites. The need for food, drink, and sexual satisfaction are all God-given, legitimate needs. However, Satan will twist them into lusts which, when coupled with enticement, lead to a life of sin and spiritual and sometimes physical death (James 1:14-16).

Remember the old commercial that advertised KOOL cigarettes? The ad (falsely) stated that "They Satisfy." Well if this were true, then we could all smoke one KOOL cigarette and our appetite would be satisfied and we would never need to indulge that appetite again. The truth is that KOOL cigarettes (as do all cigarettes) never satisfy. The appetite created with indulgence will only intensify. Indulging in any fleshly appetite only makes it stronger, never weaker.

Not too long ago, I listened to a documentary on starving children in the third world. My heart was broken as the narrator explained that though the children were starving, they do not feel the hunger pains that we feel right before dinnertime. Rather, they have suppressed their appetite for so long, that their starvation is not accompanied with the pain of hunger.

It is the same way with any fleshly desire that we struggle with. Whether it be cigarettes, drugs, alcohol, overeating, adulterous thoughts, pornography, gambling, or any other crippling appetite, if we do not feed it, do not give in to it, it will die. The only way to destroy the appetite is to starve it. That is a promise from God.

So the next time you feel that urge to indulge in a sinful fleshly desire, resign yourself to just "skip that meal." When you skip a meal, you will see that after a few minutes or hours, you have lost your appetite for that meal. You may not skip every meal, but eventually, your desire will starve itself to death and the hunger will be gone. Don't let the devil tell you if you just have one more cigarette or just one more drink or one more chocolate bar, you will be satisfied.

Ecclesiastes 5:10 *He that loveth silver shall not be satisfied with silver; nor he that loveth abundance with increase: this is also vanity.*

Principle #5-
Small Compromises lead to Great Disasters.
(Little sins lead to big sins.)

So many students and friends of the ministry have asked me questions like this, "Brother Steve, I have stayed away from my old friends, I have stopped acting the way I used to, I even go to church at least once a week, but I still ended up engaging in my addiction. Why doesn't this work?" Such a difficult question to the student, but such an easy answer from God.

I will usually ask them where they are in their Bible reading, Scripture memory, prayer life, mid-week service attendance, witnessing, and what they are doing for service to the kingdom (bus route, cleaning church, nursery work, helping others, etc.). Without fail, they have fallen away in almost everything. Oddly enough they have fallen away for only two to three weeks...then bang! The devil acquires a foothold.

How does this happen? Well, God's answer is found in Luke 16:10. *He that is faithful* (or, consistent) *in that which is least is faithful* (or, consistent) *also in much: and he that is unjust in the least is unjust also in much.* In chapter seven, we discovered that, according to this verse, if we are consistent (or, faithful) in all the little things, we will be consistent (or, faithful) in the big things (remaining victorious). However, if we are inconsistent in the little things, we will fail in the big things. The reason is simple: God loves the little things. You see, this list of small things determines our master. We cannot serve God and earthly lusts (Matthew 6:24). We will have no choice but to love one and hate the other. The more we do for God, the more we will learn to love Him (Why do we love Him? Because He first loved us!).

Remember this: Small compromises lead to great disasters. You may compromise your Bible reading or church attendance or service requirements now, but the consequences are guaranteed to be great. If you are not yielding yourself to the little requests of God, you will yield yourself to the little requests of your enemy. And him alone will you serve.   Romans 6:16 tells us, *Know ye not, that to whom ye yield yourselves servants to obey, his servants ye are to whom ye obey; whether of sin unto death, or of obedience unto righteousness?*   Commit today to do the little things every day. You will never read your Bible every day until you read your Bible on the days you don't want to.

Principle #6-
Those who do not Love the Lord will not Help us Serve the Lord.

John 15:19 *If ye were of the world, the world would love his own: but because ye are not of the world, but I have chosen you out of the world, therefore the world hateth you.*

Will my friends want anything to do with me now that I am a Christian? That was the question I asked after I gave my life to Jesus. It wasn't long before I found the answer....if I acted like them, they would accept me. When I acted like Christ, they would reject me.

I struggled to determine the correct path. You see, I wanted Christ in my life but I also wanted Christ in my friends' lives. If I broke my ties with my worldly friends, they would lose their opportunity to learn of Christ. So I tried to live as a child of God while hanging out with the devil's kids. As you would expect, more often than not, they would tempt me to do the things that I did not want to do anymore. Eventually, I would give in.

It was at this time God showed me why misery loves company. You see, if I lived right and remained right, my old friends would feel guilt and shame for their behavior. But if I lived wrong, they would prove that Christ has no affect on a person's life. The guilt for their lifestyle would be removed. They would lay the snare (temptation) and wait for me to fall. Proverbs 24:15 says, *Lay not wait, O wicked man, against the dwelling of the righteous; spoil not his resting place* They would work hard to lure me back into the world. They wanted to see that the Christian life doesn't work!

I found that when I got right and stayed right that they went left. However, when the law of sowing and reaping would kick in and they found themselves at the bottom, they would not look to their friends who did the things they did. Rather, they called on me. They would ask me what I did to change my life because my change was real. Others were not. What a blessing! I have been able to counsel with literally dozens of friends from the past, in God's timing, and tell them that Christ died for their sins. It has also led to prosperity in my Christian life and blessed happiness. Just like the Bible promises in Psalm 1:1-3 *Blessed* (or, happy) *is the man that walketh not in the counsel of the ungodly, nor standeth in the way of sinners, nor sitteth in the seat of the scornful* (listens to critical people). *But his delight is in the law of the LORD; and in his law doth he meditate day and night. And he shall be like a tree planted by the rivers of water, that bringeth forth his fruit in his season; his leaf also shall not wither; and whatsoever he doeth shall prosper.*

Principle #7-
Our Sinful Habits Do Hurt Those Who Follow Us.

Have you ever wondered if anybody cared? Have you ever thought about trying something drastic to get yourself noticed? You might say, *Maybe then they would know I needed their help!*

One of the lies from the father of lies (the devil) is that no one is watching or caring, so no one is affected by our behavior. Since the dawn of time he has deceived us into believing that our behavior will only affect, hurt, or damage ourselves. He did it in the beginning with Eve. Little did she know that her sin would then be shared by her husband, which in turn would lead to the fall of man and woman. Little did she know that a curse would be placed on herself and her husband and all generations to follow.

The devil deceived in the life of Lot. Not realizing that having day to day contact with sinners was damaging to his family, he stubbornly left his homeland. His lack of leadership over his family led to the death of his wife and uncontrolled behavior by his daughters and himself.

The devil deceived in the life of David. Little did David know that if he stayed home from battle (where he belonged at the time) that he would suffer a temptation that would lead to adultery. The consequence would be a woman would lose her husband to a plot of murder and her son would die as a newborn infant. Over and over again in scripture we see that sinful behavior has a profound effect on those who follow us.

Who, pray tell, are the ones who follow you? That is simple: Those whose lives are spent in relationship with yours. If you were to die today, would you have 100 people at your funeral? Most people would like to think so. How about 50? Or 35? Or 20? How about one? Would you have at least one person at your funeral? Yes, I believe we would all have at least one and probably closer to 100. Well, whether they actually say it to you or not, those are the people you hurt with your behavior. Those are the people affected by your sinful habit. They may not feel the pain you feel, but they feel pain. They may not say the things to you that you need said that will help you, but they think them and wish they could find the courage to say them.

Romans 14:7 says, ...*For none of us liveth to himself, and no man dieth to himself.* Your life affects others the same way your death would affect others. Choose today to let your life have a profound effect of good on others. No matter the cost. No matter the sacrifice. Make the choice. Today and tomorrow and onward from this point, your good habits will help those who follow you. Choose today to be a regular learner at Church. Choose to read your Bible. Choose to talk to God in prayer. Choose to arm yourself with memorized Bible verses that will help you overcome. Choose today to be helpful to those who come to Reformers. Choose today to make a difference in the lives of your congregation, the lives of your community, a difference in the kingdom of God. Amen!

Principle #8-
It is Not Possible to Fight a Fleshly Temptation With Fleshly Weapons.

Oh so many times we have lost students either temporarily or permanently because they believed the lie of the devil that the world had something to offer their recovery. Whether it be the patch, secular counseling, evaluation of childhood, methadone, Prozac, or any other fleshly (worldly) weapon that is intended to curb our stubborn habits and inappropriate behavior, it **will not** cure us of our affliction. Praise God, the battle is inside of us and that is exactly where Christ has chosen to take up residence in our lives! You see, the battle cannot be won with a fleshly (worldly weapon) because the battle is spiritual. Second Corinthians 10:3-5 says, *For though we walk in the flesh, we do not war after the flesh: (For the weapons of our warfare are not carnal* (or, fleshly), *but mighty through God* (or, spiritual) *to the pulling down of strong holds;) Casting down imaginations* (in your mind), *and every high thing that exalteth itself against the knowledge of God, and bringing into captivity every thought to the obedience of Christ.*

It is simple to believe but hard to apply. Whenever we have a stubborn thought, we must cast it down. Remember, as a man thinks in his heart, so is he. Principle #2 says every sin has its origin in our hearts. It is our responsibility to protect our hearts with all diligence because out of the heart are the very most important issues in life. If there is going to be any good or anything worth commending come out of our lives, we must first concentrate on things that are true, honest, just, lovely, pure and of good report (Philippians 4:8). To avoid a habitual action or reaction to our negative thoughts we must cast down the thought and bring our mind under subjection to the obedience of Christ. We will have a lot of help with this, you see, because 1 John 4:4 says, *Ye are of God, little children, and have overcome them: because greater is he that is in you, than he that is in the world.*

The world has nothing to offer you in your quest for recovery. You can believe what you are reading or you can try the world yourself. But with Christ, all things are possible, if you only believe.

Principle #9-
We Lose our Freedom to Choose when we Give in to Temptation. Our Consequences are Inevitable and Incalculable and Up to God.

When we first take hold of a vice, it is extremely pleasurable. At times, it may seem to be the only time we feel happy, the only time we experience any comfort in our lives. However, the Bible warns in Proverbs 20:17 that, *Bread of deceit is sweet to a man; but afterwards his mouth shall be filled with gravel.* You can clearly see that while deceitful and wrong actions may bring temporary pleasure, afterwards it leaves a very bad taste in your mouth. The consequences for your behavior then belong to God. Proverbs 9:17-18 indicates that, *Stolen waters are sweet, and bread eaten in secret is pleasant. But he knoweth not that the dead are there; and that her guests are in the depths of hell.* No matter how much enjoyment we may receive from our stubborn habit or addiction, we can be sure that the consequences are never worth it.

We must realize that God is watching us. He watches every single thing we do. Proverbs 5:21 says, *For the ways of man are before the eyes of the LORD, and he pondereth <u>all</u> his goings.* That word *ponders* means to "weigh, or consider." What does He consider? He considers the proper actions that should be taken against our behavior to bring a proper reaction from us. His desire is for a repentance and a dependence on Him, rather than on some vice that only brings temporal advice. Look at the warning that is given in the very next verse and ask yourself if you are in this position. *His own iniquities shall take the wicked himself, and he shall be holden with the cords of his sins* (Proverbs 5:22). This verse clearly indicates that once we grab hold of a wicked vice that it will begin to wrap itself around us. Though, at the beginning we may be able to get out of its hold, eventually, the cord will be tightened around us and we will be held in bondage with the cords of our sin. Oh, how that is what happened to me!

Next is the important warning to those of us who struggle to fight back. *He shall die without instruction; and in the greatness of his folly he shall go astray* (Proverbs 5:23). This consequence (going astray, which leads to a premature physical and spiritual death) cannot be monitored by us. It is determined by God. Until that unfortunate time that we experience this untimely demise, we will live among consequences that are designed to bring us back to God. The cure is found in Reformers Key Verse, Isaiah 55:7. *Let the wicked forsake his way* (#1), *and the unrighteous man his thoughts* (#2): *and let him return unto the LORD* (#3) *and he will have mercy upon him; and to our God, for he will abundantly pardon.* We need God's mercy (not getting what we deserve). We need God's pardon (penalty removed for what we've done) so that we may start over. That is accomplished by simply turning from our way of doing things and from our way of thinking and returning to the Lord. Reformers Unanimous is here to show you how to do this. I hope you listen to what God has to say to you.

Principle #10-
God Balances Guilt with Blame. Accept the Blame for Your Actions and God will Remove the Guilt.

As a young man trying to get away from the strongholds of my addictions, I sought the counsel and help of people in secular programs. Time and time again, they searched for hidden meaning in my behavior. They explained how my rebellion and desire to please myself was most assuredly to be blamed on my parents, that I had been forced into my sin by what they referred to as bad surroundings. Many in society today are teaching us to shift the blame for our shortcomings on our parents, our upbringing, our economic background, our race, our minority status and many other things. By shifting the blame to others, it temporarily removes the guilt.

You see, God designed us with a spiritual equilibrium. When we commit sin, we experience guilt and it throws our spirit off-balance with our emotions. When society teaches us to shift the blame (or, if we naturally shift the blame), we actually can circumvent that off balance feeling of guilt temporarily. However, when the sin returns, the guilt is so much worse. Our feelings of failure increase to even higher levels. God's design is to administer guilt through His Spirit that lives within the believer. That guilt needs to be released and God designed a formula for that to happen. It is found in 1 John 1:9. *If we confess our sins, He is faithful and just to forgive us our sins, and to cleanse us from all unrighteousness.* What a beautiful promise! *If*—big word. If we do, He will. If we don't, He won't!! If we confess (proclaim to God) our sin, He is faithful (for sure, 100% of the time, over and over again) to forgive (full pardon) our sins. He doesn't stop there. You see, we have been pardoned for our wrongdoing, but we are not cleansed from it. We still have the guilty feeling. We must be cleansed of all unrighteousness.

If my daughter got dressed for Sunday School and then went outside and fell in the mud, I would not only forgive her for playing outside when it was raining and she was dressed for Sunday school, I would also clean her. I would give her a bath and all new clothes. Why? Because when I bring her to Sunday School, I don't want anyone to know that she fell in the mud! That is what God wants to do for us. He wants to give us a full pardon for everything we've done in the past and He wants to clean us up and put us in a new set of clothes. And He is faithful! That means He wants to do this every time we sin against Him. He loves us that much. So, today, accept the blame for what you have done in your life. Confess it to God and He will clean you up. Praise God!

Afterword

I am crucified with Christ: nevertheless I live; yet not I, but Christ liveth in me: and the life which I now live in the flesh I live by the faith of the Son of God, who loved me, and gave himself for me. —Galatians 2:20

As we come to the final page of this book, let us remember the theme of *Nevertheless I Live*. The Christian life is not ours, it is Christ's. When we learn to live under His leading we will experience a life worth dying for. If you are holding onto the life that was crucified with Christ, let me encourage you to let it go and let God live His life through you. You won't ever need "will power" again. If you are willing, He will provide the power.

Just remember this truth: God is living in you. He is not only an influence, nor is He only a leading or only a revealer. He is a person. A living Person, the Holy Spirit! He is in you and you are not your own; He is now waiting to live through you. When this truth permeates every part of your conscience, you will see that the life you now live, you are living through the faith in the Son of God who gave Himself for you.

For to me to live is Christ, and to die is gain! (Philippians 1:21)

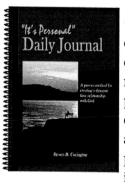

"Its Personal" Daily Journal is a daily exercise in God's five forms of communication including daily Bible reading, learning from teachers, a powerful personal prayer time unlike anything you can imagine, time with Christian friends, and being led by the Holy Spirit. It blends precisely with the RU workbooks and also includes an instructional CD by Bro. Curington explaining how to properly use this tool. It is a proven method for developing a dynamic relationship with God. (Also available in Spanish.)

Catalog Number: CE-111
Price: $15

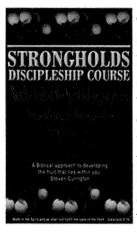

The Strongholds Discipleship Course is a biblical approach to breaking the chains of strongholds and stubborn habits. It is the four RUI workbooks conveniently contained in one. It is designed primarily for private use or as a Bible study aide. Pastors, teachers, and leaders often use the Strongholds Discipleship Course as a supplemental teaching accessory or within the RUI class format. (Also available in Spanish.)

Catalog Number: CE-103
Price: $15

Order today! *www.reformu.com*
fax: 815-986-0462   call: 815-986-0460, ext. 108

The Reformers Unanimous Student Guide is the *Nevertheless I Live* textbook in outline form. The Reformers Unanimous Program Guide can be studied or taught in about eight months and covers a wide variety of topics based only on the Bible. Space is provided for notes.

Catalog Number: CE-101
Price: $10

Onward Christian Soldiers 3-tape series is a compilation of Bro. Curington's teaching on the Christian's armor given in Ephesians 6. This will fully equip you for your daily battle of spiritual warfare.

Catalog Number: PT-101
Price: $15

With the Walkie Talkie Journal, children learn not only how to walk with God, but to talk with God as well. It is formatted so that children can easily understand it and can develop and/or strengthen a personal relationship with God by communicating with Him every day. It includes an instructional tape for the child and written instructions for the parent who will oversee the child's performance.

Catalog Number: CZ-111

Price: $8

The Fruit of the Spirit Booklets is the Kidz curriculum series. These books will teach your child the biblical definition of each fruit, they will memorize Bible verses for each fruit, and engage in activities to help develop those fruits. This includes other teaching tools, such as the Beatitudes, the Ten Commandments, the Kidz Ten Principles, the books of the Bible, and much more. This is an exciting series for the children that mirrors the adult curriculum at an elementary pace.

Catalog Number: KZ-115

Price: $25